MW00453668

# STUDENT SOLUTIONS MANUAL

*to accompany*

# BUSINESS MATHEMATICS

TWELFTH EDITION

Gary Clendenen
Stanley A. Salzman
Charles D. Miller

*Prepared by*
Deana J. Richmond
Dean R. Richmond

**Prentice Hall**

Boston Columbus Indianapolis New York San Francisco Upper Saddle River

Amsterdam Cape Town Dubai London Madrid Milan Munich Paris Montreal Toronto

Delhi Mexico City Sao Paulo Sydney Hong Kong Seoul Singapore Taipei Tokyo

Editorial Director: Vernon Anthony
Executive Acquisitions Editor: Gary Bauer
Development Editor: Linda Cupp
Editorial Assistant: Tanika Henderson
Director of Marketing: Dave Gesell
Marketing Manager: Stacey Martinez
Marketing Assistant: Les Roberts
Senior Managing Editor: JoEllen Gohr
Project Manager: Christina Taylor

Senior Operations Supervisor: Pat Tonneman
Senior Art Director: Diane Ernsberger
Cover Art: iStock
Printer/Binder: Bind-Rite Graphics / Robbinsville
Cover Printer: Lehigh-Phoenix Color/Hagerstown
Text Font: Times New Roman

Copyright © 2012 Pearson Education, Inc., publishing as Prentice Hall, One Lake Street, Upper Saddle River, New Jersey 07458. All rights reserved. Manufactured in the United States of America. This publication is protected by Copyright, and permission should be obtained from the publisher prior to any prohibited reproduction, storage in a retrieval system, or transmission in any form or by any means, electronic, mechanical, photocopying, recording, or likewise. To obtain permission(s) to use material from this work, please submit a written request to Pearson Education, Inc., Permissions Department, One Lake Street, Upper Saddle River, New Jersey 07458.

Many of the designations by manufacturers and seller to distinguish their products are claimed as trademarks. Where those designations appear in this book, and the publisher was aware of a trademark claim, the designations have been printed in initial caps or all caps.

3 4 5 6 7 8 9 10  V088  16 15 14 13 12 11

**Prentice Hall**
is an imprint of

www.pearsonhighered.com

ISBN 10: 0-13-254565-9
ISBN 13: 978-0-13-254565-5

# PREFACE

This manual provides complete solutions for the exercises in *Business Mathematics*, Twelfth Edition, by Gary Clendenen, Stanley A. Salzman, and Charles D. Miller. Solutions are provided for all odd section exercises and for all Case Studies, Case in Point Summary Exercises, Chapter Tests, and Cumulative Review exercises.

The supplement should be used as an aid to mastering the course work. Try to solve the exercises on your own before you refer to the solutions in this manual. Then, if you have difficulty, study the solutions. A conscientious effort has been made to write solutions so as to be consistent with the methods and format used in the textbook examples.

# CONTENTS

# Chapter 1 | Whole Numbers and Decimals

## 1.1 Whole Numbers

**1.** 7040
   seven thousand, forty

**3.** 37,901
   thirty-seven thousand, nine hundred one

**5.** 4,650,015
   four million, six hundred fifty thousand,
   fifteen

**7.** 2065 to the nearest ten is 2070.
   Draw a line under the tens digit.
   2065
   Since the digit to the right of that place is 5,
   increase the tens digit by 1. Change all digits
   to the right of the tens place to zero.

   2065 to the nearest hundred is 2100.
   Draw a line under the hundreds digit.
   2065
   Since the digit to the right of that place is 6,
   increase the hundreds digit by 1. Change all
   digits to the right of the hundreds place to
   zero.

   2065 to the nearest thousand is 2000.
   Draw a line under the thousands digit.
   2065
   Since the digit to the right of that place is 0,
   do not change the thousands digit. Change
   all digits to the right of the thousands place to
   zero.

**9.** 46,231 to the nearest ten is 46,230.
   Draw a line under the tens digit.
   46,231
   Since the digit to the right of that place is 1,
   do not change the tens digit. Change all
   digits to the right of the tens place to zero.

   46,231 to the nearest hundred is 46,200.
   Draw a line under the hundreds digit.
   46,231
   Since the digit to the right of that place is 3,
   do not change the hundreds digit. Change all
   digits to the right of the hundreds place to
   zero.

   46,231 to the nearest thousand is 46,000.

**9. (continued)**
   Draw a line under the thousands digit.
   46,231
   Since the digit to the right of that place is 2,
   do not change the thousands digit. Change
   all digits to the right of the thousands place to
   zero.

**11.** 106,054 to the nearest ten is 106,050.
   Draw a line under the tens digit.
   106,054
   Since the digit to the right of that place is 4,
   do not change the tens digit. Change all
   digits to the right of the tens place to zero.

   106,054 to the nearest hundred is 106,100.
   Draw a line under the hundreds digit.
   106,054
   Since the digit to the right of that place is 5,
   increase the hundreds digit by 1. Change all
   digits to the right of the hundreds place to
   zero.

   106,054 to the nearest thousand is 106,000.
   Draw a line under the thousands digit.
   106,054
   Since the digit to the right of that place is 0,
   do not change the thousands digit. Change
   all digits to the right of the thousands place to
   zero.

**13.** Answers will vary.

**15.**
$$\begin{array}{r} 75 \\ 63 \\ 45 \\ + 27 \\ \hline 210 \end{array}$$

**17.**
$$\begin{array}{r} 875 \\ 364 \\ 171 \\ + 776 \\ \hline 2186 \end{array}$$

**19.**
$$\begin{array}{r} 750 \\ 91 \\ 8 \\ 540 \\ + 7 \\ \hline 1396 \end{array}$$

**21.**     311,479
               77,631
          + 594,383
          ─────────
             983,493

**23.**     896
          − 228
          ─────
            668

**25.**   3715
        −  838
        ──────
          2877

**27.**    65,198
         − 43,652
         ────────
           21,546

**29.**  7,025,389
        −  936,490
        ──────────
          6,088,899

**31.** Adding across the rows, we get the following.

|  |  |
|---|---|
| $49,802 | $86,154 |
| $36,911 | $72,908 |
| $47,851 | $31,552 |
| $54,732 | $74,944 |
| $29,852 | $85,532 |
| + $74,119 | + $36,705 |
| $293,267 | $387,795 |

|  |  |
|---|---|
| $59,854 | $73,951 |
| $85,119 | $72,564 |
| $87,914 | $39,615 |
| $45,812 | $71,099 |
| $56,314 | $72,918 |
| + $91,856 | + $42,953 |
| $426,869 | $373,100 |

$293,267 + $387,795 + $426,869 + $373,100$
$= $1,481,031$

Adding down the columns, we get the following.

|  |  |
|---|---|
| $49,802 | $36,911 |
| $86,154 | $72,908 |
| $59,854 | $85,119 |
| + $73,951 | + $72,564 |
| $269,761 | $267,502 |

|  |  |
|---|---|
| $47,851 | $54,732 |
| $31,552 | $74,944 |
| $87,914 | $45,812 |
| + $39,615 | + $71,099 |
| $206,932 | $246,587 |

**31. (continued)**

|  |  |
|---|---|
| $29,852 | $74,119 |
| $85,532 | $36,705 |
| $56,314 | $91,856 |
| + $72,918 | + $42,953 |
| $244,616 | $245,633 |

$269,761 + $267,502 + $206,932$
$+ $246,587 + $244,616 + $245,633$
$= $1,481,031$

**33.**   218
        × 43
        ─────
         654
        872
        ─────
        9374

**35.**    1896
         ×   62
         ──────
          3792
        11376
        ───────
        117,552

**37.**     6452
          ×  263
          ───────
          19356
         38712
        12904
        ─────────
        1,696,876

**39.**    1109
         × 7311
         ──────
          1109
         1109
         3327
        7763
        ─────────
        8,107,899

**41.**
| Estimate | | Exact |
|---|---|---|
| 8000 | ⟵ | 8215 |
| 60 | ⟵ | 56 |
| 700 | ⟵ | 729 |
| + 4000 | ⟵ | + 3605 |
| 12,760 | | 12,605 |

**43.**
| Estimate | | Exact |
|---|---|---|
| 800 | ⟵ | 783 |
| − 200 | ⟵ | − 238 |
| 600 | | 545 |

**45.**
| Estimate | | Exact |
|---|---|---|
| 600 | ⟵ | 638 |
| × 50 | ⟵ | × 47 |
| 30,000 | | 29,986 |

**47.**
$$\begin{array}{r} 370 \\ \times\,180 \\ \hline \end{array} \qquad \begin{array}{r} 37 \\ \times\,18 \\ \hline 666 \ +\,2\ \text{zeros} \end{array}$$

66,600

**49.**
$$\begin{array}{r} 3760 \\ \times\,6000 \\ \hline \end{array} \qquad \begin{array}{r} 376 \\ \times\,\ \ 6 \\ \hline 2256 \ +\,4\ \text{zeros} \end{array}$$

22,560,000

**51.**
$$\begin{array}{r} 1241\frac{1}{4} \\ 4\overline{)4965} \\ \underline{4} \\ 09 \\ \underline{8} \\ 16 \\ \underline{16} \\ 05 \\ \underline{4} \\ 1 \end{array}$$

**53.**
$$\begin{array}{r} 458\frac{21}{43} \\ 43\overline{)19{,}715} \\ \underline{172} \\ 251 \\ \underline{215} \\ 365 \\ \underline{344} \\ 21 \end{array}$$

**55.** Answers will vary.

**57.**
$$180\overline{)429{,}350} \qquad \begin{array}{r} 2385\frac{5}{18} \\ 18\overline{)42{,}935} \\ \underline{36} \\ 69 \\ \underline{54} \\ 153 \\ \underline{144} \\ 95 \\ \underline{90} \\ 5 \end{array}$$

**59.**
$$1300\overline{)75{,}800} \qquad \begin{array}{r} 58\frac{4}{13} \\ 13\overline{)758} \\ \underline{65} \\ 108 \\ \underline{104} \\ 4 \end{array}$$

**61.** 24,375,300

twenty-four million, three hundred seventy-five thousand, three hundred

**63.** 3,200,000

three million, two hundred thousand

**65.** eight hundred fifty-four thousand, seven hundred ninety-five boxes

854,795 boxes

**67.** fifty-five million, five hundred seventy-two thousand, six hundred thirty-three meals

55,572,633 meals

**69.**
$$\begin{array}{r} 5000 \\ \times\ 40 \\ \hline \end{array} \qquad \begin{array}{r} 5 \\ \times\,4 \\ \hline 20 \ +\,4\ \text{zeros} \end{array}$$

There are 200,000 chips in 40 pounds.

**71.** $900 + 400 + 500 + 200 = 2000$

$2000 \div 4 = 500$

Jim restocks 500 items per hour.

**73.** A total of $6 + 15 + 10 + 5 = 36$ rafts were rented.

$$\begin{aligned} 6\times\$50 &= \$300 \\ 15\times\$72 &= \$1080 \\ 10\times\$128 &= \$1280 \\ 5\times\$143 &= \$715 \\ 36\times\$3 &= \$108 \end{aligned}$$

$\$300 + \$1080 + \$1280 + \$715 + \$108$
$= \$3483$

Total receipts were \$3483.

**75.** $3433 + 2060 + 1040 = 6533$

Combined milk production was 6533 million pounds or 6,533,000,000 pounds.

**77.** $3433 - 662 = 2771$

2771 million pounds or 2,771,000,000 pounds more milk were produced in California than in Michigan.

**79.** $6.5 \times 1000 = 6500$

There are 6500 Family Dollar retail stores.

**81.** $8.5 \times 1000 = 8500$

Dollar General has the greatest number of retail stores.

**83.** $8.5 \times 1000 = 8500$ Dollar General stores
$6 \times 1000 = 6000$ Walgreens stores

$8500 - 6000 = 2500$

Dollar General has 2500 more retail stores than Walgreens.

## 1.2   Application Problems

**1.** $602 + 935 + 1328 + 757 + 1586 = 5208$
Subway sold 5208 sandwiches.

**3.** $3020 - 2920 = 100$
100 billion fewer miles were driven.

**5.** $1050 \times 365 = 383,250$
383,250 World War II veterans are projected to die in the next year.

**7.** $8375 - 762 = 7613$
$7613 + 976 = 8589$
The weight of the boat is 8589 pounds.

**9.** $\$499 - \$435 = \$64$
The decrease in price was \$64.

**11.** $43,560 \times 140 = 6,098,400$
There are 6,098,400 square feet in 140 acres.

**13.** $\$99 - \$45 = \$54$
$7 \times \$54 = \$378$
The amount saved is \$378.

**15.** $6 \times \$1256 = \$\ \ 7,536$
$15 \times \$895 = \underline{\$13,425}$
$\text{Total} = \overline{\$20,961}$
The total cost is \$20,961.

**17.** $\$7588 - \$838 = \$6750$
\$6750 was raised.

$\$6750 \div 18 = \$375$
Each team received \$375.

**19.** $30 \times 25 = 750$
$1250 - 750 = 500$
There are 500 balcony seats

$500 \div 25 = 20$
There must be 20 seats in each row.

## 1.3   Basics of Decimals

**1.** .38
thirty-eight hundredths

**3.** 5.61
five and sixty-one hundredths

**5.** 7.408
seven and four hundred eight thousandths

**7.** 37.593
thirty-seven and five hundred ninety-three thousandths

**9.** 4.0062
four and sixty-two ten-thousandths

**11.** Answers will vary.

**13.** four hundred thirty-eight and four tenths
438.4

**15.** ninety-seven and sixty-two hundredths
97.62

**17.** one and five hundred seventy-three ten-thousandths
1.0573

**19.** three and five thousand eight hundred twenty-seven ten-thousandths
3.5827

**21.** $\$11.99 \div 2 = \$5.995 \approx \$6.00$
Zagorin pays \$6.00 for one pie.

**23.** $\$1.75 \div 3 \approx \$.58333 \approx \$.58$
Zagorin pays \$.58 for one package.

**25.** $\$3.50 \div 3 \approx \$1.1666 \approx \$1.17$
Zagorin pays \$1.17 for one bottle.

**27.** 3.5218 to the nearest tenth is 3.5.
Locate the tenths digit and draw a line.
3.5|218

Since the digit to the right of the line is 2,
leave the tenths digit alone.

3.5218 to the nearest hundredth is 3.52.
Locate the hundredths digit and draw a line.
3.52|18

Since the digit to the right of the line is 1,
leave the hundredths digit alone.

3.5218 to the nearest thousandth is 3.522.
Locate the hundredths digit and draw a line.
3.512|8

Since the digit to the right of the line is 8,
increase the thousandths digit by 1.

**29.** 2.54836 to the nearest tenth is 2.5.
Locate the tenths digit and draw a line.
2.5|4836

Since the digit to the right of the line is 4,
leave the tenths digit alone.

2.54836 to the nearest hundredth is 2.55.
Locate the hundredths digit and draw a line.
2.54|836

Since the digit to the right of the line is 8,
increase the hundredths digit by 1.

2.54836 to the nearest thousandth is 2.548.
Locate the thousandths digit and draw a line.
2.548|36

Since the digit to the right of the line is 3,
leave the thousandths digit alone.

**31.** 27.32451 to the nearest tenth is 27.3.
Locate the tenths digit and draw a line.
27.3|2451

Since the digit to the right of the line is 2,
leave the tenths digit alone.

27.32451 to the nearest hundredth is 27.32.
Locate the hundredths digit and draw a line.
27.32|451

Since the digit to the right of the line is 4,
leave the hundredths digit alone.

27.32451 to the nearest thousandths is
27.325.
Locate the thousandths digit and draw a line.
27.324|51

Since the digit to the right of the line is 5,
increase the thousandths digit by 1.

**33.** 36.47249 to the nearest tenth is 36.5.
Locate the tenths digit and draw a line.
36.4|7249

Since the digit to the right of the line is 7,
increase the tenths digit by 1.

36.47249 to the nearest hundredth is 36.47.
Locate the hundredths digit and draw a line.
36.47|249

Since the digit to the right of the line is 2,
leave the hundredths digit alone.

36.47249 to the nearest thousandths is
36.472.
Locate the thousandths digit and draw a line.
36.472|49

Since the digit to the right of the line is 4,
leave the thousandths digit alone.

**35.** .0562 to the nearest tenth is .1.
Locate the tenths digit and draw a line.
.0|562

Since the digit to the right of the line is 5,
increase the tenths digit by 1.

.0562 to the nearest hundredth is .06.
Locate the hundredths digit and draw a line.
.05|62

Since the digit to the right of the line is 6,
increase the hundredths digit by 1.

.0562 to the nearest thousandths is .056.
Locate the thousandths digit and draw a line.
.056|2

Since the digit to the right of the line is 2,
leave the thousandths digit alone.

**37.** $5.056 ≈ $5.06
Locate the digit representing the cent and
draw a vertical line.
$5.05|6

Since the digit to the right of the line is 6,
increase the cent digit by 1.

**39.** $32.493 ≈ $32.49
Locate the digit representing the cent and
draw a vertical line.
$32.49|3

Since the digit to the right of the line is 3,
leave the cent digit alone.

**41.** $382.005 ≈ $382.01

Locate the digit representing the cent and draw a vertical line.

$382.00|5

Since the digit to the right of the line is 5, increase the cent digit by 1.

**43.** $42.137 ≈ $42.14

Locate the digit representing the cent and draw a vertical line.

$42.13|7

Since the digit to the right of the line is 7, increase the cent digit by 1.

**45.** $.0015 ≈ $.00

Locate the digit representing the cent and draw a vertical line.

$.00|15

Since the digit to the right of the line is 1, leave the cent digit alone.

**47.** $1.5002 ≈ $1.50

Locate the digit representing the cent and draw a vertical line.

$1.50|02

Since the digit to the right of the line is 0, leave the cent digit alone.

**49.** $1.995 ≈ $2.00

Locate the digit representing the cent and draw a vertical line.

$1.99|5

Since the digit to the right of the line is 5, increase the cent digit by 1.

**51.** $752.798 ≈ $752.80

Locate the digit representing the cent and draw a vertical line.

$752.79|8

Since the digit to the right of the line is 8, increase the cent digit by 1.

**53.** $26.49 ≈ $26

Locate the digit representing the dollar and draw a vertical line.

$26.|49

Since the digit to the right of the line is 4, leave the dollar digit alone.

**55.** $.49 ≈ $0

Locate the digit representing the dollar and draw a vertical line.

$.|49

Since the digit to the right of the line is 4, leave the dollar digit alone.

**57.** $12,836.38 ≈ $12,836

Locate the digit representing the dollar and draw a vertical line.

$12,836.|38

Since the digit to the right of the line is 3, leave the dollar digit alone.

**59.** $395.18 ≈ $395

Locate the digit representing the dollar and draw a vertical line.

$395.|18

Since the digit to the right of the line is 1, leave the dollar digit alone.

**61.** $4699.62 ≈ $4700

Locate the digit representing the dollar and draw a vertical line.

$4699.|62

Since the digit to the right of the line is 6, increase the dollar digit by 1. $4699 increased by 1 is $4700.

**63.** $378.59 ≈ $379

Locate the digit representing the dollar and draw a vertical line.

$378.|59

Since the digit to the right of the line is 5, increase the dollar digit by 1.

**65.** $722.38 ≈ $722

Locate the digit representing the dollar and draw a vertical line.

$722.|38

Since the digit to the right of the line is 3, leave the dollar digit alone.

**67.** Answers will vary.

## 1.4 Addition and Subtraction of Decimals

**1.** Estimate    Exact

| 40 | ⟵ | 43.36 |
|---|---|---|
| 20 | ⟵ | 15.8 |
| + 9 | ⟵ | + 9.3 |
| 69 | | 68.46 |

**3.** Estimate    Exact

| 6 | ⟵ | 6.23 |
|---|---|---|
| 4 | ⟵ | 3.6 |
| 5 | ⟵ | 5.1 |
| 7 | ⟵ | 7.2 |
| + 2 | ⟵ | + 1.69 |
| 24 | | 23.82 |

**5.** Estimate    Exact

| 2000 | ⟵ | 2156.38 |
|---|---|---|
| 5 | ⟵ | 5.26 |
| 3 | ⟵ | 2.791 |
| + 7 | ⟵ | + 6.983 |
| 2015 | | 2171.414 |

**7.** Estimate    Exact

| 6000 | ⟵ | 6133.78 |
|---|---|---|
| 500 | ⟵ | 506.124 |
| 20 | ⟵ | 18.63 |
| + 8 | ⟵ | + 7.527 |
| 6528 | | 6666.061 |

**9.** Estimate    Exact

| 2000 | ⟵ | 1798.419 |
|---|---|---|
| 70 | ⟵ | 68.32 |
| 500 | ⟵ | 512.807 |
| 600 | ⟵ | 643.9 |
| + 400 | ⟵ | + 428. |
| 3570 | | 3451.446 |

**11.**

| 12.15 |
|---|
| 6.83 |
| 61.75 |
| 19.218 |
| + 73.325 |
| 173.273 |

**13.**

| 27.653 |
|---|
| 18.7142 |
| 9.7496 |
| + 3.21 |
| 59.3268 |

**15.** Answers will vary.

**17.** $1815.79 + $2367.34 + $1976.22 + $2155.81 + $1698.14 + 2885.26 + $2239.63 = $15,138.19

The total weekly sales are $15,138.19.

**19.** $6.71 − $1.39 = $5.32

The price of T-bone steak is $5.32 per pound more than turkey.

**21.** Estimate    Problem

| 20 | ⟵ | 19.74 |
|---|---|---|
| − 7 | ⟵ | − 6.58 |
| 13 | | 13.16 |

**23.** Estimate    Problem

| 50 | ⟵ | 51.215 |
|---|---|---|
| − 20 | ⟵ | − 19.708 |
| 30 | | 31.507 |

**25.** Estimate    Problem

| 300 | ⟵ | 325.053 |
|---|---|---|
| − 90 | ⟵ | − 85.019 |
| 210 | | 240.034 |

**27.** Estimate    Problem

| 8 | ⟵ | 7.8 |
|---|---|---|
| − 3 | ⟵ | − 2.952 |
| 5 | | 4.848 |

**29.** Estimate    Problem

| 5 | ⟵ | 5 |
|---|---|---|
| − 2 | ⟵ | − 1.9802 |
| 3 | | 3.0198 |

**31.** $27,282.75 + $4280.83 + $12,252.23 = $43,815.81

Edwards paid out $43,815.81.

## 1.5 Multiplication and Division of Decimals

**1.**

| Estimate | Problem |
|---|---|
| 100 ⟵ | 96.8 |
| × 4 ⟵ | × 4.2 |
| 400 | 406.56 |

**3.**

| Estimate | Problem |
|---|---|
| 30 ⟵ | 34.1 |
| × 7 ⟵ | × 6.8 |
| 210 | 231.88 |

**5.**

| Estimate | Problem |
|---|---|
| 40 ⟵ | 43.8 |
| × 2 ⟵ | × 2.04 |
| 80 | 89.352 |

**7.**

```
  .532   ⟵  3 decimals
× 3.6    ⟵  1 decimal
 3192
1596
1.9152   ⟵  4 decimals
```

**9.**

```
  21.7   ⟵  1 decimal
× .431   ⟵  3 decimals
  217
 651
868
9.3527   ⟵  4 decimals
```

**11.**

```
  .0408  ⟵  4 decimal
×  .06   ⟵  2 decimals
 2448
    0
.002448  ⟵  6 decimals
```

**13.** $18.5 \times \$8.25 = \$152.63$

**15.**

$27.9 \times \$11.42 = \$318.62$
$6.8 \times \$14.63 = \quad\$99.48$
$\qquad\qquad\qquad\quad \$418.10$

**17.**

```
        8.075
  6 )48.450
     48
     04
      0
      45
      42
       30
       30
        0
```

**19.**

```
      27.442
 15 )411.630
     30
     111
     105
      66
      60
       63
       60
        30
        30
         0
```

**21.**

```
 .65 )37.6852          57.9772
                   65 )3768.5200
 = 57.977 (rounded)    325
                       518
                       455
                       635
                       585
                       502
                       455
                       470
                       455
                       150
                       130
                        20
```

**23.** Answers will vary.

**25.** $\$246,500 \times .06 = \$14,790$

The amount of the commission was $14,790.

**27.** $519 \div 10.2 = 50.9$

The Prius got 50.9 mpg.

**29.** $\$2872.26 \div \$106.38 = 27$

It will take 27 months to pay off the balance.

**31. (a)** $.0043 \times 100 = .43$

The pile is .43 inch high.

**(b)** $.0043 \times 1000 = 4.3$

The pile is 4.3 inches high.

**33.** A total of $4 + 2 = 6$ shirts were ordered.

$4 \times \$18.95 = \$75.80$
$2 \times \$16.75 = \$33.50$
$\quad 6 \times \$2 = \$12$

$\$75.80 + \$33.50 + \$12 = \$121.30$ total price

Total price + shipping

$= \$121.30 + \$7.95 = \$129.25$
The total cost is $129.95.

**35. (a)** Add to find the total for the shirts, monograms, and gift box.

$3 \times \$14.75 = \$44.25$

$\$44.25 + \$4.95 + \$4.95 + \$4.95 + \$5$

$= \$64.10$

Total price + shipping

$= \$64.10 + \$5.95 = \$70.05$

The total cost is $70.05.

**(b)** Monogram + gift box + shipping

$= \$4.95 + \$4.95 + \$4.95 + \$5 + \$5.95$

$= \$25.80$

The monogram, gift box, and shipping added $25.80 to the cost.

## Case Study

**1.** $\$14,067 + \$3662 + \$2587 + \$2507$
$+ \$2051 + \$1955 + \$1113 + \$946$
$+ \$871 + \$407 = \$30,166$

The total is $30,166.

**2.** $\$30,166 - \$24,168 = \$5988$

A wedding in 2010 is $5988 more expensive than a wedding in 2005.

**3.** $\$6000 \div \$37 \approx 162$

You can invite 162 guests.

$\$37 \times 162 = \$5994$

$\$6000 - \$5994 = \$6$

$6 of your budgeted amount will be left over.

**4.** $\$11,000 \div 150 \approx \$73.333 \approx \$73.33$

$73.33 can be spent per person.

**5.** $\left(5 \times \$36.25\right) + \left(5 \times \$7.50\right) = \$218.75$

$\$863 - \$218.75 = \$644.25$

$644.25 remains to be spent for other floral arrangements.

## Case in Point Summary Exercise

**1.** $\$486.12 + \$1236.14 + \$364.76 + \$103.75$
$= \$2190.77$

The total is $2190.77.

**2.** $3.5 + 4.5 + 6 + \$5.5 = 19.5$

The total number of hours worked is 19.5.

$19.5 + \$8.65 = \$168.68$

The pay for the week is $168.68.

**3.** $\$2065.48 - \$1864.92 = \$200.56$

The difference between the two is $200.56.

$\$200.56 \div \$.94 \approx 213$

There are approximately 213 additional customers.

**4.** $\$168.32 \times 4 = \$673.28$

The amount spent on advertising is $673.28.

$\$10,984.76 \times 1.3 = \$14,280.19$

The revenue is approximately $14,280.19.

## Chapter 1   Test

**1.** 844 to the nearest ten is 840.
Draw a line under the tens digit.

8<u>4</u>4

Since the digit to the right of that place is 4, do not change the tens digit. Change all digits to the right of the tens place to zero.

**2.** 21,958 to the nearest hundred is 22,000.
Draw a line under the hundreds digit.

21,<u>9</u>58

Since the digit to the right of that place is 5, increase the hundreds digit by 1, which increases the thousands digit by 1. Change all digits to the right of the thousands place to zero.

**3.** 671,529 to the nearest thousand is 672,000.
Draw a line under the thousands digit.

671,<u>1</u>529

Since the digit to the right of that place is 5, increase the thousands digit by 1. Change all digits to the right of the thousands place to zero.

**4.** $50,987 \approx 50,000$

Round the first digit and change all other digits to zero.

**5.** $851,004 \approx 900,000$

Round the first digit and change all other digits to zero.

**6.** $\$124 + \$88 + \$62 + \$137 + \$195 = \$606$

Katie's total amount of commissions is $606.

**7.** $(3 \times \$1540) + (5 \times \$695) + (8 \times \$38)$
$= \$4620 + \$3475 + \$304 = \$8399$

The total cost of the equipment is **$8399.**

**8.** $\$21.0568 \approx \$21.06$

Locate the digit representing the cent and draw a vertical line.

$$\$21.05|68$$

Since the digit to the right of the line is 6, increase the cent digit by 1.

**9.** $\$364.345 \approx \$364.35$

Locate the digit representing the cent and draw a vertical line.

$$\$364.34|5$$

Since the digit to the right of the line is 5, increase the cent digit by 1.

**10.** $\$7246.49 \approx \$7246$

Locate the digit representing the dollar and draw a vertical line.

$$\$7246.|49$$

Since the digit to the right of the line is 4, leave the dollar digit alone.

**11.** $9.6 + 8.42 + 3.715 + 159.8 = 181.535$

**12.**
$$\begin{array}{r} 2.715 \\ 32.78 \\ 426.3 \\ +\ 37 \\ \hline 498.795 \end{array}$$

**13.**
$$\begin{array}{r} 341.4 \\ -\ 207.8 \\ \hline 133.6 \end{array}$$

**14.**
$$\begin{array}{r} 3.8 \\ -\ .0053 \\ \hline 3.7947 \end{array}$$

**15.**
$$\begin{array}{r} 21.98 \\ \times\ .72 \\ \hline 4396 \\ 15386 \\ \hline 15.8256 \end{array}$$
21.98 ⟵ 2 decimals
×.72 ⟵ 2 decimals
15.8256 ⟵ 4 decimals

**16.**
$$\begin{array}{r} 218.6 \\ \times .037 \\ \hline 15302 \\ 6558 \\ \hline 8.0882 \end{array}$$
218.6 ⟵ 1 decimal
×.037 ⟵ 3 decimals
8.0882 ⟵ 4 decimals

**17.** $21.8\overline{)252.008}$
$$\begin{array}{r} 11.56 \\ 218.\overline{)2520.08} \\ \underline{218} \\ 340 \\ \underline{218} \\ 1220 \\ 1090 \\ \hline 1308 \\ \underline{1308} \\ 0 \end{array}$$

**18.** $2.41\overline{)57.358}$
$$\begin{array}{r} 23.8 \\ 241.\overline{)5735.8} \\ \underline{482} \\ 915 \\ \underline{723} \\ 1928 \\ \underline{1928} \\ 0 \end{array}$$

**19.** $18.62\overline{)79.135}$
$$\begin{array}{r} 4.25 \\ 1862.\overline{)7913.50} \\ \underline{7448} \\ 4655 \\ \underline{3724} \\ 9310 \\ \underline{9310} \\ 0 \end{array}$$

**20.** $(24.8 \times \$1.89) + (38.2 \times \$2.05)$
$= \$125.182 \approx \$125.18$

The total cost is $125.18.

**21.** $\$84.52 + \$55.75 + \$9.65 = \$149.92$
The cost per square is $149.92.

$\$149.92 \times 26.3 = \$3942.896 \approx \$3942.90$
The total cost is $3942.90.

**22.** $3.4 - 1.6 = 1.8$
1.8 gallons are saved per flush.

$1.8 \times 22 \times 365 = 14,454$
14,454 gallons are saved in one year.

**23.** $(135.5 \times \$.86) + (12 \times \$2.18) = \$142.69$

The total cost was \$142.69.

$(8 \times \$20) - \$142.69 = \$17.31$

Steve received \$17.31 change.

**24.** $\$1.74 \div 2.2 = \$.7909 \approx \$.79$

The price of bananas is \$.79 per pound.

**25.** $14.674 \div .058 = 253$

253 seedlings can be fertilized.

# Chapter 2 | Fractions

## 2.1 Basics of Fractions

**1.** $3\dfrac{5}{8} = \dfrac{(8\times 3)+5}{8} = \dfrac{29}{8}$

**3.** $4\dfrac{1}{4} = \dfrac{(4\times 4)+1}{4} = \dfrac{17}{4}$

**5.** $12\dfrac{2}{3} = \dfrac{(3\times 12)+2}{3} = \dfrac{38}{3}$

**7.** $22\dfrac{7}{8} = \dfrac{(8\times 22)+7}{8} = \dfrac{183}{8}$

**9.** $7\dfrac{6}{7} = \dfrac{(7\times 7)+6}{7} = \dfrac{55}{7}$

**11.** $15\dfrac{19}{23} = \dfrac{(23\times 15)+19}{23} = \dfrac{364}{23}$

**13.** $4\overline{)13}$   $\dfrac{12}{1}$    $\dfrac{13}{4} = 3\dfrac{1}{4}$

**15.** $3\overline{)8}$   $\dfrac{6}{2}$    $\dfrac{8}{3} = 2\dfrac{2}{3}$

**17.** $10\overline{)38}$   $\dfrac{30}{8}$    $\dfrac{38}{10} = 3\dfrac{8}{10} = 3\dfrac{4}{5}$

**19.** $11\overline{)40}$   $\dfrac{33}{7}$    $\dfrac{40}{11} = 3\dfrac{7}{11}$

**21.** $63\overline{)125}$   $\dfrac{63}{62}$    $\dfrac{125}{63} = 1\dfrac{62}{63}$

**23.** $25\overline{)183}$   $\dfrac{175}{8}$    $\dfrac{183}{25} = 7\dfrac{8}{25}$

**25.** Answers will vary.

**27.** $\dfrac{8}{16} = \dfrac{8\div 8}{16\div 2} = \dfrac{1}{2}$

**29.** $\dfrac{25}{40} = \dfrac{25\div 5}{40\div 5} = \dfrac{5}{8}$

**31.** $\dfrac{27}{45} = \dfrac{27\div 9}{45\div 9} = \dfrac{3}{5}$

**33.** $\dfrac{165}{180} = \dfrac{165\div 15}{180\div 15} = \dfrac{11}{12}$

**35.** $\dfrac{24}{24} = \dfrac{24\div 24}{24\div 24} = 1$

24 Kt. gold is pure gold.

**37.** $\dfrac{14}{24} = \dfrac{14\div 2}{24\div 2} = \dfrac{7}{12}$

14 Kt. gold is $\dfrac{7}{12}$ gold.

**39.** Answers will vary.

**41.** 32 is divisible by 2 since the last digit is an even number.

32 is not divisible by 3 since $3+2=5$ is not divisible by 3.

32 is divisible by 4 since $32\div 4 = 8$.

32 is not divisible by 5 since the last digit is not 0 or 5.

32 is not divisible by 6 since $3+2=5$ is not divisible by 3.

32 is divisible by 8 since $32\div 8 = 4$.

32 is not divisible by 9 since $3+2=5$ is not divisible by 9.

32 is not divisible by 10 since the last digit is not 0.

**43.** 60 is divisible by 2 since the last digit is an even number.
60 is divisible by 3 since $6+0=6$ is divisible by 3.
60 is divisible by 4 since $60 \div 4 = 15$.
60 is divisible by 5 since the last digit is 0.
60 is divisible by 6 since 60 is even and since $6+0=6$ is divisible by 3.
60 is not divisible by 8 since $60 \div 8 \neq$ integer.
60 is not divisible by 9 since $6+0=6$ is not divisible by 9.
60 is divisible by 10 since the last digit is 0.

**45.** 90 is divisible by 2 since the last digit is an even number.
90 is divisible by 3 since $9+0=9$ is divisible by 3.
90 is not divisible by 4 since $90 \div 4 \neq$ integer.
90 is divisible by 5 since the last digit is 0.
90 is divisible by 6 since 90 is even and since $9+0=9$ is divisible by 3.
90 is not divisible by 8 since $90 \div 8 \neq$ integer.
90 is divisible by 9 since $9+0=9$ is divisible by 9.
90 is divisible by 10 since the last digit is 0.

**47.** 4172 is divisible by 2 since the last digit is an even number.
4172 is not divisible by 3 since $4+1+7+2=14$ is not divisible by 3.
4172 is divisible by 4 since 72 is divisible by 4.
4172 is not divisible by 5 since the last digit is not 0 or 5.
4172 is not divisible by 6 since $4+1+7+2=14$ is not divisible by 3.
4172 is not divisible by 8 since $172 \div 8 \neq$ integer.
4172 is not divisible by 9 since $4+1+7+2=14$ is not divisible by 9.
4172 is not divisible by 10 since the last digit is not 0.

## 2.2   Addition and Subtraction of Fractions

**1.** $\dfrac{4}{5} = \dfrac{}{20}$
$20 \div 5 = 4$
$4 \times 4 = 16$
$\dfrac{4}{5} = \dfrac{16}{20}$

**3.** $\dfrac{9}{10} = \dfrac{}{40}$
$40 \div 10 = 4$
$4 \times 9 = 36$
$\dfrac{9}{10} = \dfrac{36}{40}$

**5.** $\dfrac{6}{5} = \dfrac{}{40}$
$40 \div 5 = 8$
$8 \times 6 = 48$
$\dfrac{6}{5} = \dfrac{48}{40}$

**7.** $\dfrac{6}{7} = \dfrac{}{49}$
$49 \div 7 = 7$
$7 \times 6 = 42$
$\dfrac{6}{7} = \dfrac{42}{49}$

**9.** 3, 8, ____

$$
\begin{array}{r}
1\ \ 1 \\
3\,\overline{)3\ \ 1} \\
2\,\overline{)3\ \ 2} \\
2\,\overline{)3\ \ 4} \\
2\,\overline{)3\ \ 8} \\
\end{array}
$$
$2 \times 2 \times 2 \times 3 = 24$

**11.** 12, 18, 20, ____

$$
\begin{array}{r}
1\ \ \ 1\ \ \ 1 \\
5\,\overline{)1\ \ \ 1\ \ \ 5} \\
3\,\overline{)1\ \ \ 3\ \ \ 5} \\
3\,\overline{)3\ \ \ 9\ \ \ 5} \\
2\,\overline{)6\ \ \ 9\ \ \ 10} \\
2\,\overline{)12\ \ 18\ \ 20} \\
\end{array}
$$
$2 \times 2 \times 3 \times 3 \times 5 = 180$

**13.** 15, 24, 32, ___

$$
\begin{array}{r}
\phantom{2)}\;\;1\;\;\;1\;\;\;1 \\
5\overline{)\;5\;\;\;1\;\;\;1} \\
3\overline{)\;15\;\;\;3\;\;\;1} \\
2\overline{)\;15\;\;\;3\;\;\;2} \\
2\overline{)\;15\;\;\;3\;\;\;4} \\
2\overline{)\;15\;\;\;6\;\;\;8} \\
2\overline{)\;15\;\;12\;\;16} \\
2\overline{)\;15\;\;24\;\;32}
\end{array}
$$

$2\times2\times2\times2\times2\times3\times5=480$

**15.** 10, 35, 50, 60, ___

$$
\begin{array}{r}
\phantom{2)}\;\;1\;\;\;\;1\;\;\;\;1\;\;\;\;1 \\
7\overline{)\;1\;\;\;\;7\;\;\;\;1\;\;\;\;1} \\
5\overline{)\;1\;\;\;\;7\;\;\;\;5\;\;\;\;1} \\
5\overline{)\;5\;\;\;35\;\;25\;\;\;5} \\
3\overline{)\;5\;\;\;35\;\;25\;\;15} \\
2\overline{)\;5\;\;\;35\;\;25\;\;30} \\
2\overline{)\;10\;\;35\;\;50\;\;60}
\end{array}
$$

$2\times2\times3\times5\times5\times7=2100$

**17.** 3, 5, 8, 12, 18, ___

$$
\begin{array}{r}
\phantom{2)}\;\;1\;\;1\;\;1\;\;\;1\;\;\;1 \\
5\overline{)\;1\;\;5\;\;1\;\;\;1\;\;\;1} \\
3\overline{)\;1\;\;5\;\;1\;\;\;1\;\;\;3} \\
3\overline{)\;3\;\;5\;\;1\;\;\;3\;\;\;9} \\
2\overline{)\;3\;\;5\;\;2\;\;\;3\;\;\;9} \\
2\overline{)\;3\;\;5\;\;4\;\;\;6\;\;\;9} \\
2\overline{)\;3\;\;5\;\;8\;\;12\;\;18}
\end{array}
$$

$2\times2\times2\times3\times3\times5=360$

**19.** Answers will vary.

**21.** $\dfrac{2}{9}+\dfrac{4}{9}=\dfrac{2+4}{9}=\dfrac{6}{9}=\dfrac{2}{3}$

**23.** $\dfrac{11}{12}-\dfrac{5}{12}=\dfrac{11-5}{12}=\dfrac{6}{12}=\dfrac{1}{2}$

**25.** $\dfrac{5}{12}-\dfrac{1}{16}=\dfrac{20}{48}-\dfrac{3}{48}=\dfrac{17}{48}$

**27.** $\dfrac{3}{4}+\dfrac{5}{9}+\dfrac{1}{3}=\dfrac{27}{36}+\dfrac{20}{36}+\dfrac{12}{36}$

$=\dfrac{27+20+12}{36}=\dfrac{59}{36}=1\dfrac{23}{36}$

**29.** $\dfrac{3}{7}+\dfrac{2}{5}+\dfrac{1}{10}=\dfrac{30}{70}+\dfrac{28}{70}+\dfrac{7}{70}$

$=\dfrac{30+28+7}{70}=\dfrac{65}{70}=\dfrac{13}{14}$

**31.** $\dfrac{7}{10}+\dfrac{8}{15}+\dfrac{5}{6}=\dfrac{21}{30}+\dfrac{16}{30}+\dfrac{25}{30}$

$=\dfrac{21+16+25}{30}=\dfrac{62}{30}=2\dfrac{2}{30}=2\dfrac{1}{15}$

**33.**
$$
\begin{aligned}
\dfrac{3}{4}&=\dfrac{27}{36} \\
\dfrac{2}{3}&=\dfrac{24}{36} \\
+\dfrac{8}{9}&=\dfrac{32}{36} \\
\hline
&\;\dfrac{83}{36}=2\dfrac{11}{36}
\end{aligned}
$$

**35.**
$$
\begin{aligned}
\dfrac{8}{15}&=\dfrac{16}{30} \\
\dfrac{3}{10}&=\dfrac{9}{30} \\
+\dfrac{3}{5}&=\dfrac{18}{30} \\
\hline
&\;\dfrac{43}{30}=1\dfrac{13}{30}
\end{aligned}
$$

**37.**
$$
\begin{aligned}
\dfrac{7}{10}&=\dfrac{14}{20} \\
-\dfrac{1}{4}&=\dfrac{5}{20} \\
\hline
&\;\dfrac{9}{20}
\end{aligned}
$$

**39.**
$$
\begin{aligned}
\dfrac{5}{8}&=\dfrac{15}{24} \\
-\dfrac{1}{3}&=\dfrac{8}{24} \\
\hline
&\;\dfrac{7}{24}
\end{aligned}
$$

**41.** Answers will vary.

**43.** $\dfrac{1}{4}+\dfrac{3}{8}+\dfrac{1}{3}=\dfrac{6}{24}+\dfrac{9}{24}+\dfrac{8}{24}=\dfrac{23}{24}$

Zalia ordered $\dfrac{23}{24}$ cubic yards.

**45.** $\dfrac{1}{5}+\dfrac{1}{3}+\dfrac{1}{4}=\dfrac{12}{60}+\dfrac{20}{60}+\dfrac{15}{60}=\dfrac{47}{60}$

The total length of the bolt is $\dfrac{47}{60}$ inch.

**47.** $\dfrac{7}{8}-\dfrac{1}{4}-\dfrac{1}{3}=\dfrac{21}{24}-\dfrac{6}{24}-\dfrac{8}{24}=\dfrac{7}{24}$

$\dfrac{7}{24}$ of the contents remain.

**49.** $\dfrac{1}{8}+\dfrac{1}{3}+\dfrac{1}{4}+\dfrac{1}{12}=\dfrac{3}{24}+\dfrac{8}{24}+\dfrac{6}{24}+\dfrac{2}{24}=\dfrac{19}{24}$

$\dfrac{19}{24}$ of the debt was paid in four months.

**51.** $\dfrac{15}{16}-\dfrac{3}{8}-\dfrac{3}{8}=\dfrac{15}{16}-\dfrac{6}{16}-\dfrac{6}{16}=\dfrac{3}{16}$

The diameter of the hole is $\dfrac{3}{16}$ inch.

**53.** $\dfrac{1}{6}+\dfrac{1}{8}=\dfrac{4}{24}+\dfrac{3}{24}=\dfrac{7}{24}$

$\dfrac{7}{24}$ of the day was spent in class and study.

**55.** The greatest amount of time (the largest segment of the graph) was spent in work and travel.

$\dfrac{1}{3}+\dfrac{1}{6}=\dfrac{2}{6}+\dfrac{1}{6}=\dfrac{3}{6}=\dfrac{1}{2}$

$\dfrac{1}{2}$ of the day was spent in work and travel and in class time.

**57.** $\dfrac{3}{4}-\dfrac{1}{4}=\dfrac{2}{4}=\dfrac{1}{2}$

The difference in the width is $\dfrac{1}{2}$ inch.

**59.** $\dfrac{7}{8}-\dfrac{1}{4}-\dfrac{1}{6}-\dfrac{3}{8}$

$=\dfrac{21}{24}-\dfrac{6}{24}-\dfrac{4}{24}-\dfrac{9}{24}=\dfrac{2}{24}=\dfrac{1}{12}$

The length of the fourth side is $\dfrac{1}{12}$ mile.

## 2.3 Addition and Subtraction of Mixed Numbers

**1.**  $\begin{array}{r} 82\dfrac{3}{5} \\[2mm] +15\dfrac{1}{5} \\[2mm] \hline 97\dfrac{4}{5} \end{array}$

**3.**  $\begin{array}{r} 41\dfrac{1}{2}=41\dfrac{2}{4} \\[2mm] +39\dfrac{1}{4}=39\dfrac{1}{4} \\[2mm] \hline 80\dfrac{3}{4} \end{array}$

**5.**  $\begin{array}{r} 46\dfrac{3}{4}=46\dfrac{30}{40} \\[2mm] 12\dfrac{5}{8}=12\dfrac{25}{40} \\[2mm] +37\dfrac{4}{5}=37\dfrac{32}{40} \\[2mm] \hline 95\dfrac{87}{40}=95+2\dfrac{7}{40}=97\dfrac{7}{40} \end{array}$

**7.**  $\begin{array}{r} 32\dfrac{3}{4}=32\dfrac{18}{24} \\[2mm] 6\dfrac{1}{3}=6\dfrac{8}{24} \\[2mm] +14\dfrac{5}{8}=14\dfrac{15}{24} \\[2mm] \hline 52\dfrac{41}{24}=52+1\dfrac{17}{24}=53\dfrac{17}{24} \end{array}$

**9.**  $\begin{array}{r} 46\dfrac{5}{8}=46\dfrac{75}{120} \\[2mm] 21\dfrac{1}{6}=21\dfrac{20}{120} \\[2mm] +38\dfrac{1}{10}=38\dfrac{12}{120} \\[2mm] \hline 105\dfrac{107}{120} \end{array}$

**11.** 
$$25\frac{13}{24} = 25\frac{13}{24}$$
$$-18\frac{5}{12} = 18\frac{10}{24}$$
$$7\frac{3}{24} = 7\frac{1}{8}$$

**13.** 
$$374 = 373\frac{6}{6}$$
$$-211\frac{5}{6} = 211\frac{5}{6}$$
$$162\frac{1}{6}$$

**15.** 
$$71\frac{3}{8} = 71\frac{9}{24}$$
$$-62\frac{1}{3} = 62\frac{8}{24}$$
$$9\frac{1}{24}$$

**17.** 
$$72\frac{3}{10} = 72\frac{9}{30} = 71\frac{39}{30}$$
$$-25\frac{8}{15} = 25\frac{16}{30} = 25\frac{16}{30}$$
$$46\frac{23}{30}$$

**19.** 
$$5\frac{1}{10} = 5\frac{1}{10} = 4\frac{11}{10}$$
$$-4\frac{2}{5} = 4\frac{4}{10} = 4\frac{4}{10}$$
$$\frac{7}{10}$$

**21.** Answers will vary.

**23.** 
$$34\frac{1}{2} + 23\frac{3}{4} + 34\frac{1}{2} + 23\frac{3}{4}$$
$$= 34\frac{2}{4} + 23\frac{3}{4} + 34\frac{2}{4} + 23\frac{3}{4}$$
$$= 114\frac{10}{4} = 116\frac{1}{2}$$

The length of lead stripping needed is $116\frac{1}{2}$ inches.

**25.** 
$$107\frac{2}{3} + 150\frac{3}{4} + 138\frac{5}{8}$$
$$= 107\frac{16}{24} + 150\frac{18}{24} + 138\frac{15}{24}$$
$$= 395\frac{49}{24} = 397\frac{1}{24}$$

Length of the three sides is $397\frac{1}{24}$ feet.

$$527\frac{1}{24} - 397\frac{1}{24} = 130$$

Length of the fourth side is 130 feet.

**27.** 
$$2\frac{1}{2} + 3 + 1\frac{3}{4}$$
$$= 2\frac{2}{4} + 3 + 1\frac{3}{4}$$
$$= 6\frac{5}{4} = 7\frac{1}{4}$$

$7\frac{1}{4}$ cubic yards has been unloaded.

$$8\frac{7}{8} - 7\frac{1}{4} = 8\frac{7}{8} - 7\frac{2}{8} = 1\frac{5}{8}$$

$1\frac{5}{8}$ cubic yards of concrete remain in the truck.

**29.** 
$$3\frac{3}{8} + 5\frac{1}{2} + 4\frac{3}{4} + 3\frac{1}{4} + 6$$
$$= 3\frac{3}{8} + 5\frac{4}{8} + 4\frac{6}{8} + 3\frac{2}{8} + 6$$
$$= 21\frac{15}{8} = 22\frac{7}{8}$$

$7\frac{1}{4}$ Loren worked $22\frac{7}{8}$ hours altogether.

## 2.4 Multiplication and Division of Fractions

**1.** $\dfrac{3}{\cancel{4}_{2}} \times \dfrac{\overset{1}{\cancel{2}}}{5} = \dfrac{3 \times 1}{2 \times 5} = \dfrac{3}{10}$

**3.** $\dfrac{9}{10} \times \dfrac{11}{16} = \dfrac{9 \times 11}{10 \times 16} = \dfrac{99}{160}$

**5.** $\dfrac{9}{\cancel{22}_{2}} \times \dfrac{\overset{1}{\cancel{11}}}{16} = \dfrac{9 \times 1}{2 \times 16} = \dfrac{9}{32}$

**7.** $1\dfrac{1}{4} \times 3\dfrac{1}{2} = \dfrac{5}{4} \times \dfrac{7}{2} = \dfrac{5 \times 7}{4 \times 2} = \dfrac{35}{8} = 4\dfrac{3}{8}$

**9.** $3\dfrac{1}{9} \times 3 = \dfrac{28}{\cancel{9}_{3}} \times \dfrac{\overset{1}{\cancel{3}}}{1} = \dfrac{28 \times 1}{3 \times 1} = \dfrac{28}{3} = 9\dfrac{1}{3}$

**11.** $\dfrac{1}{4} \times 6\dfrac{2}{3} \times \dfrac{1}{5} = \dfrac{1}{\cancel{4}_{1}} \times \dfrac{\overset{\overset{1}{\cancel{5}}}{\cancel{20}}}{3} \times \dfrac{1}{\cancel{5}_{1}}$

$= \dfrac{1 \times 1 \times 1}{1 \times 3 \times 1} = \dfrac{1}{3}$

**13.** $\dfrac{5}{9} \times 2\dfrac{1}{4} \times 3\dfrac{2}{3} = \dfrac{5}{\cancel{9}} \times \dfrac{\overset{1}{\cancel{9}}}{4} \times \dfrac{11}{3}$

$= \dfrac{5 \times 1 \times 11}{1 \times 4 \times 3} = \dfrac{55}{12} = 4\dfrac{7}{12}$

**15.** $5\dfrac{3}{5} \times 1\dfrac{5}{9} \times \dfrac{10}{49} = \dfrac{\overset{4}{\cancel{28}}}{\cancel{5}_{1}} \times \dfrac{\overset{2}{\cancel{14}}}{9} \times \dfrac{\overset{2}{\cancel{10}}}{\cancel{49}_{7}}$

$= \dfrac{4 \times 2 \times 2}{1 \times 9 \times 1} = \dfrac{16}{9} = 1\dfrac{7}{9}$

**17.** $\dfrac{3}{8} \div \dfrac{5}{8} = \dfrac{3}{\cancel{8}_{1}} \times \dfrac{\overset{1}{\cancel{8}}}{5} = \dfrac{3 \times 1}{1 \times 5} = \dfrac{3}{5}$

**19.** $\dfrac{9}{10} \div \dfrac{3}{5} = \dfrac{\overset{3}{\cancel{9}}}{\cancel{10}_{2}} \times \dfrac{\overset{1}{\cancel{5}}}{\cancel{3}_{1}} = \dfrac{3 \times 1}{2 \times 1} = \dfrac{3}{2} = 1\dfrac{1}{2}$

**21.** $2\dfrac{1}{2} \div 3\dfrac{3}{4} = \dfrac{5}{2} \div \dfrac{15}{4} = \dfrac{\overset{1}{\cancel{5}}}{\cancel{2}_{1}} \times \dfrac{\overset{2}{\cancel{4}}}{\cancel{15}_{3}} = \dfrac{1 \times 2}{1 \times 3} = \dfrac{2}{3}$

**23.** $5 \div 1\dfrac{7}{8} = 5 \div \dfrac{15}{8} = \dfrac{\overset{1}{\cancel{5}}}{1} \times \dfrac{8}{\cancel{15}_{3}} = \dfrac{1 \times 8}{1 \times 3} = \dfrac{8}{3} = 2\dfrac{2}{3}$

**25.** $\dfrac{3}{8} \div 2\dfrac{1}{2} = \dfrac{3}{8} \div \dfrac{5}{2} = \dfrac{3}{\cancel{8}_{4}} \times \dfrac{\overset{1}{\cancel{2}}}{5} = \dfrac{3 \times 1}{4 \times 5} = \dfrac{3}{20}$

**27.** $2\dfrac{5}{8} \div \dfrac{5}{16} = \dfrac{21}{8} \div \dfrac{5}{16}$

$= \dfrac{21}{\cancel{8}_{1}} \times \dfrac{\overset{2}{\cancel{16}}}{5} = \dfrac{21 \times 2}{1 \times 5} = \dfrac{42}{5} = 8\dfrac{2}{5}$

**29.** Answers will vary.

**31.** $\$8 \times 1\dfrac{1}{2} = \dfrac{\$\overset{4}{\cancel{8}}}{1} \times \dfrac{3}{\cancel{2}_{1}}$

$= \dfrac{\$4 \times 3}{1 \times 1} = \$12$

**33.** $\$12.50 \times 1\dfrac{1}{2} = \dfrac{\$25}{2} \times \dfrac{3}{2}$

$= \dfrac{\$25 \times 3}{2 \times 2} = \dfrac{\$75}{4} = \$18.75$

**35.** Answers will vary.

**37.** $30 \times \dfrac{1}{5} = \dfrac{\overset{6}{\cancel{30}}}{1} \times \dfrac{1}{\cancel{5}_{1}} = \dfrac{6 \times 1}{1 \times 1} = 6$

The cost of operating the hair dryer for 30 minutes is 6 cents.

**39.** $16 \times 2\frac{1}{4} = \frac{\overset{4}{\cancel{16}}}{1} \times \frac{9}{\cancel{4}} = \frac{4 \times 9}{1 \times 1} = 36$

Matthew needs 36 yards of ribbon.

**41.** $1314 \div 109\frac{1}{2} = \frac{1314}{1} \div \frac{219}{2}$

$= \frac{\overset{6}{\cancel{1314}}}{1} \times \frac{2}{\cancel{219}} = \frac{6 \times 2}{1 \times 1} = 12$

12 homes can be fitted with cabinet trim.

**43.** $135 \times 19\frac{1}{2} = \frac{135}{1} \times \frac{39}{2}$

$= \frac{135 \times 39}{1 \times 2} = \frac{5265}{2} = 2632\frac{1}{2}$

$2632\frac{1}{2}$ inches of steel tubing are needed.

**45.** $25,730 \div 10\frac{3}{8} = 25,730 \div \frac{83}{8}$

$= \frac{\overset{310}{\cancel{25,730}}}{1} \times \frac{8}{\cancel{83}} = \frac{310 \times 8}{1 \times 1} = 2480$

2480 anchors can be manufactured.

**47.** $28 \times 12\frac{3}{4} = \frac{\overset{7}{\cancel{28}}}{1} \times \frac{51}{\cancel{4}} = \frac{7 \times 51}{1 \times 1} = 357$

$16 \times 7\frac{1}{8} = \frac{\overset{2}{\cancel{16}}}{1} \times \frac{57}{\cancel{8}} = \frac{2 \times 57}{1 \times 1} = 114$

$357 + 114 = 471$

471 gallons of fuel are used.

**49.** $11 \div \frac{1}{8} = 11 \times 8 = 88$

88 dispensers can be filled.

**51.** $40 \div 8\frac{1}{2} = 40 \div \frac{17}{2}$

$= \frac{40}{1} \times \frac{2}{17} = \frac{40 \times 2}{1 \times 17} = \frac{80}{17} = 4\frac{12}{17} \approx 5$

Approximately 5 round trips are required.

## 2.5 Converting Decimals to Fractions and Fractions to Decimals

**1.** $.75 = \frac{75}{100} = \frac{3}{4}$

**3.** $.24 = \frac{24}{100} = \frac{6}{25}$

**5.** $.73 = \frac{73}{100}$

**7.** $.85 = \frac{85}{100} = \frac{17}{20}$

**9.** $.34 = \frac{34}{100} = \frac{17}{50}$

**11.** $.444 = \frac{444}{1000} = \frac{111}{250}$

**13.** $.625 = \frac{625}{1000} = \frac{5}{8}$

**15.** $.805 = \frac{805}{1000} = \frac{161}{200}$

**17.** $.096 = \frac{96}{1000} = \frac{12}{125}$

**19.** $.0375 = \frac{375}{10,000} = \frac{3}{80}$

**21.** $.1875 = \frac{1875}{10,000} = \frac{3}{16}$

**23.** $.0016 = \frac{16}{10,000} = \frac{1}{625}$

**25.** Answers will vary.

**27.** $\dfrac{1}{4} = .25$

$$\begin{array}{r} .25 \\ 4\overline{)1.00} \\ \underline{8} \\ 20 \\ \underline{20} \\ 0 \end{array}$$

**29.** $\dfrac{3}{8} = .375$

$$\begin{array}{r} .375 \\ 8\overline{)3.000} \\ \underline{24} \\ 60 \\ \underline{56} \\ 40 \\ \underline{40} \\ 0 \end{array}$$

**31.** $\dfrac{2}{3} = .667$

$$\begin{array}{r} .6666 \\ 3\overline{)2.0000} \\ \underline{18} \\ 20 \\ \underline{18} \\ 20 \\ \underline{18} \\ 20 \\ \underline{18} \\ 2 \end{array}$$

**33.** $\dfrac{7}{9} = .778$

$$\begin{array}{r} .7777 \\ 9\overline{)7.0000} \\ \underline{63} \\ 70 \\ \underline{63} \\ 70 \\ \underline{63} \\ 70 \\ \underline{63} \\ 7 \end{array}$$

**35.** $\dfrac{7}{11} = .636$

$$\begin{array}{r} .6363 \\ 11\overline{)7.0000} \\ \underline{66} \\ 40 \\ \underline{33} \\ 70 \\ \underline{66} \\ 40 \\ \underline{33} \\ 7 \end{array}$$

**37.** $\dfrac{22}{25} = .88$

$$\begin{array}{r} .88 \\ 25\overline{)22.00} \\ \underline{200} \\ 200 \\ \underline{200} \\ 0 \end{array}$$

**39.** $\dfrac{181}{205} = .883$

$$\begin{array}{r} .8829 \\ 205\overline{)181.0000} \\ \underline{1640} \\ 1700 \\ \underline{1640} \\ 600 \\ \underline{410} \\ 1900 \\ \underline{1845} \\ 55 \end{array}$$

**41.** $\dfrac{148}{149} = .993$

$$\begin{array}{r} .9932 \\ 149\overline{)148.0000} \\ \underline{1341} \\ 1390 \\ \underline{1341} \\ 490 \\ \underline{447} \\ 430 \\ \underline{298} \\ 132 \end{array}$$

**43. (a)** $\dfrac{2}{3} = .667$

$$\begin{array}{r} .6666 \\ 3\overline{)2.0000} \\ \underline{18} \\ 20 \\ \underline{18} \\ 20 \\ \underline{18} \\ 20 \\ \underline{18} \\ 2 \end{array}$$

**(b)** $\dfrac{2}{3} \times 272 = \dfrac{2}{3} \times \dfrac{272}{1} = \dfrac{2 \times 272}{3 \times 1}$

$\qquad = \dfrac{544}{3} = 181\dfrac{1}{3} \approx 181$

181 people continued to smoke.

$272 - 181 = 91$

91 people quit smoking.

## Case Study

1. Multiply each monthly amount by 12.
   Salaries: $\$10,000 \times 12 = \$120,000$
   Rent: $\$6000 \times 12 = \$72,000$
   Utilities: $\$2000 \times 12 = \$24,000$
   Insurance: $\$1500 \times 12 = \$18,000$
   Advertising: $\$1500 \times 12 = \$18,000$
   Miscellaneous: $\$3000 \times 12 = \$36,000$

   $\$120,000 + \$72,000 + \$24,000$
   $+\$18,000 + \$18,000 + \$36,000 = \$288,000$
   The total annual operating expenses are
   $\$288,000$.

2. Divide each annual amount by the total
   annual operating expenses.
   Salaries: $\dfrac{\$120,000}{\$288,000} = \dfrac{5}{12}$

   Rent: $\dfrac{\$72,000}{\$288,000} = \dfrac{1}{4}$

   Utilities: $\dfrac{\$24,000}{\$288,000} = \dfrac{1}{12}$

   Insurance: $\dfrac{\$18,000}{\$288,000} = \dfrac{1}{16}$

   Advertising: $\dfrac{\$18,000}{\$288,000} = \dfrac{1}{16}$

   Miscellaneous: $\dfrac{\$36,000}{\$288,000} = \dfrac{1}{8}$

3.

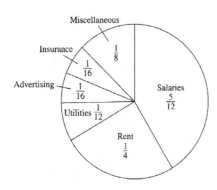

4. Multiply each fraction by $360°$.
   Salaries: $\dfrac{5}{12} \times 360° = 150°$

   Rent: $\dfrac{1}{4} \times 360° = 90°$

   Utilities: $\dfrac{1}{12} \times 360° = 30°$

   Insurance: $\dfrac{1}{16} \times 360° = 22.5°$

   Advertising: $\dfrac{1}{16} \times 360° = 22.5°$

   Miscellaneous: $\dfrac{1}{8} \times 360° = 45°$

## Case in Point Summary Exercise

1. $6 \times 32\dfrac{1}{4} = \dfrac{\cancel{6}^{\,3}}{1} \times \dfrac{129}{\cancel{4}_{\,2}}$

   $= \dfrac{3 \times 129}{1 \times 2} = \dfrac{387}{2} = 193\dfrac{1}{2}$

   $193\dfrac{1}{2}$ inches of cherry wood are needed.

2. $32\dfrac{1}{4} \times 14\dfrac{1}{2} = \dfrac{129}{4} \times \dfrac{29}{2}$

   $= \dfrac{129 \times 29}{4 \times 2} = \dfrac{3741}{8} = 467\dfrac{5}{8}$

   The area of each panel is $467\dfrac{5}{8}$ square
   inches.

3. $467\dfrac{5}{8} \times 6 = \dfrac{3741}{\cancel{8}} \times \dfrac{\cancel{6}^{\,3}}{1}$

   $= \dfrac{3741 \times 3}{4 \times 1} = \dfrac{11,223}{4} = 2805\dfrac{3}{4}$

   A total area of $2805\dfrac{3}{4}$ square inches of
   cherry wood is needed.

4. $2250 \div 467\dfrac{5}{8} = \dfrac{2250}{1} \div \dfrac{3741}{8}$

   $= \dfrac{\cancel{2250}^{\,750}}{1} \times \dfrac{8}{\cancel{3741}_{\,1247}} = \dfrac{750 \times 8}{1 \times 1247} = \dfrac{6000}{1247}$

   $= 4\dfrac{1012}{1247}$, which must be rounded to 4.

   4 side panels can be made.

## Chapter 2   Test

**1.** $\dfrac{25}{30} = \dfrac{25 \div 5}{30 \div 5} = \dfrac{5}{6}$

**2.** $\dfrac{875}{1000} = \dfrac{875 \div 125}{1000 \div 125} = \dfrac{7}{8}$

**3.** $\dfrac{84}{132} = \dfrac{84 \div 12}{132 \div 12} = \dfrac{7}{11}$

**4.** $8\overline{)65} \quad \dfrac{8}{\phantom{)}}$ ... $\begin{array}{r} 8 \\ 8\overline{)65} \\ \underline{64} \\ 1 \end{array} \qquad \dfrac{65}{8} = 8\dfrac{1}{8}$

**5.** $\begin{array}{r} 4 \\ 12\overline{)56} \\ \underline{48} \\ 8 \end{array} \qquad \dfrac{56}{12} = 4\dfrac{8}{12} = 4\dfrac{2}{3}$

**6.** $\begin{array}{r} 2 \\ 45\overline{)120} \\ \underline{90} \\ 30 \end{array} \qquad \dfrac{120}{45} = 2\dfrac{30}{45} = 2\dfrac{2}{3}$

**7.** $7\dfrac{3}{4} = \dfrac{(4 \times 7) + 3}{4} = \dfrac{31}{4}$

**8.** $18\dfrac{4}{5} = \dfrac{(5 \times 18) + 4}{5} = \dfrac{94}{5}$

**9.** $18\dfrac{3}{8} = \dfrac{(8 \times 18) + 3}{8} = \dfrac{147}{8}$

**10.** 2, 6, 5, ___

$\begin{array}{r} \phantom{5)}1 \quad 1 \quad 1 \\ 5\overline{)1 \quad 1 \quad 5} \\ 3\overline{)1 \quad 3 \quad 5} \\ 2\overline{)2 \quad 6 \quad 5} \end{array}$

$2 \times 3 \times 5 = 30$

**11.** 6, 8, 15, ___

$\begin{array}{r} \phantom{5)}1 \quad 1 \quad 1 \\ 5\overline{)1 \quad 1 \quad 5} \\ 3\overline{)3 \quad 1 \quad 15} \\ 2\overline{)3 \quad 2 \quad 15} \\ 2\overline{)3 \quad 4 \quad 15} \\ 2\overline{)6 \quad 8 \quad 15} \end{array}$

$2 \times 2 \times 2 \times 3 \times 5 = 120$

**12.** 6, 9, 12, 24, ___

$\begin{array}{r} \phantom{3)}1 \quad 1 \quad 1 \quad 1 \\ 3\overline{)1 \quad 3 \quad 1 \quad 1} \\ 3\overline{)3 \quad 9 \quad 3 \quad 3} \\ 2\overline{)3 \quad 9 \quad 3 \quad 6} \\ 2\overline{)3 \quad 9 \quad 6 \quad 12} \\ 2\overline{)6 \quad 9 \quad 12 \quad 24} \end{array}$

$2 \times 2 \times 2 \times 3 \times 3 = 72$

**13.**

$\begin{aligned} \dfrac{1}{5} &= \dfrac{8}{40} \\[4pt] \dfrac{3}{10} &= \dfrac{12}{40} \\[4pt] + \dfrac{3}{8} &= \dfrac{15}{40} \\ \hline & \dfrac{35}{40} = \dfrac{7}{8} \end{aligned}$

**14.**

$\begin{aligned} 32\dfrac{5}{16} &= 32\dfrac{5}{16} \\[4pt] - 17\dfrac{1}{4} &= 17\dfrac{4}{16} \\ \hline & 15\dfrac{1}{16} \end{aligned}$

**15.** $126\dfrac{3}{16} = 126\dfrac{3}{16} = 125\dfrac{19}{16}$

$\quad - 89\dfrac{7}{8} = \phantom{1}89\dfrac{14}{16} = \phantom{12}89\dfrac{14}{16}$

$\qquad\qquad\qquad\qquad\qquad\quad 36\dfrac{5}{16}$

**16.** $67\dfrac{1}{2} \times \dfrac{8}{15} = \dfrac{\overset{9}{\cancel{135}}}{\underset{1}{\cancel{2}}} \times \dfrac{\overset{4}{\cancel{8}}}{\underset{1}{\cancel{15}}} = \dfrac{9 \times 4}{1 \times 1} = 36$

**17.** $33\dfrac{1}{3} \div \dfrac{200}{9} = \dfrac{100}{3} \div \dfrac{20}{9}$

$= \dfrac{\overset{1}{\cancel{100}}}{\underset{1}{\cancel{3}}} \times \dfrac{\overset{3}{\cancel{9}}}{\underset{2}{\cancel{200}}} = \dfrac{1 \times 3}{1 \times 2} = \dfrac{3}{2} = 1\dfrac{1}{2}$

**18.** $23\frac{1}{2}+34\frac{3}{4}+17\frac{5}{8}=23\frac{4}{8}+34\frac{6}{8}+17\frac{5}{8}$

$=74\frac{15}{8}=75\frac{7}{8}$

Becky used $75\frac{7}{8}$ pounds of sugar.

$(2\times50)-75\frac{7}{8}=100-75\frac{7}{8}$

$=99\frac{8}{8}-75\frac{7}{8}=24\frac{1}{8}$

$24\frac{1}{8}$ pounds of sugar remain.

**19.** $\$1275\times\frac{1}{3}=\$425$ rent

$\$1275-\$425=\$850$

$\$850\times\frac{3}{5}=\$510$

food, utilities, transportation

$\$1275-\$425-\$510=\$340$

Rhonda has $340 left.

**20.** $68\frac{1}{2}+37\frac{3}{8}+5\frac{3}{4}=68\frac{4}{8}+37\frac{3}{8}+5\frac{6}{8}$

$=110\frac{13}{8}=111\frac{5}{8}$

$111\frac{5}{8}$ gallons of paint were used.

$$147\frac{1}{2} \;=\; 147\frac{4}{8} \;=\; 146\frac{12}{8}$$

$$-\,111\frac{5}{8} \;=\; 111\frac{5}{8} \;=\; 111\frac{5}{8}$$

$$35\frac{7}{8}$$

There are $35\frac{7}{8}$ gallons of paint remaining.

**21.** $80\frac{1}{2}\div1\frac{1}{4}=\frac{161}{2}\div\frac{5}{4}$

$=\frac{161}{\cancel{2}}\times\frac{\cancel{4}}{5}=\frac{161\times2}{1\times5}=\frac{322}{5}=64\frac{2}{5}$

64 blouses can be made.

**22.** $.625=\frac{625}{100}=\frac{5}{8}$

**23.** $.82=\frac{82}{100}=\frac{41}{50}$

**24.** 
$$\begin{array}{r}.25\phantom{0}\\4\overline{)1.00}\\\underline{8}\phantom{00}\\20\\\underline{20}\\0\end{array}$$
    .25 inch

**25.** 
$$\begin{array}{r}.875\\8\overline{)7.000}\\\underline{64}\phantom{00}\\60\\\underline{56}\phantom{0}\\40\\\underline{40}\\0\end{array}$$
    .875 inch

# Chapter 3 | Percent

## 3.1 Writing Decimals and Fractions as Percents

To write a decimal as a percent, move the decimal point two places to the right and attach a percent sign (%). Change a percent to a decimal by moving the decimal point two places to the left and dropping the percent sign (%).

**1.** $.25 = 25\%$

**3.** $.72 = 72\%$

**5.** $2.034 = 203.4\%$

**7.** $3.625 = 362.5\%$

**9.** $.875 = 87.5\%$

**11.** $.0005 = .05\%$

**13.** $3.45 = 345\%$

**15.** $.0308 = 3.08\%$

**17.** $\dfrac{5}{8} = .625$

**19.** $65\% = .65$

**21.** $\dfrac{1}{8} = .125$

**23.** $12\dfrac{1}{2}\% = 12.5\% = .125$

**25.** $\dfrac{1}{400} = .0025$

**27.** $84\dfrac{3}{4}\% = 84.75\% = .8475$

**29.** $1\dfrac{3}{4} = 1.75$

**31.** $\dfrac{1}{2} = .5 = 50\%$

**33.** $\dfrac{7}{8} = .875 = 87.5\%$

**35.** $\dfrac{1}{125} = .008 = .8\%$

**37.** $10\dfrac{1}{2} = 10.5 = 1050\%$

**39.** $\dfrac{13}{20} = .65 = 65\%$

**41.** $\dfrac{1}{200} = .005 = .5\%$

**43.** $\dfrac{1}{3} = .33\overline{3} = 33\dfrac{1}{3}\%$

**45.** $2\dfrac{1}{2} = 2.5 = 250\%$

**47.** $\dfrac{17}{400} = .0425 = 4.25\% = 4\dfrac{1}{4}\%$

**49.** $\dfrac{3}{200} = .015 = 1.5\%$

**51.** $10\dfrac{3}{8} = 10.375 = 1037.5\%$

**53.** $\dfrac{1}{400} = .0025 = .25\%$

**55.** $\dfrac{3}{8} = .375 = 37.5\% = 37\dfrac{1}{2}\%$

**57.** Answers will vary.

**59.** Answers will vary.

## 3.2   Finding Part

**1.** 10% of 620 homes

$P = B \times R$
$P = 620 \times 10\%$
$P = 620 \times .10$
$P = 62$ homes

**3.** 75.5% of $800

$P = B \times R$
$P = \$800 \times 75.5\%$
$P = \$800 \times .755$
$P = \$604$

**5.** 4% of 120 feet

$P = B \times R$
$P = 120 \times 4\%$
$P = 120 \times .04$
$P = 4.8$ feet

**7.** 175% of 5820 miles

$P = B \times R$
$P = 5820 \times 175\%$
$P = 5820 \times 1.75$
$P = 10,185$ miles

**9.** 17.5% of 1040 cell phones

$P = B \times R$
$P = 1040 \times 17.5\%$
$P = 1040 \times .175$
$P = 182$ cell phones

**11.** 118% of 125.8 yards

$P = B \times R$
$P = 125.8 \times 118\%$
$P = 125.8 \times 1.18$
$P = 148.444 \approx 148.44$ yards

**13.** $90\frac{1}{2}\%$ of $5930

$P = B \times R$
$P = \$5930 \times 90\frac{1}{2}\%$
$P = \$5930 \times 90.5\%$
$P = \$5930 \times .905$
$P = \$5366.65$

**15.** Answers will vary.

**17.** $P = B \times R$
$P = 350 \times 68\%$
$P = 350 \times .68$
$P = 238$
238 people said they prefer the Caribbean.

**19.** $P = B \times R$
$P = \$399 \times 7.75\%$
$P = \$399 \times .0775$
$P = \$30.9225 \approx \$30.92$
Sales tax is $30.92.

$\$399 + \$30.92 = \$429.92$
The total price including the sales tax is
$429.92 .

**21.** $P = B \times R$
$P = 335 \times 13\%$
$P = 335 \times .13$
$P = 43.55 \approx 44$

There are 44 female crew members.

**23.** $P = B \times R$
$P = 9 \times 99\frac{44}{100}\%$
$P = 9 \times 99.44\%$
$P = 9 \times .9944$
$P = 8.9496 \approx 8.95$

Approximately 8.95 ounces are pure.

**25.** $P = B \times R$
$P = 16,450 \times 29.5\%$
$P = 16,450 \times .295$
$P = 4852.75 \approx 4853$

4853 crashes would be caused by driver distractions.

**27.** (a) If 71.4% of lawyers are male, then
$100\% - 71.4\% = 28.6\%$  are female.

   (b) $P = B \times R$
$P = 1,094,751 \times 28.6\%$
$P = 1,094,751 \times .286$
$P = 313,098.786 \approx 313,099$
313,099 lawyers are female.

**29.** $P = B \times R$
$P = \$319 \times 25\%$
$P = \$319 \times .25$
$P = \$79.75$
The markdown is $79.75.

$\$319 - \$75.79 = \$239.25$
The price after markdown is $239.25.

**31.** If 86% failed to reach their business objectives, then $100\% - 86\% = 14\%$ did reach their objectives.

$P = B \times R$
$P = 15,401 \times 14\%$
$P = 15,401 \times .14$
$P = 2156.14 \approx 2156$

2156 products did reach their objectives.

**33.** $P = B \times R$
$P = 1,180,358 \times 38\%$
$P = 1,180,358 \times .38$
$P = 448,536.04 \approx 448,536$

Increase in sales is 448,536.

$1,180,358 + 448,536 = 1,628,894$

This year's sales are 1,628,894 units.

**35.** $P = B \times R$

$P = \$48,680 \times 6\frac{1}{2}\%$

$P = \$48,680 \times 6.5\%$
$P = \$48,680 \times .065$
$P = \$3164.20$

The sales tax is \$3164.20.

$\$48,680 + \$3164.20 = \$51,844.20$

The combined amount of sales and tax is \$51,844.20.

**37.** $P = B \times R$
$P = \$174,900 \times 6\%$
$P = \$174,900 \times .06$
$P = \$10,494$

The total commission is \$10,494.

$P = B \times R$
$P = \$10,494 \times 60\%$
$P = \$10,494 \times .60$
$P = \$6296.40$

The amount received by Dugally is \$6296.40.

**39.** $P = B \times R$
$P = (6 \times \$29.99) \times 5\%$
$P = (6 \times \$29.99) \times .05$
$P = \$8.997 \approx \$9.00$

Sales tax is \$9.00.

$(6 \times \$29.99) + \$9.00 + \$10.95 = \$199.89$

The total cost is \$199.89.

**41.** $P = B \times R$
$P = \left[(3 \times \$9.99) + (4 \times \$10.99)\right] \times 5\%$
$P = \left[(3 \times \$9.99) + (4 \times \$10.99)\right] \times .05$
$P = \$3.6965 \approx \$3.70$

Sales tax is \$3.70.

$\left[(3 \times \$9.99) + (4 \times \$10.99)\right] + \$3.70 + \$9.95$
$= \$87.58$

The total cost is \$87.58.

## 3.3 Finding Base

**1.** 530 firms is 25% of _____ firms.

$B = \dfrac{P}{R}$

$B = \dfrac{530}{.25}$

$B = 2120$

530 firms is 25% of 2120 firms.

**3.** 130 salads is 40% of _____ salads.

$B = \dfrac{P}{R}$

$B = \dfrac{130}{.40}$

$B = 325$

130 salads is 40% of 325 salads.

**5.** 110 lab tests is 5.5% of _____ lab tests.

$B = \dfrac{P}{R}$

$B = \dfrac{110}{.055}$

$B = 2000$

110 lab tests is 5.5% of 2000 lab tests.

**7.** 36 students is .75% of _____ students.

$B = \dfrac{P}{R}$

$B = \dfrac{36}{.0075}$

$B = 4800$

36 students is .75% of 4800 students.

**9.** 66 files is .15% of _____ files.

$$B = \frac{P}{R}$$

$$B = \frac{66}{.0015}$$

$$B = 44,000$$

66 files is .15% of <u>44,000</u> files.

**11.** 50 doors is .25% of _____ doors.

$$B = \frac{P}{R}$$

$$B = \frac{50}{.0025}$$

$$B = 20,000$$

50 doors is .25% of <u>20,000</u> doors.

**13.** $33,870 is $37\frac{1}{2}$% of _____.

$$B = \frac{P}{R}$$

$$B = \frac{\$33,870}{.375}$$

$$B = \$90,320$$

$33,870 is $37\frac{1}{2}$ of <u>$90,320</u>.

**15.** $12\frac{1}{2}$% of _____ people is 135 people.

$$B = \frac{P}{R}$$

$$B = \frac{135}{.125}$$

$$B = 1080$$

$12\frac{1}{2}$% of <u>1080</u> people is 135 people.

**17.** 375 crates is .12% of _____ crates.

$$B = \frac{P}{R}$$

$$B = \frac{375}{.0012}$$

$$B = 312,500$$

375 crates is .12% of <u>312,500</u> crates.

**19.** .5% of _____ homes is 327 homes.

$$B = \frac{P}{R}$$

$$B = \frac{327}{.005}$$

$$B = 65,400$$

.5% of <u>65,400</u> homes is 327 homes.

**21.** 12 audits is .03% of _____ audits.

$$B = \frac{P}{R}$$

$$B = \frac{12}{.0003}$$

$$B = 40,000$$

12 audits is .03% of <u>40,000</u> audits.

**23.** Answers will vary.

**25.** $B = \frac{P}{R}$

$$B = \frac{72.6 \text{ million}}{.678}$$

$$B \approx 107.1 \text{ million}$$

The total number of U.S. households is approximately 107.1 million.

**27.** $B = \frac{P}{R}$

$$B = \frac{1785}{.23}$$

$$B \approx 7761$$

Total enrollment is about 7761 students.

**29.** $B = \frac{P}{R}$

$$B = \frac{\$1350}{.3}$$

$$B = \$4500$$

The minimum monthly income required is $4500.

**31.** $28\% + 15\% + 11\% + 15\% + 11\% + 7\% = 87\%$
87% of his income is spent.

$100\% - 87\% = 13\%$
13% of his income is saved.

$B = \dfrac{P}{R}$

$B = \dfrac{\$266.50}{.13}$

$B = \$2050$
His monthly earnings are $2050.

**33.** $B = \dfrac{P}{R}$

$B = \dfrac{901}{.34}$

$B = 2650$
There were 2650 dog owners in the survey.

$2650 - 901 = 1749$
1749 dog owners do not take their dogs on vacation.

**35.** If the payback is 97.4%, then
$100\% - 97.4\% = 2.6\%$ is retained.

$B = \dfrac{P}{R}$

$B = \dfrac{\$4823}{.026}$

$B = \$185,500$
The total amount played on the slot machines is $185,500.

## Supplementary Application Exercises on Base and Part

**1.** $B = \dfrac{P}{R}$

$B = \dfrac{12.5}{.78}$

$B \approx 16$

The size of the bottle is 16 ounces.

**3.** $P = B \times R$
$P = \$423,750 \times 68\%$
$P = \$423,750 \times .68$
$P = \$288,150$

The insurance coverage is $288,150.

**5.** $B = \dfrac{P}{R}$

$B = \dfrac{220,917}{.462}$

$B \approx 478,175$

478,175 Mustangs were sold in 1967.

**7.** $P = B \times R$
$P = 270 \times 60\%$
$P = 270 \times .6$
$P = 162$

162 calories come from fat.

**9.** $B = \dfrac{P}{R}$

$B = \dfrac{\$308.75}{.095}$

$B = \$3250$
Erin's monthly income is $3250.

$\$3250 \times 12 = \$39,000$
Erin's annual earnings are $39,000.

**11.** $P = B \times R$
$P = 501 \times 46\%$
$P = 501 \times .46$
$P = 230.46 \approx 230$
999999230 companies renovated the workplace.

**13.** $P = B \times R$
$P = 501 \times 11\%$
$P = 501 \times .11$
$P = 55.11 \approx 55$
55 companies changed worker hours.

## 3.4    Finding Rate

**1.**  ____% of 2760 listings is 276 listings.

$$R = \frac{P}{B}$$

$$R = \frac{276}{2760}$$

$$R = .10 = 10\%$$

<u>10</u>% of 2760 listings is 276 listings.

**3.**  35 rail cars is ____% of 70 rail cars.

$$R = \frac{P}{B}$$

$$R = \frac{35}{70}$$

$$R = .50 = 50\%$$

35 rail cars is <u>50</u>% of 70 rail cars.

**5.**  ____% of 78.57 ounces is 22.2 ounces.

$$R = \frac{P}{B}$$

$$R = \frac{22.2}{78.57}$$

$$R \approx .283 = 28.3\%$$

<u>28.3</u>% of 78.57 ounces is 22.2 ounces.

**7.**  114 tuxedos is ____% of 150 tuxedos.

$$R = \frac{P}{B}$$

$$R = \frac{114}{150}$$

$$R = .76 = 76\%$$

114 tuxedos is <u>76</u>% of 150 tuxedos.

**9.**  ____% of $53.75 is $2.20.

$$R = \frac{P}{B}$$

$$R = \frac{\$2.20}{\$53.75}$$

$$R \approx .041 = 4.1\%$$

<u>4.1</u>% of $53.75 is $2.20.

**11.**  46 shirts is ____% of 780 shirts.

$$R = \frac{P}{B}$$

$$R = \frac{46}{780}$$

$$R \approx .059 = 5.9\%$$

46 shirts is <u>5.9</u>% of 780 shirts.

**13.**  ____% of 600 acres is 7.5 acres.

$$R = \frac{P}{B}$$

$$R = \frac{7.5}{600}$$

$$R = .0125 \approx .013 = 1.3\%$$

<u>1.3</u>% of 600 acres is 7.5 acres.

**15.**  170 cartons is ____% of 68 cartons.

$$R = \frac{P}{B}$$

$$R = \frac{170}{68}$$

$$R = 2.5 = 250\%$$

170 cartons is 250% of 68 cartons.

**17.**  ____% of $330 is $91.74.

$$R = \frac{P}{B}$$

$$R = \frac{\$91.74}{\$330}$$

$$R = .278 = 27.8\%$$

<u>27.8</u>% of $330 is $91.74.

**19.**  Answers will vary.

**21.**  $$R = \frac{P}{B}$$

$$R = \frac{\$19,567.20}{\$315,600}$$

$$R = .062 = 6.2\%$$

6.2% of last month's income was spent on advertising.

**23.** $R = \dfrac{P}{B}$

$R = \dfrac{960}{48,000}$

$R = .02 = 2\%$

2% of these jobs were filled by women.

**25.** $\$2250 + \$954 + \$1950$
$+ \$1425 + \$1605 + \$2775 = \$10,959$
Total advertising expenses were $10,959.

$R = \dfrac{P}{B}$

$R = \dfrac{\$954}{\$10,959}$

$R \approx .087 = 8.7\%$

8.7% of the total advertising expenditures is spent on radio advertising.

**27.** $R = \dfrac{P}{B}$

$R = \dfrac{559}{860}$

$R = .65 = 65\%$

65% were under age 28.

**29.** $R = \dfrac{P}{B}$

$R = \dfrac{159}{230}$

$R \approx .691 = 69.1\%$

69.1% were unhappy with their jobs.

## Supplementary Application Exercises on Rate, Base, and Part

**1.** $P = B \times R$
$P = 571 \times 17\%$
$P = 571 \times .17$
$P = 97.07 \approx 97$

97 people felt that they had made this mistake.

**3.** $R = \dfrac{P}{B}$

$R = \dfrac{20}{50}$

$R = .40 = 40\%$

40% of states require motorcycle riders to wear helmets.

**5.** $B = \dfrac{P}{R}$

$B = \dfrac{88}{.08}$

$B = 1100$

There were 1100 boaters in the survey.

**7.** $P = B \times R$
$P = \$398 \times 7\%$
$P = \$398 \times .07$
$P = \$27.86$
The markdown is $27.86.

$\$398 - \$27.86 = \$370.14$
The reduced price is $370.14.

**9.** $P = B \times R$
$P = \$18,960 \times 3\%$
$P = \$18,960 \times .03$
$P = \$568.80$

The commission for Strong is $568.80.

**11.** $R = \dfrac{P}{B}$

$R = \dfrac{\$707.20}{\$17,680}$

$R \approx .04 = 4\%$

The rate of commission for Keyes is 4%.

**13.** $B = \dfrac{P}{R}$

$B = \dfrac{2.48 \text{ million}}{.62}$

$B = 4 \text{ million}$

There are 4 million motorcycle riders.

**15.** $R = \dfrac{P}{B}$

$R = \dfrac{257}{414}$

$R \approx .621 = 62.1\%$

62.1% of students drop out before graduating.

**17.** China:

$$R = \frac{P}{B}$$

$$R = \frac{150}{1267}$$

$$R \approx .12 = 12\%$$

India:

$$R = \frac{P}{B}$$

$$R = \frac{571}{1043}$$

$$R \approx .55 = 55\%$$

United States:

$$R = \frac{P}{B}$$

$$R = \frac{116}{288}$$

$$R \approx .40 = 40\%$$

Indonesia:

$$R = \frac{P}{B}$$

$$R = \frac{80}{205}$$

$$R \approx .39 = 39\%$$

Brazil:

$$R = \frac{P}{B}$$

$$R = \frac{43}{174}$$

$$R \approx .25 = 25\%$$

Pakistan:

$$R = \frac{P}{B}$$

$$R = \frac{187}{148}$$

$$R \approx 1.26 = 126\%$$

**19.** China: 1,417,000,000
$1267 + 150 = 1417$

India: 1,614,000,000
$1043 + 571 = 1614$

**21.** $B = \dfrac{P}{R}$

$$B = \frac{1440}{.25}$$

$$B = 5760$$

A total of 5760 items were sold in the vending machines.

**23.** $100\% - 25\% - 22\% - 12\% - 32\% = 9\%$
Annual savings are 9% of total income.

$$P = B \times R$$

$$P = \$5450 \times 9\%$$

$$P = \$5450 \times .09$$

$$P = \$490.50$$

Monthly savings are $490.50.

$\$490.50 \times 12 = \$5886$
Annual savings are $5886.

**25.** $100\% - 35\% - 17\% - 40\% = 8\%$
Annual savings are 8% of total income.

$$P = B \times R$$

$$P = \$6800 \times 8\%$$

$$P = \$6800 \times .08$$

$$P = \$544$$

Monthly savings are $544.

$\$544 \times 12 = \$6528$
Annual savings are $6528.

**27.** $P = B \times R$
$P = 9000 \times 63.8\%$
$P = 9000 \times .638$
$P = 5742$

5742 deaths would have been prevented.

**29.** **(a)** $R = \dfrac{P}{B}$

$$R = \frac{18}{50}$$

$$R = .36 = 36\%$$

36% of the top 50 companies were Japanese companies.

**(b)** $100\% - 36\% = 64\%$
64% of the top 50 companies were not Japanese companies.

## 3.5   Increase and Decrease Problems

**1.** $100\% + 20\% = 120\%$

$$B = \frac{P}{R}$$

$$B = \frac{\$450}{120\%}$$

$$B = \frac{\$450}{1.2}$$

$$B = \$375$$

**3.** $100\% + 10\% = 110\%$

$$B = \frac{P}{R}$$

$$B = \frac{\$30.70}{110\%}$$

$$B = \frac{\$30.70}{1.1}$$

$$B \approx \$27.91$$

**5.** $100\% - 20\% = 80\%$

$$B = \frac{P}{R}$$

$$B = \frac{\$20}{80\%}$$

$$B = \frac{\$20}{.8}$$

$$B = \$25$$

**7.** $100\% - 30\% = 70\%$

$$B = \frac{P}{R}$$

$$B = \frac{\$598.15}{70\%}$$

$$B = \frac{\$598.15}{.7}$$

$$B = \$854.50$$

**9.** Answers will vary.

**11.** $100\% + 5\% = 105\%$

$$B = \frac{P}{R}$$

$$B = \frac{\$205,275}{105\%}$$

$$B = \frac{\$205,275}{1.05}$$

$$B = \$195,500$$

Last year's selling price was $195,500.

**13. (a)** $100\% + 8\% = 108\%$

$$B = \frac{P}{R}$$

$$B = \frac{\$1026}{108\%}$$

$$B = \frac{\$1026}{1.08}$$

$$B = \$950$$

Santiago's sales, not including sales tax, were $950.

**(b)** $\$1026 - \$950 = \$76$

The sales tax is $76.

**15.** $B = \frac{P}{R}$

$$B = \frac{177,000}{21\%}$$

$$B = \frac{177,000}{.21}$$

$$B \approx 842,857$$

There are approx. 842,857 restaurants.

**17.** $100\% + 10\% = 110\%$

$$B = \frac{P}{R}$$

$$B = \frac{\$80}{110\%}$$

$$B = \frac{\$80}{1.1}$$

$$B = \$72.73$$

The cost one year ago was $72.73.

$100\% + 10\% = 110\%$

$$B = \frac{P}{R}$$

$$B = \frac{\$72.73}{110\%}$$

$$B = \frac{\$72.73}{1.1}$$

$$B = \$66.12$$

The cost two years ago was $66.12.

**19.** $100\% + 220\% = 320\%$

$$B = \frac{P}{R}$$

$$B = \frac{11,000,000}{320\%}$$

$$B = \frac{11,000,000}{3.2}$$

$$B = 3,437,500$$

There were 3,437,500 subscribers 5 years ago.

**21.** $100\% + 9.4\% = 109.4\%$

$$B = \frac{P}{R}$$

$$B = \frac{23.4 \text{ million}}{109.4\%}$$

$$B = \frac{23.4 \text{ million}}{1.094}$$

$$B = 21.4 \text{ million}$$

The number of auto sales in Asia last year was 21.4 million.

**23.** $\$5750 + \$4186 = \$9936$

Sales during the first two days were $9936.

$100\% - 28\% = 72\%$

$$B = \frac{P}{R}$$

$$B = \frac{\$9936}{72\%}$$

$$B = \frac{\$9936}{.72}$$

$$B = \$13,800$$

The original value of all equipment is $13,800.

$\$13,800 - \$9936 = \$3864$

Value of the surplus equipment is $3864.

**25.** $100\% - 16\% = 84\%$

$$B = \frac{P}{R}$$

$$B = \frac{\$122 \text{ million}}{84\%}$$

$$B = \frac{\$122 \text{ million}}{.84}$$

$$B \approx \$145.24 \text{ million}$$

Earnings were $145.24 million.

**27.** $100\% - 2\% = 98\%$

$$B = \frac{P}{R}$$

$$B = \frac{50.2 \text{ million}}{98\%}$$

$$B = \frac{50.2 \text{ million}}{.98}$$

$$B \approx 51.2 \text{ million}$$

51.2 million acres were planted last year.

**29.** $100\% + 6\% = 106\%$

$$B = \frac{P}{R}$$

$$B = \frac{33,708}{106\%}$$

$$B = \frac{33,708}{1.06}$$

$$B = 31,800$$

Student enrollment last year was 31,800.

$100\% + 6\% = 106\%$

$$B = \frac{P}{R}$$

$$B = \frac{31,800}{106\%}$$

$$B = \frac{31,800}{1.06}$$

$$B = 30,000$$

Student enrollment two years ago was 30,000.

**31.** $100\% + 70\% = 170\%$

$$B = \frac{P}{R}$$

$$B = \frac{1181}{170\%}$$

$$B = \frac{1181}{1.7}$$

$$B \approx 695$$

There were 695 deaths five years ago.

**33.** $P = B \times R$

$P = 1,340,200 \times 8.2\%$

$P = 1,340,200 \times .082$

$P \approx 109,896$

109,896 workers were unemployed last year.

$P = B \times R$

$P = 1,340,200 \times 7.1\%$

$P = 1,340,200 \times .071$

$P \approx 95,154$

95,154 workers were unemployed this year.

$109,896 - 95,154 = 14,742$

14,742 fewer workers were unemployed this year than last year.

## Case Study

**1.** Amazon.com

$\$85.72 - \$84.36 = \$1.36$

$\dfrac{-\$1.36}{\$85.72} \approx -.016 = -1.6\%$

**2.** Medico Health Solutions

$\$48.27 \times 11.3\% = \$48.27 \times .113 \approx \$5.45$

$\$48.27 + \$5.45 = \$53.72$

**3.** McDonald's

$100\% - 9.8\% = 90.2\%$

$\dfrac{\$55.15}{90.2\%} = \dfrac{\$55.15}{.902} = \$61.14$

**4.** Wal-Mart Stores

$\$60.05 \times 17.9\% = \$60.05 \times .179 = \$10.75$

$\$60.05 - \$10.75 = \$49.30$

## Case in Point Summary Exercise

**1.** $\$892,680 - \$865,000 = \$27,680$

The increase in value is $27,680.

$R = \dfrac{P}{B}$

$R = \dfrac{\$27,680}{\$865,000}$

$R = .032 = 3.2\%$

The percent increase in value is 3.2%.

**2.** $P = B \times R$

$P = \$1,145,000 \times 3.2\%$

$P = \$1,145,000 \times .032$

$P = \$36,640$

The increase in value is $36,640.

$\$1,145,000 + \$36,640 = \$1,181,640$

The current value of this property is $1,181,640.

**3.** $100\% + 3.2\% = 103.2\%$

$B = \dfrac{P}{R}$

$B = \dfrac{\$435,000}{103.2\%}$

$B = \dfrac{\$435,000}{1.032}$

$B \approx \$421,512$

The home price one year ago was $421,512.

$\$435,000 - \$421,512 = \$13,488$

The home price increased by $13,488.

**4.** $100\% - 65\% = 35\%$

$P = B \times R$

$P = \$237,075 \times 35\%$

$P = \$237,075 \times .35$

$P = \$82,976.25$

The real estate office keeps $82,976.25.

## Chapter 3  Test

**1.** $\dfrac{3}{8} = .375 = 37.5\%$

**2.** $\dfrac{7}{20} = .35 = 35\%$

**3.** $\dfrac{3}{125} = .024 = 2.4\%$

**4.** $\dfrac{7}{50} = .14 = 14\%$

**5.** $5\dfrac{7}{8} = 5.875 = 587.5\%$

**6.** 36 homes sales is 12% of what number of home sales?

$B = \dfrac{P}{R}$

$B = \dfrac{36}{.12}$

$B = 300$

36 homes sales is 12% of 300 home sales.

**7.** What is $\frac{1}{4}$% of $1260?

$P = R \times B$

$P = \frac{1}{4}\% \times \$1260$

$P = .25\% \times \$1260$

$P = .0025 \times \$1260$

$P = \$3.15$

$3.15 is $\frac{1}{4}$% of $1260?

**8.** $24\% = .24 = \frac{24}{100} = \frac{6}{25}$

**9.** 48 purchase orders is $2\frac{1}{2}$% of how many purchase orders?

$B = \frac{P}{R}$

$B = \frac{48}{.025}$

$B = 1920$

48 purchase orders is $2\frac{1}{2}$% of 1920 purchase orders?

**10.** $87.5\% = .875 = \frac{875}{1000} = \frac{7}{8}$

**11.** $P = B \times R$

$P = \$29.60 \times 1.8\%$

$P = \$29.60 \times .018$

$P = \$.5328 \approx \$.53$

The dividend per share is $.53.

**12.** $B = \frac{P}{R}$

$B = \frac{1120}{.005}$

$B = 224,000$

The total monthly production is 224,000 units.

**13.** $P = B \times R$

$P = \$25,189 \times 18\%$

$P = \$25,189 \times .18$

$P = \$4534.02$

The discount is $4534.02.

$25,189 - \$4534.02 = \$20,654.98$

The sale price is $20,654.98.

**14.** $B = \frac{P}{R}$

$B = \frac{41 \text{ million}}{.13}$

$B \approx 315.4$ million

The total population of the United States is approximately 315.4 million.

**15. (a)** $100\% - (22\% + 38\% + 14\% + 15\%)$
$= 11\%$

They plan to spend 11% on bumper stickers.

**(b)** $P = B \times R$

$P = \$3400 \times 11\%$

$P = \$3400 \times .11$

$P = \$374$

$\$374 \times 12 = \$4488$

They plan to spend $4488 on bumper stickers for the entire year.

**16.** $R = \frac{P}{B}$

$R = \frac{225 \text{ million}}{300 \text{ million}}$

$R = .75 = 75\%$

75% of the lost golf balls are recovered and resold.

**17.** $100\% - 20\% = 80\%$

$B = \frac{P}{R}$

$B = \frac{\$149}{.8}$

$B = \$186.25$

The original price of the media player was $186.25.

**18.** $100\% + 10\% = 110\%$

$$B = \frac{P}{R}$$

$$B = \frac{1452}{110\%}$$

$$B = \frac{1452}{1.1}$$

$$B = 1320$$

1320 backpacks were sold last year.

$$B = \frac{P}{R}$$

$$B = \frac{1320}{110\%}$$

$$B = \frac{1320}{1.1}$$

$$B = 1200$$

1200 backpacks were sold two years ago.

**19.** $379 - 357 = 22$

The increase was 22.

$$R = \frac{P}{B}$$

$$R = \frac{22}{357}$$

$$R \approx .062 = 6.2\%$$

The percent of increase was 6.2%.

**20.** $100\% + 20\% = 120\%$

$$B = \frac{P}{R}$$

$$B = \frac{\$1.76 \text{ billion}}{120\%}$$

$$B = \frac{\$1.76 \text{ billion}}{1.2}$$

$$B = \$1.4\overline{6} \text{ billion} \approx \$1.47 \text{ billion}$$

Earnings in the previous quarter were $1.47 billion.

# Chapter 4 | Equations and Formulas

## 4.1 Solving Equations

**1.**
$$s + 12 = 15$$
$$s + 12 - 12 = 15 - 12$$
$$s = 3$$

**3.**
$$b - 7 = 24$$
$$b - 7 + 7 = 24 + 7$$
$$b = 31$$

**5.**
$$12 = b + 9$$
$$12 - 9 = b + 9 - 9$$
$$3 = b$$

**7.** $8k = 56$
$$\frac{8k}{8} = \frac{56}{8}$$
$$k = 7$$

**9.** $60 = 30m$
$$\frac{60}{30} = \frac{30m}{30}$$
$$2 = m$$

**11.** $\dfrac{m}{5} = 6$
$$\frac{m}{5} \cdot 5 = 6 \cdot 5$$
$$m = 30$$

**13.** $\dfrac{2}{3}a = 5$
$$\frac{2}{3}a \cdot \frac{3}{2} = 5 \cdot \frac{3}{2}$$
$$a = \frac{15}{2} = 7\frac{1}{2} = 7.5$$

**15.** $\dfrac{9}{5}r = 18$
$$\frac{9}{5}r \cdot \frac{5}{9} = 18 \cdot \frac{5}{9}$$
$$r = \frac{90}{9} = 10$$

**17.**
$$3m + 5 = 17$$
$$3m + 5 - 5 = 17 - 5$$
$$3m = 12$$
$$\frac{3m}{3} = \frac{12}{3}$$
$$m = 4$$

**19.**
$$4r + 3 = 9$$
$$4r + 3 - 3 = 9 - 3$$
$$4r = 6$$
$$\frac{4r}{4} = \frac{6}{4}$$
$$r = \frac{3}{2} = 1.5$$

**21.**
$$11r - 5r + 6r = 84$$
$$(11 - 5 + 6)r = 84$$
$$12r = 84$$
$$\frac{12r}{12} = \frac{84}{12}$$
$$r = 7$$

**23.**
$$3(2x + 3) = 3x + 12$$
$$6x + 9 = 3x + 12$$
$$6x + 9 - 9 = 3x + 12 - 9$$
$$6x = 3x + 3$$
$$6x - 3x = 3x + 3 - 3x$$
$$3x = 3$$
$$\frac{3x}{3} = \frac{3}{3}$$
$$x = 1$$

**25.** Answers will vary.

## 4.2   Applications of Equations

**1.** 27 plus a number
$27 + x$

**3.** a number added to 22
$22 + x$

**5.** 4 less than a number
$x - 4$

**7.** subtract $3\frac{1}{2}$ from a number

$x - 3\frac{1}{2}$

**9.** triple a number
$3x$

**11.** three-fifths of a number
$\frac{3}{5}x$

**13.** the quotient of 9 and a number
$\frac{9}{x}$

**15.** 16 divided by a number
$\frac{16}{x}$

**17.** the product of 2.1 and the sum of 4 and a number
$2.1(4 + x)$

**19.** 7 times the difference of a number and 3
$7(x - 3)$

**21.** The cost of 12 CDs at $y$ dollars each is $12y$.

**23.** The amount that should be ordered is $472 - x$.

**25.** $73 - x$ employees are not union members.

**27.** The cost of one textbook is $\frac{20,210}{x}$.

**29.** Robin has $21 - x$ books left.

**31.** 4 times a number, plus 6 equals 58
$4 \ \times \quad n \quad + 6 \ = \ 58$

Solve the equation.
$4n + 6 = 58$
$4n = 52$
$n = 13$

**33.** 6 times quantity 4 minus a number is 15
$6 \ \times \qquad (4 \ - \quad n) \ = 15$

Solve the equation.
$6(4 - n) = 15$
$24 - 6n = 15$
$-6n = -9$
$n = \frac{3}{2} = 1.5$

**35.** 6 added to a number is 7 times the number.
$6 \ + \quad n \ = 7 \times \quad n$

Solve the equation.
$6 + n = 7n$
$6 = 6n$
$1 = n$

**37.** 5 times number added to twice number is 10
$5 \ \times \ n \quad + \qquad 2n \qquad = 10$

Solve the equation.
$5n + 2n = 10$
$7n = 10$
$n = \frac{10}{7} = 1\frac{3}{7}$

**39.**     $x$ = stereos sold by Jamison
$x - 17$ = stereos sold by other salesperson

sold by Jamison + sold by other = total sold
$x \qquad + \ (x - 17) \ = \quad 101$

Solve the equation.
$x + (x - 17) = 101$
$x + x - 17 = 101$
$2x - 17 = 101$
$2x = 118$
$x = 59$
Jamison sold 59 stereos.

**41.**    $x$ = employees building ships

$x - 185$ = other employees

building + other   = total employees

   $x$    $+ x - 185$ =    229

Solve the equation.

$x + (x - 185) = 229$

$x + x - 185 = 229$

$2x - 185 = 229$

$2x = 414$

$x = 207$

207 employees work building the ships.

**43.**    $p$ = original price

$\dfrac{9}{10} p$ = sale price

Solve the equation.

$$\$18,450 = \frac{9}{10} p$$

$$\frac{10}{9} \cdot \$18,450 = \frac{10}{9} \cdot \frac{9}{10} p$$

$$\$20,500 = p$$

The original price was $20,500.

**45.**    $x$ = number of deluxe models

$\dfrac{3}{2} x$ = number of economy models

deluxe + economy = total homes

   $x$    +    $\dfrac{3}{2} x$    =    105

Solve the equation.

$$x + \frac{3}{2} x = 105$$

$$\frac{5}{2} x = 105$$

$$\frac{2}{5} \cdot \frac{5}{2} x = \frac{2}{5} \cdot 105$$

$$x = 42$$

$$\frac{3}{2} x = \frac{3}{2} \cdot 42 = 63$$

There were 42 deluxe models.
There were 63 economy models.

**47.**    $a$ = amount spent on all other employees

$\dfrac{3}{5} a$ = amount spent on announcers

other employees + announcers = total

   $a$    +    $\dfrac{3}{5} a$    = \$21,000

Solve the equation.

$$a + \frac{3}{5} a = \$21,000$$

$$\frac{8}{5} a = \$21,000$$

$$\frac{5}{8} \cdot \frac{8}{5} a = \frac{5}{8} \cdot \$21,000$$

$$a = \$13,125$$

$$\frac{3}{5} a = \frac{3}{5} \cdot \$13,125 = \$7875$$

$7875 was spent on announcers.
$13,125 was spent on other employees.

**49.**    $r$ = rent from offices

$3\dfrac{1}{2} r$ = rent from retail stores

offices + retail stores = total annual rent

   $r$    +    $3\dfrac{1}{2} r$    =    \$135,000

Solve the equation.

$$r + 3\frac{1}{2} r = \$135,000$$

$$\frac{2}{2} r + \frac{7}{2} r = \$135,000$$

$$\frac{9}{2} r = \$135,000$$

$$\frac{2}{9} \cdot \frac{9}{2} r = \frac{2}{9} \cdot \$135,000$$

$$r = \$30,000$$

$$3\frac{1}{2} r = 3\frac{1}{2} \cdot \$30,000 = \$105,000$$

She expects rent of $30,000 from office space.
She expects rent of $105,000 from retail stores.

**51.**    $n =$ number of new employees

$22 - n =$ number of experienced employees

new wage + experienced wage = total wage

$$\$9.50n \; + \; \$12.90(22 - n) \; = \$273.60$$

Solve the equation.

$$\$9.50n + \$12.90(22 - n) = \$273.60$$
$$\$9.50n + \$283.80 - \$12.90n = \$273.60$$
$$-\$3.40n + \$283.80 = \$273.60$$
$$-\$3.40n = -\$10.20$$
$$n = 3$$

$22 - n = 22 - 3 = 19$

There are 3 new employees.

There are 19 experienced employees.

**53.**    $n =$ number of Altimas

$120 - n =$ number of Sentras

Altimas profit + Sentras profit = total profit

$$\$1200n \quad + \$850(120 - n) = \$130,350$$

Solve the equation.

$$\$1200n + \$850(120 - n) = \$130,350$$
$$\$1200n + \$102,000 - \$850n = \$130,350$$
$$\$350n + \$102,000 = \$130,350$$
$$\$350n = \$28,350$$
$$n = 81$$

$120 - n = 120 - 81 = 39$

81 Altimas were sold.

39 Sentras were sold.

**55.** Answers will vary.

## 4.3  Business Formulas

**1.** $I = PRT$; $P = \$4600, R = .085, T = 1\frac{1}{2}$

$$I = \$4600 \times .085 \times 1.5$$
$$I = \$586.50$$

**3.** $P = B \times R$; $B = \$168,000, R = .06$

$$P = \$168,000 \times .06$$
$$P = \$10,080$$

**5.** $s = c + m$; $c = \$14, m = \$2.50$

$$s = \$14 + \$2.50$$
$$s = \$16.50$$

**7.** $P = 2L + 2W$; $P = 40, W = 6$

$$40 = 2L + 2 \cdot 6$$
$$40 = 2L + 12$$
$$28 = 2L$$
$$14 = L$$

**9.** $P = \dfrac{I}{RT}$; $T = 3, I = \$540, R = .08$

$$P = \frac{\$540}{.08(3)}$$
$$P = \frac{\$540}{.24}$$
$$P = \$2250$$

**11.** $y = mx^2 + c$; $m = 3, x = 7, c = 4.2$

$$y = 3(7)^2 + 4.2$$
$$y = 3(49) + 4.2$$
$$y = 147 + 4.2$$
$$y = 151.2$$

**13.** $M = P(1 + i)^n$; $P = \$640, i = .02, n = 8$

$$M = \$640(1 + .02)^8$$
$$M = \$640(1.02)^8$$
$$M \approx \$640(1.171659381)$$
$$M \approx \$749.86$$

**15.** $E = mc^2$; $m = 7.5, c = 1$

$E = 7.5(1)^2$

$E = 7.5(1)$

$E = 7.5$

**17.** $A = \dfrac{1}{2}(b+B)h$; $A = 105, b = 19, B = 11$

$105 = \dfrac{1}{2}(19+11)h$

$105 = \dfrac{1}{2}(30)h$

$105 = 15h$

$7 = h$

**19.** $P = \dfrac{S}{1+RT}$; $S = 24{,}600, R = .06, T = \dfrac{5}{12}$

$P = \dfrac{24{,}600}{1 + .06\left(\dfrac{5}{12}\right)}$

$P = \dfrac{24{,}600}{1 + .025}$

$P = \dfrac{24{,}600}{1.025}$

$P = 24{,}000$

**21.** $A = LW$; for $L$

$\dfrac{A}{W} = \dfrac{LW}{W}$     *Divide by* W.

$\dfrac{A}{W} = L$

**23.** $PV = nRT$; for $V$

$\dfrac{PV}{P} = \dfrac{nRT}{P}$     *Divide by* P.

$V = \dfrac{nRT}{P}$

**25.** $M = P(1+i)^n$; for $P$

$\dfrac{M}{(1+i)^n} = \dfrac{P(1+i)^n}{(1+i)^n}$     *Divide by* $(1+i)^n$.

$\dfrac{M}{(1+i)^n} = P$

**27.** $P = \dfrac{A}{1+i}$; for $i$.

$P(1+i) = \dfrac{A}{1+i}(1+i)$     *Multiply by* $(1+i)$.

$P(1+i) = A$

$P + Pi = A$     *Distribute.*

$Pi = A - P$     *Subtract* P.

$\dfrac{Pi}{P} = \dfrac{A-P}{P}$     *Divide by* P.

$i = \dfrac{A-P}{P}$

**29.** $P = M(1-DT)$; for $D$

$P = M - MDT$     *Distribute.*

$P - M = -MDT$     *Subtract* M.

$\dfrac{P-M}{-MT} = \dfrac{-MDT}{-MT}$     *Divide by* $-MT$.

$\dfrac{M-P}{MT} = D$

**31.** $A = \dfrac{1}{2}(b+B)h$; for $h$

$2 \cdot A = 2 \cdot \dfrac{1}{2}(b+B)h$     *Multiply by* 2.

$2A = (b+B)h$

$\dfrac{2A}{(b+B)} = \dfrac{(b+B)h}{(b+B)}$     *Divide by* $(b+B)$.

$\dfrac{2A}{(b+B)} = h$

**33.** $x =$ the cost per stuffed animal

$1800x = 4320$

$\dfrac{1800x}{1800} = \dfrac{4320}{1800}$

$x = 2.4$

The cost per stuffed animal is $2.40.

**35.** $x =$ the cost for a set of bongo drums

$6x + 7 \cdot 269 = 2445.80$

$6x + 1883 = 2445.80$

$6x = 562.80$

$x = 93.8$

The cost for a set of bongo drums is $93.80.

**37.** Use the formula $S = 280 + .05x$, where $x$ is the employee's total sales for the week and $S$ is the salary.

(a) $x = \$2940$

$$S = 280 + .05(2940)$$
$$S = 280 + 147$$
$$S = \$427$$

(b) $x = \$4450$

$$S = 280 + .05(4450)$$
$$S = 280 + 222.50$$
$$S = \$502.50$$

**39.** $x = $ gross sales

$\dfrac{1}{40}x = $ returns

net sales $=$ gross sales $-$ returns

$$230 \quad = \quad x \quad - \quad \dfrac{1}{40}x$$

Solve the equation.

$$230 = x - \dfrac{1}{40}x$$
$$230 = \dfrac{40}{40}x - \dfrac{1}{40}x$$
$$230 = \dfrac{39}{40}x$$
$$\dfrac{40}{39} \cdot 230 = \dfrac{40}{39} \cdot \dfrac{39}{40}x$$
$$236 \approx x$$

Gross sales are approximately $236 million.

**41.** $x = $ cost of chocolate-covered raisins

$\dfrac{3}{4}x = $ markup

selling price $=$ cost $+$ markup

$$4 \quad = \quad x \quad + \quad \dfrac{3}{4}x$$

Solve the equation.

$$4 = x + \dfrac{3}{4}x$$
$$4 = \dfrac{4}{4}x + \dfrac{3}{4}x$$
$$4 = \dfrac{7}{4}x$$
$$\dfrac{4}{7} \cdot 4 = \dfrac{4}{7} \cdot \dfrac{7}{4}x$$
$$2.29 \approx x$$

The cost, to the nearest cent, is $2.29.

**43.** $x = $ revenue

$\dfrac{5}{6}x = $ expenses

profit $=$ revenue $-$ expenses

$$107,400 = \quad x \quad - \quad \dfrac{5}{6}x$$

Solve the equation.

$$107,400 = x - \dfrac{5}{6}x$$
$$107,400 = \dfrac{6x}{6} - \dfrac{5}{6}x$$
$$107,400 = \dfrac{1}{6}x$$
$$6 \cdot 107,400 = 6 \cdot \dfrac{1}{6}x$$
$$644,400 = x$$

The total revenue was $644,400.

**45.** $I = PRT$; $P = \$5200, R = .075, T = 1$

$$I = \$5200 \times .075 \times 1$$
$$I = \$390$$

The interest would be $390.

**47.** $I = PRT$; $P = \$22,000, T = 2, I = \$5720$

$$\$5720 = \$22,000 \times R \times 2$$
$$\$5720 = \$44,000R$$
$$\dfrac{\$5720}{\$44,000} = \dfrac{\$44,000R}{\$44,000}$$
$$.013 = R$$

The rate of interest was .013 or 13%.

**49.** $I = PRT$;

$$P = \$5850, R = .03, I = \$702$$
$$\$702 = \$5850 \times .03 \times T$$
$$\$702 = \$175.50T$$
$$\dfrac{\$702}{\$175.50} = \dfrac{\$175.50T}{\$175.50}$$
$$4 = T$$

The time for the loan is 4 years.

**51.** $M = P(1 + RT)$;

$$M = \$4560, R = .07, T = 2$$
$$\$4560 = P(1 + .07 \cdot 2)$$
$$\$4560 = P(1 + .14)$$
$$\$4560 = P(1.14)$$
$$\dfrac{\$4560}{1.14} = \dfrac{1.14P}{1.14}$$
$$\$4000 = P$$

John initially deposited $4000.

**53.** $M = P(1+i)^n$;

$M = \$5989.50$, $i = .1$, $n = 3$

$\$5989.50 = P(1+.1)^3$

$\$5989.50 = P(1.1)^3$

$\$5989.50 = P(1.331)$

$\dfrac{\$5989.50}{1.331} = \dfrac{1.331P}{1.331}$

$\$4500 = P$

The amount borrowed was $4500.

**55.** Answers will vary.

## 4.4   Ratios and Proportions

**1.** 18 kilometers to 64 kilometers

$\dfrac{18}{64} = \dfrac{9}{32}$

**3.** 216 students to 8 faculty

$\dfrac{216}{8} = \dfrac{27}{1}$

**5.** 8 men to 6 women

$\dfrac{8}{6} = \dfrac{4}{3}$

**7.** 30 kilometers (30,000 meters) to 8 meters

$\dfrac{30,000}{8} = \dfrac{3750}{1}$

**9.** 90 dollars to 40 cents

90 dollars = 9000 cents

$\dfrac{9000}{40} = \dfrac{225}{1}$

**11.** 4 dollars to 10 quarters

4 dollars = 16 quarters

$\dfrac{16}{10} = \dfrac{8}{5}$

**13.** 20 hours to 5 days

5 days = 120 hours

$\dfrac{20}{120} = \dfrac{1}{6}$

**15.** $0.80 to $3

$\dfrac{0.8}{3} = \dfrac{8}{30} = \dfrac{4}{15}$

**17.** $3.24 to $0.72

$\dfrac{3.24}{0.72} = \dfrac{324}{72} = \dfrac{9}{2}$

**19.** $\dfrac{3}{5} = \dfrac{21}{35}$

$3 \cdot 35 = 5 \cdot 21$

$105 = 105$

The proportion is true.

**21.** $\dfrac{9}{7} = \dfrac{720}{480}$

$9 \cdot 480 = 7 \cdot 720$

$4320 \neq 5040$

The proportion is false.

**23.** $\dfrac{69}{320} = \dfrac{7}{102}$

$69 \cdot 102 = 320 \cdot 7$

$7038 \neq 2240$

The proportion is false.

**25.** $\dfrac{19}{32} = \dfrac{33}{77}$

$19 \cdot 77 = 32 \cdot 33$

$1463 \neq 1056$

The proportion is false.

**27.** $\dfrac{110}{18} = \dfrac{160}{27}$

$110 \cdot 27 = 18 \cdot 160$

$2970 \neq 2880$

The proportion is false.

**29.** $\dfrac{32}{75} = \dfrac{61}{108}$

$32 \cdot 108 = 75 \cdot 61$

$3456 \neq 4575$

The proportion is false.

**31.** $\dfrac{7.6}{10} = \dfrac{76}{100}$

$7.6 \cdot 100 = 10 \cdot 76$

$760 = 760$

The proportion is true.

**33.**
$$\frac{2\frac{1}{4}}{5} = \frac{9}{20}$$
$$2\frac{1}{4} \cdot 20 = 5 \cdot 9$$
$$45 = 45$$
The proportion is true.

**35.**
$$\frac{4\frac{1}{5}}{6\frac{1}{8}} = \frac{27}{41}$$
$$4\frac{1}{5} \cdot 41 = 6\frac{1}{8} \cdot 27$$
$$4.2 \cdot 41 = 6.125 \cdot 27$$
$$172.2 \neq 165.375$$
The proportion is false.

**37.**
$$\frac{8.15}{2.03} = \frac{61.125}{15.225}$$
$$8.15 \cdot 15.225 = 2.03 \cdot 61.125$$
$$124.08375 = 124.08375$$
The proportion is true.

**39.**
$$\frac{x}{15} = \frac{49}{105}$$
$$x \cdot 105 = 15 \cdot 49$$
$$105x = 735$$
$$\frac{105x}{105} = \frac{735}{105}$$
$$x = 7$$

**41.**
$$\frac{6}{9} = \frac{r}{108}$$
$$6 \cdot 108 = 9 \cdot r$$
$$648 = 9r$$
$$\frac{648}{9} = \frac{9r}{9}$$
$$72 = r$$

**43.**
$$\frac{63}{s} = \frac{3}{5}$$
$$63 \cdot 5 = s \cdot 3$$
$$315 = 3s$$
$$\frac{315}{3} = \frac{3s}{3}$$
$$105 = s$$

**45.**
$$\frac{1}{2} = \frac{r}{7}$$
$$1 \cdot 7 = 2 \cdot r$$
$$7 = 2r$$
$$\frac{7}{2} = \frac{2r}{2}$$
$$3\frac{1}{2} = r$$

**47.**
$$\frac{\frac{3}{4}}{6} = \frac{3}{x}$$
$$\frac{3}{4} \cdot x = 6 \cdot 3$$
$$\frac{3}{4}x = 18$$
$$\frac{4}{3} \cdot \frac{3}{4}x = \frac{4}{3} \cdot 18$$
$$x = 24$$

**49.**
$$\frac{12}{P} = \frac{23.571}{15.714}$$
$$12 \cdot 15.714 = P \cdot 23.571$$
$$188.568 = 23.571P$$
$$\frac{188.568}{23.571} = \frac{23.571P}{23.571}$$
$$8 = P$$

**51.** Answers will vary.

**53.** $x$ = number of tickets it can expect to sell in 9 days
Set up and solve a proportion.
$$\frac{2}{9} = \frac{350}{x}$$
$$2 \cdot x = 9 \cdot 350$$
$$2x = 3150$$
$$x = 1575$$
It can expect to sell 1575 tickets in 9 days.

**55.** $x$ = cost for a 12-unit apartment house
Set up and solve a proportion.
$$\frac{5}{12} = \frac{215,000}{x}$$
$$5 \cdot x = 12 \cdot 215,000$$
$$5x = 2,580,000$$
$$x = 516,000$$
The cost for a 12-unit apartment house is $516,000.

**57.** $x$ = cost of 12 dresses
Set up and solve a proportion.
$$\frac{22}{12} = \frac{660}{x}$$
$$22 \cdot x = 12 \cdot 660$$
$$22x = 7920$$
$$x = 360$$
The cost of 12 dresses is $360.

**59.** $x$ = increase in global average temperature
Set up and solve a proportion.
$$\frac{380 - 315}{1} = \frac{550 - 380}{x}$$
$$\frac{65}{1} = \frac{170}{x}$$
$$65 \cdot x = 1 \cdot 170$$
$$65x = 170$$
$$x \approx 2.6$$
There is a further increase of $2.6°$ F.

**61.** $x$ = distance between the two other cities
Set up and solve a proportion.
$$\frac{2}{17} = \frac{120}{x}$$
$$2 \cdot x = 17 \cdot 120$$
$$2x = 2040$$
$$x = 1020$$
The cities are 1020 miles apart.

**63.** $x$ = sales for the entire 52-week year
Set up and solve a proportion.
$$\frac{20}{52} = \frac{\$274,312}{x}$$
$$20 \cdot x = 52 \cdot \$274,312$$
$$20x = \$14,264,224$$
$$x = \$713,211.20$$
Sales for the entire year are $713,211.20.

**65.** $x$ = profits for the second partner
Set up and solve a proportion.
$$\frac{3}{8} = \frac{48,000}{x}$$
$$3 \cdot x = 8 \cdot 48,000$$
$$3x = 384,000$$
$$x = 128,000$$
The second partner earned $128,000.

**67.** $x$ = distance eider ducks migrate in the amount of time it takes songbirds to migrate 200 miles
Set up and solve a proportion.
$$\frac{20}{35} = \frac{200}{x}$$
$$20 \cdot x = 35 \cdot 200$$
$$20x = 7000$$
$$x = 350$$
Eider ducks migrate 350 miles in the amount of time it takes songbirds to migrate 200 miles.

**69.** $x$ = amount of an iceberg that is under water
Set up and solve a proportion.
$$\frac{\frac{1}{8}}{\frac{7}{8}} = \frac{500,000}{x}$$
$$\frac{1}{8} \cdot x = \frac{7}{8} \cdot 500,000$$
$$\frac{1}{8} x = 437,500$$
$$8 \cdot \frac{1}{8} x = 8 \cdot 437,500$$
$$x = 3,500,000$$
3,500,000 cubic meters of the iceberg is under water.

**71.** $x$ = number of U.S. dollars he will receive
Set up and solve a proportion.
$$\frac{\$1}{95 \text{ yen}} = \frac{x \text{ dollars}}{20,355 \text{ yen}}$$
$$1 \cdot 20,355 = 95 \cdot x$$
$$20,355 = 95x$$
$$214.26 \approx x$$
Benjamin will receive $214.26 U.S.

## Case Study

1. Sales = $6500 + $4.95 \cdot$ Advertising
   Sales = $6500 + $4.95 \cdot $800 = $10,460$
   Sales = $6500 + $4.95 \cdot $2000 = $16,400$

2. $50\% \cdot $6000 = .5 \cdot $6000 = $3000$
   The increased gross profit is $3000.

3. Answers will vary.

## Case in Point Summary Exercise

1. Answers will vary, but here are some obvious things: Sales of light trucks have increased dramatically since 1985, but sales of cars have fallen off. Sales of both light trucks and cars fell sharply in 2009. General Motors has a lot of competition and was only slightly larger than Ford or Toyota in 2009.

2. Sales $= 34.8 + 5.3 \cdot 6.2 + 485 \cdot .028 - 34.2 \cdot .6$
   $= 34.8 + 32.86 + 13.58 - 20.52$
   $= 60.72$ or $60,720$ vehicles

3. Sales $= 50.9 + 9.6 \cdot 5.3 + 720 \cdot .065 - 28.7 \cdot .7$
   $= 50.9 + 50.88 + 46.8 - 20.09$
   $= 128.49$ or $128,490$ vehicles

4. $\dfrac{23,850}{36,400} = \dfrac{14,910}{x}$
   $23,850 \cdot x = 36,400 \cdot 14,910$
   $23,850x = 542,724,000$
   $\dfrac{23,850x}{23,850} = \dfrac{542,724,000}{23,850}$
   $x \approx 22,756$

## Chapter 4   Test

1. $x + 45 = 96$
   $x + 45 - 45 = 96 - 45$   *Subtract* 45.
   $x = 51$

2. $r - 36 = 14.7$
   $r - 36 + 36 = 14.7 + 36$   *Add* 36.
   $r = 50.7$

3. $8t + 45 = 175.4$
   $8t + 45 - 45 = 175.4 - 45$   *Subtract* 45.
   $8t = 130.4$
   $\dfrac{8t}{8} = \dfrac{130.4}{8}$   *Divide by* 8.
   $t = 16.3$

4. $4t - 6 = 15$
   $4t - 6 + 6 = 15 + 6$   *Add* 6.
   $4t = 21$
   $\dfrac{4t}{4} = \dfrac{21}{4}$   *Divide by* 4.
   $t = 5\dfrac{1}{4} = 5.25$

5. $\dfrac{s}{6} = 43$
   $\dfrac{s}{6} \cdot 6 = 43 \cdot 6$   *Multiply by* 6.
   $s = 258$

6. $\dfrac{5z}{8} = 85$
   $\dfrac{8}{5} \cdot \dfrac{5z}{8} = \dfrac{8}{5} \cdot 85$   *Multiply by* $\dfrac{8}{5}$.
   $z = 136$

7. $\dfrac{m}{4} - 5 = 9$
   $\dfrac{m}{4} - 5 + 5 = 9 + 5$   *Add* 5.
   $\dfrac{m}{4} = 14$
   $\dfrac{m}{4} \cdot 4 = 14 \cdot 4$   *Multiply by* 4.
   $m = 56$

**8.**
$$5(x-3) = 3(x+4)$$
$$5x - 15 = 3x + 12 \qquad \textit{Distribute.}$$
$$5x - 15 + 15 = 3x + 12 + 15 \quad \textit{Add } 15.$$
$$5x = 3x + 27$$
$$5x - 3x = 3x - 3x + 27 \quad \textit{Subtract } 3x.$$
$$2x = 27$$
$$\frac{2x}{2} = \frac{27}{2} \qquad \textit{Divide by } 2.$$
$$x = \frac{27}{2} = 13\frac{1}{2}$$

**9.**
$$6y = 2y + 28$$
$$6y - 2y = 2y - 2y + 28 \quad \textit{Subtract } 2y.$$
$$4y = 28$$
$$\frac{4y}{4} = \frac{28}{4} \qquad \textit{Divide by } 4.$$
$$y = 7$$

**10.**
$$3r - 7 = 2(4 - 3r)$$
$$3r - 7 = 8 - 6r \qquad \textit{Distribute.}$$
$$3r - 7 + 7 = 8 + 7 - 6r \qquad \textit{Add } 7.$$
$$3r = 15 - 6r$$
$$3r + 6r = 15 - 6r + 6r \quad \textit{Add } 6r.$$
$$9r = 15$$
$$\frac{9r}{9} = \frac{15}{9} \qquad \textit{Divide by } 9.$$
$$r = \frac{15}{9} = 1\frac{2}{3}$$

**11.**
$$0.15(2x - 3) = 5.85$$
$$0.3x - .45 = 5.85$$
$$\textit{Distribute.}$$
$$0.3x - .45 + .45 = 5.85 + .45$$
$$\textit{Add } .45.$$
$$.3x = 6.3$$
$$\frac{.3x}{.3} = \frac{6.3}{.3}$$
$$\textit{Divide by } .3.$$
$$x = 21$$

**12.**
$$.6(y - 3) = .1y$$
$$.6y - 1.8 = .1y$$
$$\textit{Distribute.}$$
$$.6y - 1.8 - .1y = .1y - .1y$$
$$\textit{Subtract } .1y.$$
$$.5y - 1.8 = 0$$
$$.5y - 1.8 + 1.8 = 0 + 1.8$$
$$\textit{Add } 1.8.$$
$$.5y = 1.8$$
$$\frac{.5y}{.5} = \frac{1.8}{.5}$$
$$\textit{Divide by } .5.$$
$$y = 3.6$$

**13.** $I = PRT$
$$I = 2800 \times .09 \times 2$$
$$I = 504$$

**14.** $S = C + M$
$$S = 275 + 49$$
$$S = 324$$

**15.** $G = NP$
$$G = 840 \times 3.79$$
$$G = 3183.6$$

**16.** $M = P(1 + RT)$
$$M = 420\left(1 + .07 \cdot 2\frac{1}{2}\right)$$
$$M = 420(1 + .175)$$
$$M = 420(1.175)$$
$$M = 493.50$$

**17.** $R = \dfrac{D}{1 - DT}$
$$R = \frac{.04}{1 - .04(5)}$$
$$R = \frac{.04}{1 - .2}$$
$$R = \frac{.04}{.8}$$
$$R = .05$$

**18.** $A = \dfrac{S}{1+RT}$

$A = \dfrac{12{,}600}{1+.12 \cdot \dfrac{5}{12}}$

$A = \dfrac{12{,}600}{1+.05}$

$A = \dfrac{12{,}600}{1.05}$

$A = 12{,}000$

**19.** $T = \dfrac{D}{S}$

$100 = \dfrac{D}{2}$

$100 \cdot 2 = \dfrac{D}{2} \cdot 2$

$200 = D$

**20.** $\dfrac{I}{PR} = T$, or $I = PRT$

$I = 1000 \times .05 \times 1\dfrac{1}{2}$

$I = 7.5$

**21.** $d = rt$

$d = .07 \times 12$

$d = .84$

**22.** $I = PRT$

$I = 500 \times .08 \times 3$

$I = 120$

**23.** $A = LW$

$\dfrac{A}{L} = \dfrac{LW}{L}$

$\dfrac{A}{L} = W$

**24.** $d = rt$

$\dfrac{d}{t} = \dfrac{rt}{t}$

$\dfrac{d}{t} = r$

**25.** $I = PRT$

$\dfrac{I}{PR} = \dfrac{PRT}{PR}$

$\dfrac{I}{PR} = T$

**26.** $P = 1 + RT$

$P - 1 = 1 + RT - 1$

$P - 1 = RT$

$\dfrac{P-1}{T} = \dfrac{RT}{T}$

$\dfrac{P-1}{T} = R$

**27.** $A = P + PRT$

$A - P = P - P + PRT$

$A - P = PRT$

$\dfrac{A-P}{PR} = \dfrac{PRT}{PR}$

$\dfrac{A-P}{PR} = T$

**28.** $R(1 - DT) = D$

$\dfrac{R(1-DT)}{1-DT} = \dfrac{D}{1-DT}$

$R = \dfrac{D}{1-DT}$

**29.** $\dfrac{250 \text{ pesos}}{1250 \text{ pesos}} = \dfrac{1}{5}$

**30.** $\dfrac{45 \text{ women}}{110 \text{ men}} = \dfrac{9}{22}$

**31.** $\dfrac{\$1.20}{75 \text{ cents}} \times \dfrac{100 \text{ cents}}{\$1} = \dfrac{120}{75} = \dfrac{8}{5}$

**32.** $\dfrac{20 \text{ hours}}{5 \text{ days}} \times \dfrac{1 \text{ day}}{24 \text{ hours}} = \dfrac{20}{120} = \dfrac{1}{6}$

**33.** $\dfrac{35 \text{ dimes}}{6 \text{ dollars}} \times \dfrac{1 \text{ dollar}}{10 \text{ dimes}} = \dfrac{35}{60} = \dfrac{7}{12}$

**34.** $\dfrac{30 \text{ inches}}{5 \text{ yards}} \times \dfrac{1 \text{ yard}}{36 \text{ inches}} = \dfrac{30}{180} = \dfrac{1}{6}$

**35.** $\dfrac{2}{3} = \dfrac{42}{63}$

$2 \times 63 = 3 \times 42$

$126 = 126$

The proportion is true.

**36.** $\dfrac{6}{9} = \dfrac{36}{52}$

$6 \times 52 = 9 \times 36$

$312 \neq 324$

The proportion is false.

**37.** $\dfrac{18}{20} = \dfrac{56}{60}$

$18 \times 60 = 20 \times 56$

$1080 \neq 1120$

The proportion is false.

**38.** $\dfrac{12}{18} = \dfrac{8}{12}$

$12 \times 12 = 18 \times 8$

$144 = 144$

The proportion is true.

**39.** $\dfrac{420}{600} = \dfrac{14}{20}$

$420 \times 20 = 600 \times 14$

$8400 = 8400$

The proportion is true.

**40.** $\dfrac{7.6}{10} = \dfrac{76}{100}$

$7.6 \times 100 = 10 \times 76$

$7602 = 760$

The proportion is true.

**41.** $\dfrac{y}{35} = \dfrac{25}{5}$

$y \cdot 5 = 35 \cdot 25$

$5y = 875$

$\dfrac{5y}{5} = \dfrac{875}{5}$

$y = 175$

**42.** $\dfrac{15}{s} = \dfrac{45}{117}$

$15 \cdot 117 = s \cdot 45$

$1755 = 45s$

$\dfrac{1755}{45} = \dfrac{45s}{45}$

$39 = s$

**43.** $\dfrac{a}{25} = \dfrac{4}{20}$

$a \cdot 20 = 25 \cdot 4$

$20a = 100$

$\dfrac{20a}{20} = \dfrac{100}{20}$

$a = 5$

**44.** $\dfrac{6}{x} = \dfrac{4}{18}$

$6 \cdot 18 = x \cdot 4$

$108 = 4x$

$\dfrac{108}{4} = \dfrac{4x}{4}$

$27 = x$

**45.** $\dfrac{z}{20} = \dfrac{80}{200}$

$z \cdot 200 = 20 \cdot 80$

$200z = 1600$

$\dfrac{200z}{200} = \dfrac{1600}{200}$

$z = 8$

**46.** $\dfrac{25}{100} = \dfrac{8}{m}$

$25 \cdot m = 100 \cdot 8$

$25m = 800$

$\dfrac{25m}{25} = \dfrac{800}{25}$

$m = 32$

**47.** $\dfrac{1}{2} = \dfrac{r}{7}$

$1 \cdot 7 = 2 \cdot r$

$7 = 2r$

$\dfrac{7}{2} = \dfrac{2r}{2}$

$\dfrac{7}{2} = r$

$r = \dfrac{7}{2} = 3\dfrac{1}{2}$

**48.** $\dfrac{2}{3} = \dfrac{5}{s}$

$2 \cdot s = 3 \cdot 5$

$2s = 15$

$\dfrac{2s}{2} = \dfrac{15}{2}$

$s = \dfrac{15}{2} = 7\dfrac{1}{2}$

**49.** $x + 8 = 20$
$x + 8 - 8 = 20 - 8$
$x = 12$

**50.** $4 + x = 51$
$4 + x - 4 = 51 - 4$
$x = 47$

**51.** $30x = 1800$
$\dfrac{30x}{30} = \dfrac{1800}{30}$
$x = 60$

**52.** $24 = 3x$
$\dfrac{24}{3} = \dfrac{3x}{3}$
$8 = x$

**53.** $3x + 5 = 50$
$3x + 5 - 5 = 50 - 5$
$3x = 45$
$\dfrac{3x}{3} = \dfrac{45}{3}$
$x = 15$

**54.** $4 + 7x = 18$
$4 + 7x - 4 = 18 - 4$
$7x = 14$
$\dfrac{7x}{7} = \dfrac{14}{7}$
$x = 2$

**55.** $x + (x + 1) = 91$
$x + x + 1 = 91$
$2x + 1 = 91$
$2x + 1 - 1 = 91 - 1$
$2x = 90$
$\dfrac{2x}{2} = \dfrac{90}{2}$
$x = 45$
$x + 1 = 46$

**56.** $x + (x + 2) = 240$
$x + x + 2 = 240$
$2x + 2 = 240$
$2x + 2 - 2 = 240 - 2$
$2x = 238$
$\dfrac{2x}{2} = \dfrac{238}{2}$
$x = 119$
$x + 2 = 121$

**57.** $x + 2x = 2.61$
$3x = 2.61$
$\dfrac{3x}{3} = \dfrac{2.61}{3}$
$x = .87$
$2x = 1.74$
Joe placed \$1.74 on the table.

**58.** $x + (x + 9) = 47$
$x + x + 9 = 47$
$2x + 9 = 47$
$2x + 9 - 9 = 47 - 9$
$2x = 38$
$\dfrac{2x}{2} = \dfrac{38}{2}$
$x = 19$
$x + 9 = 28$
There were 19 men in the class.
There were 28 women in the class.

**59.** $5 \cdot 1742 + 3 \cdot x = 14,878$
$8710 + 3x = 14,878$
$8710 - 8710 + 3x = 14,878 - 8710$
$3x = 6168$
$\dfrac{3x}{3} = \dfrac{6168}{3}$
$x = 2056$
The cost of a skiff is \$2056.

**60.** $\dfrac{\$172,000}{4} = \dfrac{x}{10}$
$\$172,000 \cdot 10 = 4 \cdot x$
$\$1,720,000 = 4x$
$\dfrac{\$1,720,000}{4} = \dfrac{4x}{4}$
$\$430,000 = x$

The cost of a 10-unit apartment house is \$2056.

**61.** $\dfrac{40}{3} = \dfrac{160}{x}$
$40 \cdot x = 3 \cdot 160$
$40x = 480$
$\dfrac{40x}{40} = \dfrac{480}{40}$
$x = 12$
The tax on a \$160 item is \$12.

**62.** $\dfrac{17}{1942.25} = \dfrac{1}{x}$

$\qquad 17 \cdot x = 1942.25 \cdot 1$

$\qquad 17x = 1942.25$

$\qquad \dfrac{17x}{17} = \dfrac{1942.25}{17}$

$\qquad x = 114.25$

The cost of one set is \$114.25.

**63.** $\qquad C = S - \dfrac{1}{4} \cdot C$

$\qquad\quad C = 20 - \dfrac{1}{4}C$

$\quad C + \dfrac{1}{4}C = 20 - \dfrac{1}{4}C + \dfrac{1}{4}C$

$\qquad\quad \dfrac{5}{4}C = 20$

$\quad \dfrac{5}{4}C \cdot \dfrac{4}{5} = 20 \cdot \dfrac{4}{5}$

$\qquad\qquad C = 16$

The cost is \$16.

**64.** $P = \dfrac{M}{1 + RT}$

$P = \dfrac{\$1368}{1 + .08 \cdot 1\frac{3}{4}}$

$P = \dfrac{\$1368}{1.14}$

$P = \$1200$

**65.** Answers will vary.

**66.** Answers will vary.

# Chapters 1-4 | Cumulative Review

**1.** 65,462 to the nearest hundred is 65,500.
Draw a line under the hundreds digit.

65,4̲62

Since the digit to the right of that place is 6,
increase the hundreds digit by 1. Change all
digits to the right of the hundreds place to zero.

**2.** 4,732,489 to the nearest thousand is 4,732,000.
Draw a line under the thousands digit.

4,732̲,489

Since the digit to the right of that place is 4, do
not change the thousands digit. Change all
digits to the right of the thousands place to zero.

**3.** 78.35 to the nearest tenth is 78.4.
Locate the tenths digit and draw a line.

78.3|5

Since the digit to the right of the line is 5,
increase the tenths digit by 1.

**4.** 328.2849 to the nearest hundredth is 328.28.
Locate the hundredths digit and draw a line.

328.28|49

Since the digit to the right of the line is 4, leave
the hundredths digit alone.

**5.**
```
   351
   763
  2478
+   17
  3609
```

**6.**
```
  45,867
- 37,985
   7882
```

**7.**
```
    634
  ×  38
   5072
  1902
  24,092
```

**8.**
```
  2450        245
× 320       ×  32
             490
             735
             7840    + 2 zeros
784,000
```

**9.**
```
      85
74)6290
   592
   370
   370
     0
```

**10.**
```
         224.5
102)22,899.0
    20 4
     2 49
     2 04
       459
       408
       510
       510
         0
```

**11.**
```
    .46
   9.2
   8
+ 17.514
  35.174
```

**12.**
```
   45.36
-  23.7
   21.66
```

**13.**
```
   29.8   ←——— 1 decimal
 × .41    ←——— 2 decimals
   298
  1192
  12.218  ←——— 3 decimals
```

**14.**
```
                             18.2
21.8)396.76         218)3967.6
                       218
                      1787
                      1744
                       436
                       436
                         0
```

**15.** $700 + $325 + $420 + $182 + $300 = $1927
$2025 - $1927 = $98

Felix Schmid's savings are $98.

**16.** $12 \times 16 = 192$
Clancy Strock has written 192 articles.

**17.** $\$29,742.18 + (\$14,096.18 + \$6529.42)$
$- \$18,709.51 = \$31,658.27$

The firm's checking account balance at the end of April is $\$31,658.27$.

**18.** $\$4099.52 \div \$128.11 = 32$
It will take 32 months.

**19.** $\dfrac{48}{54} = \dfrac{48 \div 6}{54 \div 6} = \dfrac{8}{9}$

**20.** $8\dfrac{1}{8} = \dfrac{(8 \times 8) + 1}{8} = \dfrac{65}{8}$

**21.** $15\overline{)107}$   $\dfrac{107}{15} = 7\dfrac{2}{15}$
$\phantom{15)}\dfrac{\phantom{0}7}{\phantom{0}}$
$\phantom{15)1}\underline{105}$
$\phantom{15)10}2$

**22.** $\phantom{+}1\dfrac{2}{3} = 1\dfrac{8}{12}$
$\underline{+2\dfrac{3}{4} = 2\dfrac{9}{12}}$
$\phantom{+2}3\dfrac{17}{12} = 4\dfrac{5}{12}$

**23.** $\phantom{+}5\dfrac{7}{8} = 5\dfrac{21}{24}$
$\underline{+7\dfrac{2}{3} = 7\dfrac{16}{24}}$
$\phantom{+}12\dfrac{37}{24} = 13\dfrac{13}{24}$

**24.** $\phantom{-}6\dfrac{1}{3} = 6\dfrac{4}{12} = 5\dfrac{16}{12}$
$\underline{-4\dfrac{7}{12} = 4\dfrac{7}{12} = 4\dfrac{7}{12}}$
$\phantom{-4}1\dfrac{9}{12} = 1\dfrac{3}{4}$

**25.** $8\dfrac{1}{2} \times \dfrac{9}{17} \times \dfrac{2}{3} = \dfrac{\overset{1}{\cancel{17}}}{\cancel{2}} \times \dfrac{\overset{3}{\cancel{9}}}{\cancel{17}} \times \dfrac{\overset{1}{\cancel{2}}}{\cancel{3}}$
$= \dfrac{1 \times 3 \times 1}{1 \times 1 \times 1} = 3$

**26.** $3\dfrac{3}{4} \div \dfrac{27}{16} = \dfrac{15}{4} \div \dfrac{27}{16}$
$= \dfrac{\overset{5}{\cancel{15}}}{\cancel{4}} \times \dfrac{\overset{4}{\cancel{16}}}{\cancel{27}} = \dfrac{5 \times 4}{1 \times 9} = \dfrac{20}{9} = 2\dfrac{2}{9}$

**27.** $5 \times 6\dfrac{1}{2} = \dfrac{5}{1} \times \dfrac{13}{2} = \dfrac{5 \times 13}{1 \times 2} = \dfrac{65}{2} = 32\dfrac{1}{2}$

The area of a shark cage is $32\dfrac{1}{2}$ square feet.

$5 \times 9 = 45$
The area of a prison cell is 45 square feet.

$45 - 32\dfrac{1}{2} = 44\dfrac{2}{2} - 32\dfrac{1}{2} = 12\dfrac{1}{2}$

A prison cell is $12\dfrac{1}{2}$ square feet larger than a shark cage.

**28.** $5\dfrac{1}{2} + 6\dfrac{1}{4} + 3\dfrac{3}{4} + 7 = 5\dfrac{2}{4} + 6\dfrac{1}{4} + 3\dfrac{3}{4} + 7$
$= 21\dfrac{6}{4} = 22\dfrac{2}{4} = 22\dfrac{1}{2}$

Mia studied $22\dfrac{1}{2}$ hours altogether.

**29.** $527\dfrac{1}{24} - \left(107\dfrac{2}{3} + 150\dfrac{3}{4} + 138\dfrac{5}{8}\right)$
$= 527\dfrac{1}{24} - \left(107\dfrac{16}{24} + 150\dfrac{18}{24} + 138\dfrac{15}{24}\right)$
$= 527\dfrac{1}{24} - \left(395\dfrac{49}{24}\right)$
$= 527\dfrac{1}{24} - \left(397\dfrac{1}{24}\right)$
$= 130$

The length of the fourth side is 130 feet.

**30.** $\dfrac{2}{3} \div 8 = \dfrac{\overset{1}{\cancel{2}}}{3} \times \dfrac{1}{\underset{4}{\cancel{8}}} = \dfrac{1 \times 1}{3 \times 4} = \dfrac{1}{12}$

Each store manager will receive $\dfrac{1}{12}$ of the total profits.

**31.** $.65 = \dfrac{65}{100} = \dfrac{13}{20}$

**32.** $\dfrac{2}{3} = .666\overline{6} \approx .667$

$$\begin{array}{r} .6666 \\ 3\overline{)2.0000} \\ \underline{18} \\ 20 \\ \underline{18} \\ 20 \\ \underline{18} \\ 20 \\ \underline{18} \\ 2 \end{array}$$

**33.** $\dfrac{7}{8} = .875 = 87.5\%$

**34.** $.25\% = .0025$

**35.** 35% of 6200 home loans

$P = B \times R$
$P = 6200 \times 35\%$
$P = 6200 \times .35$
$P = 2170$ home loans

**36.** 134% of $80

$P = B \times R$
$P = \$80 \times 134\%$
$P = \$80 \times 1.34$
$P = \$107.20$

**37.** 275 sales is what percent of 1100 sales?

$R = \dfrac{P}{B}$

$R = \dfrac{275}{1100}$

$R = .25 = 25\%$

275 sales is 25% of 1100 sales?

**38.** 375 patients is what percent of 250 patients?

$R = \dfrac{P}{B}$

$R = \dfrac{375}{250}$

$R = 1.5 = 150\%$

375 patients is 150% of 250 patients?

**39.** $R = \dfrac{P}{B}$

$R = \dfrac{400}{38,990}$

$R \approx .0103 = 1.03\%$

About 1.03% will be added.

**40.** $P = B \times R$
$P = \$2499.99 \times 15\%$
$P = \$2499.99 \times .15$
$P = \$374.9985 \approx \$375$
The discount is $375.

$\$2499.99 - \$375 = \$2124.99$
The sale price is $2124.99.

**41.** $100\% + 13.7\% = 113.7\%$

$B = \dfrac{P}{R}$

$B = \dfrac{111,150}{113.7\%}$

$B = \dfrac{111,150}{1.137}$

$B \approx 97,757$

Last year's sales were 97,757 copies.

**42.** $100\% - 11.8\% = 88.2\%$

$B = \dfrac{P}{R}$

$B = \dfrac{\$35,138.88}{88.2\%}$

$B = \dfrac{\$35,138.88}{.882}$

$B = \$39,840$

Hornor's sales were $39,840.

**43.** $450 = 450 \times 100\% = 45,000\%$
Sales increased 45,000%.

**44.** $\dfrac{1}{6} \times 100\% \approx 16.7\%$

The value today is approximately 16.7% of the past value.

**45. (a)**   $45\% + 23\% + 15\% = 83\%$

83% of the exported beef was shipped to Japan, Mexico, and South Korea.

**(b)**   $P = B \times R$
$P = 2.3 \text{ billion} \times 83\%$
$P = 2.3 \text{ billion} \times .83$
$P = 1.909 \text{ billion}$

1.909 billion pounds was exported to these three countries.

**46. (a)**   $10\% + 7\% = 17\%$

17% of the exported beef was shipped to countries other than Japan, Mexico, and South Korea.

**(b)**   $P = B \times R$
$P = 2.3 \text{ billion} \times 17\%$
$P = 2.3 \text{ billion} \times .17$
$P = .391 \text{ billion}$

.391 billion pounds was exported to countries other than Japan, Mexico, and South Korea.

**47.**   $P = B \times R$
$P = 2.3 \text{ billion} \times 45\%$
$P = 2.3 \text{ billion} \times .45$
$P = 1.035 \text{ billion}$
1.035 billion pounds to Japan

$P = B \times R$
$P = 2.3 \text{ billion} \times 15\%$
$P = 2.3 \text{ billion} \times .15$
$P = .345 \text{ billion}$
.345 billion pounds to South Korea

$1.035 - .345 = .69$
.69 billion pounds more beef was exported to Japan than to South Korea.

**48.**   $P = B \times R$
$P = 2.3 \text{ billion} \times 23\%$
$P = 2.3 \text{ billion} \times .23$
$P = .529 \text{ billion}$
.529 billion pounds to Mexico

$P = B \times R$
$P = 2.3 \text{ billion} \times 10\%$
$P = 2.3 \text{ billion} \times .1$
$P = .23 \text{ billion}$
.23 billion pounds to Canada

$.529 - .23 = .299$
.299 billion pounds more beef was exported to Mexico than to Canada.

**49.**   $9r - 23 = 31$
$9r - 23 + 23 = 31 + 23$
$9r = 54$
$\dfrac{9r}{9} = \dfrac{54}{9}$
$r = 6$

**50.**   $\dfrac{3}{4}t = 120$
$\dfrac{3}{4}t \cdot \dfrac{4}{3} = 120 \cdot \dfrac{4}{3}$
$t = \dfrac{480}{3} = 160$

**51.**   $5y - 10 = 26$
$5y - 10 + 10 = 26 + 10$
$5y = 36$
$\dfrac{5y}{5} = \dfrac{36}{5}$
$y = 7\dfrac{1}{5}$

**52.**   $20 + 5x = 83 - x$
$20 + 5x - 20 = 83 - x - 20$
$5x = 63 - x$
$5x + x = 63 - x + x$
$6x = 63$
$\dfrac{6x}{6} = \dfrac{63}{6}$
$x = 10\dfrac{3}{6} = 10\dfrac{1}{2}$

**53.**   $I = PRT;\ P = \$45,000, R = .015, T = .5$
$I = \$45,000 \times .015 \times .5$
$I = \$337.50$

**54.**   $d = rt;\ r = 378, t = 8.5$
$d = 378 \times 8.5$
$d = 3213$

**55.**   $A = P + PRT;\ A = 1368,\ P = 1200,\ T = 2$
$1368 = 1200 + 1200 \times R \times 2$
$1368 = 1200 + 2400R$
$1368 - 1200 = 1200 + 2400R - 1200$
$168 = 2400R$
$.07 = R$

**56.** $M = P(1+i)^n$; $n = 6$, $i = 0.02$,

$M = \$42,231.09$

$$\$42,231.09 = P(1+.02)^6$$

$$\$42,231.09 = P(1.02)^6$$

$$\frac{\$42,231.09}{(1.02)^6} = \frac{P(1.02)^6}{(1.02)^6}$$

$$\frac{\$42,231.09}{(1.126162419)} \approx P$$

$$\$37,500 \approx P$$

**57.** $I = PRT$; for T

$$\frac{I}{PR} = \frac{PRT}{PR} \qquad \textit{Divide by PR.}$$

$$\frac{I}{PR} = T$$

**58.** $PV = nRT$; for P

$$\frac{PV}{V} = \frac{nRT}{V} \qquad \textit{Divide by V.}$$

$$P = \frac{nRT}{V}$$

**59.** $M = P(1+i)^n$; for P

$$\frac{M}{(1+i)^n} = \frac{P(1+i)^n}{(1+i)^n} \qquad \textit{Divide by } (1+i)^n.$$

$$\frac{M}{(1+i)^n} = P$$

**60.** $A = \dfrac{S}{1+RT}$; for R

$$A(1+RT) = S \qquad \textit{Multiply by } (1+RT).$$

$$A + ART = S \qquad \textit{Distribute.}$$

$$ART = S - A \qquad \textit{Subtract A.}$$

$$\frac{ART}{AT} = \frac{S-A}{AT} \qquad \textit{Divide by AT.}$$

$$R = \frac{S-A}{AT}$$

**61.** 500 euros to 725 dollars

$$\frac{500}{725} = \frac{20}{29}$$

**62.** 24 ounces to 15 gallons

$$\frac{24}{15} = \frac{8}{5}$$

**63.** 14 lockers to 40 minutes

$$\frac{14}{40} = \frac{7}{20}$$

**64.** 630 apples to 168 cans

$$\frac{630}{168} = \frac{15}{4}$$

**65.** $\qquad x + 47 = 93$

$$x + 47 - 47 = 93 - 47$$

$$x = 46$$

**66.** $x + (x+2) = 228$

$$2x + 2 = 228$$

$$2x + 2 - 2 = 228 - 2$$

$$2x = 226$$

$$x = 113$$

$$x + 2 = 113 + 2 = 115$$

**67.** $C + .42C = \$159$

$$1.42C = \$159$$

$$C \approx \$111.97$$

The cost to the bookstore is \$111.97.

**68.** $\qquad x = $ number of men

$x + 9 = $ number of women

men + women = total students

$\quad x \ + \ x + 9 \ = \qquad 21$

Solve the equation.

$$x + (x + 9) = 47$$

$$2x + 9 = 47$$

$$2x + 9 - 9 = 47 - 9$$

$$2x = 38$$

$$x = 19$$

There are 19 men.

$$x + 9 = 19 + 9 = 28$$

There are 28 women.

**69.** $x =$ cost to replace the roof on a 2400 square foot house

Set up and solve a proportion.

$$\frac{1450}{6600} = \frac{2400}{x}$$

$$1450 \cdot x = 6600 \cdot 2400$$

$$1450x = 15{,}840{,}000$$

$$x \approx 10{,}924$$

The cost is approximately \$10,924.

**70.** $x =$ total monthly rent generated by a 70 unit complex

Set up and solve a proportion.

$$\frac{32}{21{,}920} = \frac{70}{x}$$

$$32 \cdot x = 21{,}920 \cdot 70$$

$$32x = 1{,}534{,}400$$

$$x = 47{,}950$$

The total monthly rent generated is \$47,950.

# Chapter 5 | Bank Services

## 5.1 Checking Accounts and Check Registers

**1.** $\$5.00 + (92 \times \$.10) = \$5.00 + \$9.20 = \$14.20$

**3.** $\$12.00 + (40 \times \$.20) = \$12.00 + \$8.00 = \$20.00$

**5.** $\$7.50 + (48 \times \$.20) = \$7.50 + \$9.60 = \$17.10$

**7.** $\$7.50 + (72 \times \$.20) = \$7.50 + \$14.40 = \$21.90$

**9.**

| 857 | | |
|---|---|---|
| _Mar. 8_ 20____ | | |
| Amount _$380.71_ | | |
| To _Nola Akala_ | | |
| For _Tutoring_ | | |
| Bal. Bro't. For'd. | 3971 | 28 |
| Am't. Deposited | 79 | 26 |
| Total | 4050 | 54 |
| Am't. this Check | 380 | 71 |
| Balance For'd. | 3669 | 83 |

**11.**

| 735 | | |
|---|---|---|
| _Dec. 4_ 20____ | | |
| Amount _$37.52_ | | |
| To _Paul's Pools_ | | |
| For _Chemicals_ | | |
| Bal. Bro't. For'd. | 1126 | 73 |
| Am't. Deposited | | |
| Total | 1126 | 73 |
| Am't. this Check | 37 | 52 |
| Balance For'd. | 1089 | 21 |

**13.** Answers will vary.

**15.** Answers will vary.

**17.**

| 5312 | | |
|---|---|---|
| _Oct. 10_ 20____ | | |
| Amount _$39.12_ | | |
| To _County Clerk_ | | |
| For _License_ | | |
| Bal. Bro't. For'd. | 5972 | 89 |
| Am't. Deposited | 752 | 18 |
| | 23 | 32 |
| Total | 6748 | 39 |
| Am't. this Check | 39 | 12 |
| Balance For'd. | 6709 | 27 |

**19.** Balance Brought Forward = $9628.35

$\$\ 9,628.35 - \$\ \ 215.71 = \$\ 9,412.64$
$\$\ 9,412.64 - \$\ \ 573.78 = \$\ 8,838.68$
$\$\ 8,838.68 - \$\ \ 112.15 = \$\ 8,726.71$
$\$\ 8,726.71 + \$\ \ 753.28 = \$\ 9,479.99$
$\$\ 9,479.99 + \$1475.69 = \$10,955.68$
$\$10,955.68 - \$\ \ 426.55 = \$10,529.13$
$\$10,529.13 - \$\ \ 637.93 = \$\ 9,891.20$
$\$\ 9,891.20 - \$\ \ \ 65.62 = \$\ 9,825.58$
$\$\ 9,825.58 - \$\ \ 248.17 = \$\ 9,577.41$
$\$\ 9,577.41 + \$\ \ 335.85 = \$\ 9,913.26$
$\$\ 9,913.26 - \$\ \ 450.50 = \$\ 9,462.76$

**21.** Balance Brought Forward = $832.15

$\$832.15 - \$257.29 = \$\ 574.86$
$\$574.86 - \$190.50 = \$\ 384.36$
$\$384.36 + \$\ \ 78.29 = \$\ 462.65$
$\$462.65 + \$157.42 = \$\ 620.07$
$\$620.07 - \$\ \ 38.76 = \$\ 581.31$
$\$581.31 - \$175.88 = \$\ 405.43$
$\$405.43 + \$379.28 = \$\ 784.71$
$\$784.71 - \$197.20 = \$\ 587.51$
$\$587.51 - \$\ \ 25.10 = \$\ 562.41$
$\$562.41 - \$\ \ 75.00 = \$\ 487.41$
$\$487.41 + \$722.35 = \$1209.76$

## 5.2 Checking Services and Credit-Card Transactions

1. $66.68 + $119.63 + $53.86 + $178.62
   $+ $219.78 + $18.95 + $496.28 + $21.85$
   $+ $242.78 + $176.93 = $1595.36$
   The total of the credit card sales is $1595.36.

3. $1595.36 − $207.69 = $1387.67
   The credit card sales less refunds are
   $1387.67.

5. $1387.67 − $34.69 = $1352.98
   The amount of credit given is $1352.98.

7. $29.76 + $102.15 + $71.95 = $203.86
   The total of the credit refunds is $203.86.

9. $2215.90 × .03 = $66.48
   The charge at the statement date is $66.48.

11. $7.84 + $33.18 + $50.76 + $12.72 + $9.36
    $+ $118.68 + $98.56 + $318.72 + $116.35$
    $+ $23.78 + $38.95 + $235.82 = $1064.72$
    The total of the credit card sales is $1064.72.

13. $1064.72 − $72.83 = $991.89
    The credit card sales less refunds are $991.89.

15. $991.89 − $19.84 = $972.05
    The amount of credit given is $972.05.

17. $43.15 + $17.06 = $60.21
    The total of the credit refunds is $60.21.

19. $1184.99 × .025 ≈ $29.62
    The charge at the statement date is $29.62.

21. Answers will vary.

## 5.3 Bank Statement Reconciliation

1. Balance:
   $4572.15

   Deposits:
   $816.14 + $571.28 = $1387.42

   Checks Outstanding:
   $225.23 + $97.68 + $418.25 + $348.17
   $= $1089.33$

   Current Balance
   $=$ Balance $+$ Deposits $−$ Checks Outstanding
   $= $4572.15 + $1387.42 − $1089.33$
   $= $4870.24$

3. Balance:
   $7911.42

   Deposits:
   $492.80 + $38.72 = $531.52

   Checks Outstanding:
   $52.38 + $95.42 + $528.02 + $76.50
   $= $752.32$

   Current Balance
   $=$ Balance $+$ Deposits $−$ Checks Outstanding
   $= $7911.42 + $531.52 − $752.32$
   $= $7690.62$

5. Balance:
   $19,523.20

   Deposits:
   $6724.93 + $78.81 = $6803.74

   Checks Outstanding:
   $6853.60 + $795.77 + $340.00 + $22.85
   $= $8012.22$

   Current Balance
   $=$ Balance $+$ Deposits $−$ Checks Outstanding
   $= $19,523.20 + $6803.74 − $8012.22$
   $= $18,314.72$

7. Answers will vary.

9. Answers will vary.

**11.**

| Checks Outstanding | | |
|---|---|---|
| Number | Amount | |
| 421 | 371 | 52 |
| 424 | 429 | 07 |
| 427 | 883 | 69 |
| 429 | 35 | 62 |
| | | |
| | | |
| Total | $1719 | 90 |

Compare the list of checks paid by the bank with your records. List and total the checks not yet paid.

(1) Enter new balance from bank statement:     $6875.09

(2) List any deposits made by you and not yet recorded by the bank:
+ 701.56
+ 421.78
+ 689.35
+ _____

(3) Add all numbers from lines above. Total:     $8687.78

(4) Write total of checks outstanding:     − 1719.90

(5) Subtract (4) from (3). This is adjusted bank balance:     $6967.88

**To reconcile your records:**

(6) List your checkbook balance:     $6965.92

(7) Write the total of any fees or charges deducted by the bank and not yet subtracted by you from your checkbook:     − 8.75

(8) Subtract line (7) from line (6):     $6957.17

(9) Enter interest credit: (Add to your checkbook)     + 10.71

(10) Add line (9) to line (8). Adjusted checkbook balance:     $6967.88

New balance of your account; this number should be same as (5).

**13.**

| Checks Outstanding | | |
|---|---|---|
| Number | Amount | |
| 767 | 63 | 24 |
| 771 | 135 | 76 |
| | | |
| | | |
| | | |
| | | |
| Total | $199 | 00 |

Compare the list of checks paid by the bank with your records. List and total the checks not yet paid.

(1) Enter new balance from bank statement:     $5636.51

(2) List any deposits made by you and not yet recorded by the bank:
+ 220.16
+ _____
+ _____
+ _____

(3) Add all numbers from lines above. Total:     $5856.67

(4) Write total of checks outstanding:     − 199.00

(5) Subtract (4) from (3). This is adjusted bank balance:     $5657.67

**To reconcile your records:**

(6) List your checkbook balance:     $5858.85

(7) Write the total of any fees or charges deducted by the bank and not yet subtracted by you from your checkbook:     − 209.30

(8) Subtract line (7) from line (6):     $5649.55

(9) Enter interest credit: (Add to your checkbook)     + 8.12

(10) Add line (9) to line (8). Adjusted checkbook balance:     $5657.67

New balance of your account; this number should be same as (5).

## Case Study

1. Net deposit:
   $$\$8752.40 - \$573.94 = \$8178.46$$

2. Fee on net credit-card sales:
   $$\$8178.46 \times .025 = \$204.46$$

3. Total checks outstanding:
   $$\$758.14 + \$38.37 + \$1671.88$$
   $$+\$120.13 + \$2264.75 + \$78.11$$
   $$+\$3662.73 + \$816.25 + \$400 = \$9810.36$$

4. Total deposits not recorded:
   $$\$458.23 + \$771.18 + \$235.71 + \$1278.55$$
   $$+\$663.52 + \$1475.39 = \$4882.58$$

5. Current balance:
   $$\$4228.34 + \$7974 - \$9810.36 + \$4882.58$$
   $$= \$7274.56$$

## Case in Point Summary Exercise

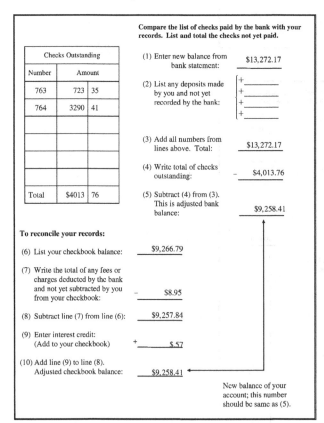

## Chapter 5   Test

1.  $\$7.50 + (62 \times \$.20) = \$7.50 + \$12.40 = \$19.90$

2.  $\$5.00 + (44 \times \$.10) = \$5.00 + \$4.40 = \$9.40$

3.  $\$12.00 + (27 \times \$.20) = \$12.00 + \$5.40 = \$17.40$

4.

| 2261 | | |
|---|---|---|
| *Aug. 6*                    20_____ | | |
| Amount  *$6892.12* | | |
| To  *WBC Broadcasting* | | |
| For  *Airtime* | | |
| Bal. Bro't. For'd. | *16,409* | *82* |
| Am't. Deposited | | |
| Total | *16,409* | *82* |
| Am't. this Check | *6,892* | *12* |
| Balance For'd. | *9,517* | *70* |

5.

| 2262 | | |
|---|---|---|
| *Aug. 8*                    20_____ | | |
| Amount  *$1258.36* | | |
| To  *Lakeland Weekly* | | |
| For  *Space buy* | | |
| Bal. Bro't. For'd. | *9,517* | *70* |
| Am't. Deposited | *1,572* | *00* |
| Total | *11,089* | *70* |
| Am't. this Check | *1,258* | *36* |
| Balance For'd. | *9,831* | *34* |

6.

| 2263 | | |
|---|---|---|
| *Aug. 14*                    20_____ | | |
| Amount  *$416.14* | | |
| To  *W. Wilson* | | |
| For  *Freelance Art* | | |
| Bal. Bro't. For'd. | *9,831* | *34* |
| Am't. Deposited | *10,000* | *00* |
| Total | *19,831* | *34* |
| Am't. this Check | *416* | *14* |
| Balance For'd. | *19,415* | *20* |

7.  $\$218.68 + \$37.84 + \$33.18 + \$20.76$
    $+ \$12.72 + \$8.97 + \$135.82 + \$67.45$
    $+ \$461.82 + \$116.35 + \$23.78 + \$572.18$
    $= \$1709.55$
    The total amount of credit sales is $1709.55.

8.  $\$45.63 + \$36.36 = \$81.99$
    The total amount of refunds is $81.99.

9.  $\$1709.55 - \$81.99 = \$1627.56$
    The credit card sales less refunds are $1627.56.

10. $\$1627.56 \times .035 \approx \$56.96$
    The charge at the statement date is $56.96.

11. $\$1627.56 - \$56.96 = \$1570.60$
    The amount of credit given is $1570.60.

**12.**

Compare the list of checks paid by the bank with your records. List and total the checks not yet paid.

| Checks Outstanding | |
|---|---|
| Number | Amount |
| 3221 | 82 \| 74 |
| 3229 | 69 \| 08 |
| 3230 | 124 \| 73 |
| 3232 | 51 \| 20 |
|  |  |
|  |  |
| Total | $327 \| 75 |

(1) Enter new balance from bank statement:     $4721.30

(2) List any deposits made by you and not yet recorded by the bank:
+ 758.06
+ 32.51
+ 298.06
+ _____

(3) Add all numbers from lines above. Total:    $5809.93

(4) Write total of checks outstanding:    − 327.75

(5) Subtract (4) from (3). This is adjusted bank balance:    $5482.18

**To reconcile your records:**

(6) List your checkbook balance:    $5474.60

(7) Write the total of any fees or charges deducted by the bank and not yet subtracted by you from your checkbook:    − 2.00

(8) Subtract line (7) from line (6):    $5472.60

(9) Enter interest credit: (Add to your checkbook)    + 9.58

(10) Add line (9) to line (8). Adjusted checkbook balance:    $5482.18

New balance of your account; this number should be same as (5).

# Chapter 6 | Payroll

## 6.1 Gross Earnings: Wages and Salaries

1. $7+4+7+10+8+4=40$
   40 regular hours
   0 overtime hours
   Overtime rate: $1\frac{1}{2} \times \$8.10 = \$12.15$

3. $3+5+8.25+9+8.5+5=38.75$
   38.75 regular hours
   0 overtime hours
   Overtime rate: $1\frac{1}{2} \times \$18.70 = \$28.05$

5. $9.5+7+9+9.25+10.5=45.25$
   40 regular hours
   $45.25-40=5.25$ overtime hours
   Overtime rate: $1\frac{1}{2} \times \$11.48 = \$17.22$

7. 
   | | |
   |---|---|
   | 40 hours × \$8.24 | = \$329.60 |
   | 7.5 O.T. hours × \$12.36 | = + 92.70 |
   | Gross Earnings | \$422.30 |

9. 
   | | |
   |---|---|
   | 40 hours × \$9.50 | = \$380.00 |
   | 11.25 O.T. hours × \$14.25 | = + 160.31 |
   | Gross Earnings | \$540.31 |

11. Overtime rate: $1\frac{1}{2} \times \$8.80 = \$13.20$

    | | |
    |---|---|
    | 39.5 hours × \$8.80 | = \$347.60 |
    | 0 O.T. hours × \$13.20 | = + 0 |
    | Gross Earnings | \$347.60 |

13. Overtime rate: $1\frac{1}{2} \times \$14.40 = \$21.60$

    | | |
    |---|---|
    | 40 hours × \$14.40 | = \$576.00 |
    | 4.5 O.T. hours × \$21.60 | = + 97.20 |
    | Gross Earnings | \$673.20 |

15. Overtime rate: $1\frac{1}{2} \times \$9.18 = \$13.77$

    | | |
    |---|---|
    | 40 hours × \$9.18 | = \$367.20 |
    | 4.25 O.T. hours × \$13.77 | = + 58.52 |
    | Gross Earnings | \$425.72 |

17. $7.75+10+5+9.75+8+10=50.5$
    40 regular hours
    10.5 overtime hours
    Overtime premium rate: $\frac{1}{2} \times \$9.50 = \$4.75$

    | | |
    |---|---|
    | 50.5 hours × \$9.50 | = \$479.75 |
    | 10.5 O.T. hours × \$4.75 | = + 49.88 |
    | Gross Earnings | \$529.63 |

19. $8.5+5.5+10+12+10.5+7=53.5$
    40 regular hours
    13.5 overtime hours
    Overtime premium rate: $\frac{1}{2} \times \$12.50 = \$6.25$

    | | |
    |---|---|
    | 53.5 hours × \$12.50 | = \$668.75 |
    | 13.5 O.T. hours × \$6.25 | = + 84.38 |
    | Gross Earnings | \$753.13 |

21. $8+8+8+6+5=35$ regular hours
    $2+1+3=6$ overtime hours
    Overtime rate: $1\frac{1}{2} \times \$9.40 = \$14.10$

    | | |
    |---|---|
    | 35 hours × \$9.40 | = \$329.00 |
    | 6 O.T. hours × \$14.10 | = + \$84.60 |
    | Gross Earnings | \$413.60 |

23. $7.5+8+8+8+8=39.5$ regular hours
    $1+2.75=3.75$ overtime hours
    Overtime rate: $1\frac{1}{2} \times \$10.80 = \$16.20$

    | | |
    |---|---|
    | 39.5 hours × \$10.80 | = \$426.60 |
    | 3.75 O.T. hours × \$16.20 | = + \$60.75 |
    | Gross Earnings | \$487.35 |

25. $8+8+7.75+8+8=39.75$ regular hours
    $1.5+0.5+1.5=3.5$ overtime hours
    Overtime rate: $1\frac{1}{2} \times \$21.50 = \$32.25$

    | | |
    |---|---|
    | 39.75 hours × \$21.50 | = \$854.63 |
    | 3.5 O.T. hours × \$32.25 | = + \$112.88 |
    | Gross Earnings | \$967.51 |

27. Answers will vary.

**29.** $\$960 \times 24 = \$23,040$     annually
$\$23,040 \div 12 = \$1920$     monthly
$\$23,040 \div 26 = \$886.15$     biweekly
$\$23,040 \div 52 = \$443.08$     weekly

**31.** $5200 \times 12 = \$62,400$     annually
$\$62,400 \div 24 = \$2600$     semimonthly
$\$62,400 \div 26 = \$2400$     biweekly
$\$62,400 \div 52 = \$1200$     weekly

**33.** $(\$830 \times 52 = \$43,160$ annually
$\$43,160 \div 12 = \$3596.67$ monthly
$\$43,160 \div 24 = \$1798.33$ semimonthly
$\$43,160 \div 26 = \$1660$ biweekly

**35.** $\$360 \div 40 = \$9$ per hour

Overtime rate: $1\frac{1}{2} \times \$9 = \$13.50$

Overtime hours: $42 - 40 = 2$

| Salary | $= \$360$ |
|---|---|
| 2 O.T. hours $\times \$13.50 =$ | $+ \ 27$ |
| Gross Earnings | $\$387$ |

**37.** $\$420 \div 40 = \$10.50$ per hour

Overtime rate: $1\frac{1}{2} \times \$10.50 = \$15.75$

Overtime hours: $43 - 40 = 3$

| Salary | $= \$420.00$ |
|---|---|
| 3 O.T. hours $\times \$15.75 =$ | $+\$47.25$ |
| Gross Earnings | $\$467.25$ |

**39.** $\$640 \div 40 = \$16$ per hour

Overtime rate: $1\frac{1}{2} \times \$16 = \$24$

Overtime hours: $48 - 40 = 8$

| Salary | $= \$640$ |
|---|---|
| 8 O.T. hours $\times \$24 =$ | $+\$192$ |
| Gross Earnings | $\$832$ |

**41.** 40 regular hours
$52 - 40 = 12$ overtime hours

Overtime rate: $1\frac{1}{2} \times \$13.60 = \$20.40$

| 40 hours $\times \$13.60$ | $= \ \ \$544.00$ |
|---|---|
| 12 O.T. hours $\times \$20.40 =$ | $+ \ 244.80$ |
| Gross Earnings | $\$788.80$ |

**43.** $8+8+5.5+8+7.25 = 36.75$  regular hours
$2+1.75+4 = 7.75$ overtime hours

Overtime rate: $1\frac{1}{2} \times \$11.50 = \$17.25$

| 36.75 hours $\times \$11.50$ | $= \ \ \ \$422.63$ |
|---|---|
| 7.75 O.T. hours $\times \$17.25 =$ | $+ \ 133.69$ |
| Gross Earnings | $\$556.32$ |

**45. (a)** $\$630 \times 2 = \$1260$ biweekly

**(b)** $(\$630 \times 52) \div 24 = \$1365$ semimonthly

**(c)** $(\$630 \times 52) \div 12 = \$2730$ monthly

**(d)** $\$630 \times 52 = \$32,760$ annually

**47.** Answers will vary.

## 6.2   Gross Earnings:
## Piecework and Commission

**1.** $194 \times \$.48 = \$93.12$

**3.** $320 \times \$.48 = \$153.60$

**5.**
| (Total units) | 820 | | |
|---|---|---|---|
| (First 500 units) | $- \ 500$ | at \$.05 each $=$ | \$25.00 |
| | 320 | | |
| (Next 200 units) | $- \ 200$ | at \$.07 each $=$ | \$14.00 |
| (Over 700 units) | 120 | at \$.09 each $=$ | \$10.80 |
| | | | \$49.80 |

**7.**
| (Total units) | 852 | | |
|---|---|---|---|
| (First 500 units) | $- \ 500$ | at \$.05 each $=$ | \$25.00 |
| | 352 | | |
| (Next 200 units) | $- \ 200$ | at \$.07 each $=$ | \$14.00 |
| (Over 700 units) | 152 | at \$.09 each $=$ | \$13.68 |
| | | | \$52.68 |

**9.** Answers will vary.

**11.** Hourly Rate: $8 \times \$8.20 = \$65.60$

| Monday | $95 \times \$.75 = \$71.25$ |
|---|---|
| Tuesday | $90 \times \$.75 = \$67.50$ |
| Wednesday | $74 \times \$.75$   \$65.60 (hourly) |
| Thursday | $98 \times \$.75 = \$73.50$ |
| Friday | $101 \times \$.75 = \$75.75$ |
| | \$353.60 |

**13.** Hourly Rate: $8 \times \$8.80 = \$70.40$

Monday $\quad 98 \times \$.75 = \$73.50$

Tuesday $\quad 92 \times \$.75 \quad \$70.40$ (hourly)

Wednesday $\ 102 \times \$.75 = \$76.50$

Thursday $\quad 96 \times \$.75 = \$72.00$

Friday $\qquad 106 \times \$.75 = \underline{\$79.50}$

$\qquad\qquad\qquad\qquad \$371.90$

**15.** Gross Earnings

$= 430 \times \$.76 + \left(62 \times 1.5 \times \$.76\right)$

$= \$326.80 + \$70.68$

$= \$397.48$

**17.** Gross Earnings

$= 470 \times \$.82 + \left(70 \times 1.5 \times \$.82\right)$

$= \$385.40 + \$86.10$

$= \$471.50$

**19.** Gross earnings $= \left(\$6210 - \$129\right) \times 10\%$

$= \$6081 \times .1$

$= \$608.10$

**21.** Gross earnings $= \left(\$2875 - \$64\right) \times 15\%$

$= \$2811 \times .15$

$= \$421.65$

**23.** (Total sales) $\quad \$18,550$

(First \$7500) $\quad \underline{-\$7,500}$ at 6% $= \$450$

$\qquad\qquad\qquad \$11,050$

(Next \$7500) $\quad \underline{-\$7,500}$ at 8% $= \$600$

(Over \$15,000) $\quad \$3,550$ at 10% $= \underline{\$355}$

Total commissions $\qquad\quad \$1405$

**25.** (Total sales) $\quad \$10,480$

(First \$7500) $\quad \underline{-\$7,500}$ at 6% $= \$450.00$

(Next \$7500) $\quad \$2,980$ at 8% $= \underline{\$238.40}$

Total commissions $\qquad\qquad \$688.40$

**27.** Gross Earnings

$=$ Salary $+$ Commission

$= \$452 + \left(\$2900 \times .009\right)$

$= \$452 + \$26.10$

$= \$478.10$

**29.** Gross Earnings

$=$ Salary $+$ Commission

$= \$452 + \left(\$10,000 \times .009\right) + \left(\$7874 \times .011\right)$

$= \$452 + \$90 + \$86.61$

$= \$628.61$

## 6.3 Social Security, Medicare, and Other Taxes

**1.** Social Security tax

$= \$420 \times 6.2\%$

$= \$420 \times .062$

$= \$26.04$

Medicare tax

$= \$420 \times 1.45\%$

$= \$420 \times .0145$

$= \$6.09$

**3.** Social Security tax

$= \$463.24 \times 6.2\%$

$= \$463.24 \times .062$

$= \$28.72$

Medicare tax

$= \$463.24 \times 1.45\%$

$= \$463.24 \times .0145$

$= \$6.72$

**5.** Social Security tax

$= \$854.71 \times 6.2\%$

$= \$854.71 \times .062$

$= \$52.99$

Medicare tax

$= \$854.71 \times 1.45\%$

$= \$854.71 \times .0145$

$= \$12.39$

**7.** $\quad \$110,000.00$

$\quad \underline{-\$106,945.32}$

$\qquad\quad \$3,054.68$

Social Security tax

$= \$3054.68 \times 6.2\%$

$= \$3054.68 \times .062$

$= \$189.39$

**9.** $\quad \$110,000.00$

$\quad \underline{-\$105,016.22}$

$\qquad\quad \$4,983.78$

Social Security tax

$= \$4983.78 \times 6.2\%$

$= \$4983.78 \times .062$

$= \$308.99$

**11.**  $110,000.00
$\underline{-\$109,329.75}$
$670.25

Social Security tax
$= \$670.25 \times 6.2\%$
$= \$670.25 \times .062$
$= \$41.56$

**13.**  $40 \times \$9.22 = \$368.80$      regular

$5.5 \times 1\frac{1}{2} \times \$9.22 = \$76.07$      overtime

$\$368.80 + \$76.07 = \$444.87$      gross

$\$444.87 \times 6.2\% = \$27.58$      FICA

$\$444.87 \times 1.45\% = \$6.45$      Medicare

$\$444.87 \times 1\% = \$4.45$      SDI

**15.**  $40 \times \$14.20 = \$568$      regular

$5 \times 1\frac{1}{2} \times \$14.20 = \$106.50$      overtime

$\$568 + \$106.50 = \$674.50$      gross

$\$674.50 \times 6.2\% = \$41.82$      FICA

$\$674.50 \times 1.45\% = \$9.78$      Medicare

$\$674.50 \times 1\% = \$6.75$      SDI

**17.**  $40 \times \$11.68 = \$467.20$      regular

$7 \times 1\frac{1}{2} \times \$11.68 = \$122.64$      overtime

$\$467.20 + \$122.64 = \$589.84$      gross

$\$589.84 \times 6.2\% = \$36.57$      FICA

$\$589.84 \times 1.45\% = \$8.55$      Medicare

$\$589.84 \times 1\% = \$5.90$      SDI

**19.**  $40 \times \$8.58 = \$343.20$      regular

$3.5 \times 1\frac{1}{2} \times \$8.58 = \$45.05$      overtime

$\$343.20 + \$45.05 = \$388.25$      gross

  **(a)**  $\$388.25 \times 6.2\% = \$24.07$      FICA

  **(b)**  $\$388.25 \times 1.45\% = \$5.63$      Medicare

**21.**  Commission $= (\$19,482 - \$193) \times 8\%$
$= \$19,289 \times .08$
$= \$1543.12$

  **(a)**  $\$1543.12 \times 6.2\% = \$95.67$      FICA

  **(b)**  $\$1543.12 \times 1.45\% = \$22.38$      Medicare

  **(c)**  $\$1543.12 \times 1\% = \$15.43$      SDI

**23.**  Social Security tax
$= \$58,238.74 \times 12.4\%$
$= \$58,238.74 \times 0.124$
$= \$7221.60$

Medicare tax
$= \$58,238.74 \times 2.9\%$
$= \$58,238.74 \times 0.029$
$= \$1688.92$

**25.**  Social Security tax
$= \$29,104.80 \times 12.4\%$
$= \$29,104.80 \times .124$
$= \$3609$

Medicare tax
$= \$29,104.80 \times 2.9\%$
$= \$29,104.80 \times .029$
$= \$844.04$

**27.**  Social Security tax
$= \$26,843.60 \times 12.4\%$
$= \$26,843.60 \times .124$
$= \$3328.61$

Medicare tax
$= \$26,843.60 \times 2.9\%$
$= \$26,843.60 \times .029$
$= \$778.46$

**29.**  Answers will vary.

## 6.4  Income Tax Withholding

For problems #1-11, use the wage bracket method and Figures 6.9 and 6.10 to find the federal withholding tax.

  **1.**  $101

  **3.**  $22

  **5.**  $85

  **7.**  $39

  **9.**  $11

**11.**  $33

**13.**  $2.8\% \times \$245.18 = .028 \times \$245.18 = \$6.87$

**15.** $6\% \times \$466.71 = .06 \times \$466.71 = \$28.00$

**17.** $4.3\% \times \$1607.23 = .043 \times \$1607.23 = \$69.11$

**19.** Federal withholding tax
$\$70.19 \times 4 = \$280.76$
$\$576.28 - \$280.76 = \$295.52$
Not over \$303
\$0

| | |
|---|---|
| FICA tax $(\$576.28 \times 6.2\%)$ | \$35.73 |
| Medicare $(\$576.28 \times 1.45\%)$ | \$8.36 |
| Federal withholding tax | \$0 |
| Total deductions | \$44.09 |

$\$576.28 - \$44.09 = \$532.19$ net pay

**21.** Federal withholding tax
$\$304.17 \times 1 = \$304.17$
$\$3512.53 - \$304.17 = \$3208.36$
$\$3208.36 - \$3017 = \$191.36$
$\$349.40 + (25\% \times \$191.36) = \$397.24$

| | |
|---|---|
| FICA tax $(\$3512.53 \times 6.2\%)$ | \$217.78 |
| Medicare $(\$3512.53 \times 1.45\%)$ | \$50.93 |
| Federal withholding tax | \$397.24 |
| Total deductions | \$665.95 |

$\$3512.53 - \$665.95 = \$2846.58$ net pay

**23.** Federal withholding tax
$\$152.08 \times 3 = \$456.24$
$\$2276.83 - \$456.24 = \$1820.59$
$\$1820.59 - \$1019 = \$801.59$
$\$36.30 + (15\% \times \$801.59) = \$156.54$

| | |
|---|---|
| FICA tax $(\$2276.83 \times 6.2\%)$ | \$141.16 |
| Medicare $(\$2276.83 \times 1.45\%)$ | \$33.01 |
| Federal withholding tax | \$156.54 |
| Total deductions | \$330.71 |

$\$2276.83 - \$330.71 = \$1946.12$ net pay

**25.** Federal withholding tax
$\$152.08 \times 6 = \$912.48$
$\$2971.06 - \$912.48 = \$2058.58$
$\$2058.58 - \$1019 = \$1039.58$
$\$36.30 + (15\% \times \$1039.58) = \$192.24$

| | |
|---|---|
| FICA tax $(\$2971.06 \times 6.2\%)$ | \$184.21 |
| Medicare $(\$2971.06 \times 1.45\%)$ | \$43.08 |
| Federal withholding tax | \$192.24 |
| Total deductions | \$419.53 |

$\$2971.06 - \$419.53 = \$2551.53$ net pay

**27.** Federal withholding tax
$\$140.38 \times 3 = \$421.14$
$\$3753.18 - \$421.14 = \$3332.04$
$\$3332.04 - \$2559 = \$773.04$
$\$452.95 + (28\% \times \$773.04) = \$669.40$

| | |
|---|---|
| FICA tax $(\$3753.18 \times 6.2\%)$ | \$232.70 |
| Medicare $(\$3753.18 \times 1.45\%)$ | \$54.42 |
| Federal withholding tax | \$669.40 |
| Total deductions | \$956.52 |

$\$3753.18 - \$956.52 = \$2796.66$ net pay

**29.** Federal withholding tax
$\$70.19 \times 1 = \$70.19$
$\$1786.44 - \$70.19 = \$1716.25$
$\$1716.25 - \$1279 = \$437.25$
$\$226.35 + (28\% \times \$437.25) = \$348.78$

| | |
|---|---|
| FICA tax $(\$1786.44 \times 6.2\%)$ | \$110.76 |
| Medicare $(\$1786.44 \times 1.45\%)$ | \$25.90 |
| Federal withholding tax | \$348.78 |
| Total deductions | \$485.44 |

$\$1786.44 - \$485.44 = \$1301.00$ net pay

**31.** Answers will vary.

**33.** Answers will vary.

**35.** $1483.59
1483.59
342.37
342.37
5096.13
——————
$8748.05

The total amount owed to the Internal Revenue Service is $8748.05.

**37.** $8,212.18
8,212.18
1,895.37
1,895.37
33,117.42
——————
$53,332.52

The total amount owed to the Internal Revenue Service is $53,332.52.

**39.** $7,271.39
7,271.39
1,678.24
1,678.24
26,423.84
——————
$44,323.10

The total amount owed to the Internal Revenue Service is $44,323.10.

**41.** Federal withholding tax
$70.19 \times 4 = $280.76
$975 - $280.76 = $694.24
$16.70 + .15($694.24 - $470) = $50.34

| | |
|---|---|
| FICA tax $($975 \times 6.2\%)$ | $60.45 |
| Medicare $($975 \times 1.45\%)$ | $14.14 |
| Federal withholding tax | $50.34 |
| SDI $($975 \times 1\%)$ | $9.75 |
| State tax $($975 \times 3.4\%)$ | $33.15 |
| Union dues | $15.50 |
| Credit union savings | $100.00 |
| Total deductions | $283.33 |

$975 - $283.33 = $691.67
Horwitz's net pay is $691.67.

**43.** Salary
$= $410 + 7\%($11,284 - $424.50 - $5000)$
$= $410 + .07($5859.50)$
$= $410 + $410.17$
$= $820.17$

Federal withholding tax
$70.19 \times 2 = $140.38
$820.17 - $140.38 = $679.79
$6.20 + .15($679.79 - $200) = $78.17

| | |
|---|---|
| FICA tax $($820.17 \times 6.2\%)$ | $50.85 |
| Medicare $($820.17 \times 1.45\%)$ | $11.89 |
| Federal withholding tax | $78.17 |
| SDI $($820.17 \times 1\%)$ | $8.20 |
| State tax $($820.17 \times 3.4\%)$ | $27.89 |
| Credit union savings | $50.00 |
| Salvation Army contribution | $10.00 |
| Professional dues | $15.00 |
| Total deductions | $252.00 |

$820.17 - $252.00 = $568.17  net pay
Jordan's net pay is $568.17.

**45.** Salary
$4200 + ($42,618 \times 1.5\%)$
$= $4200 + ($42,618 \times .015)$
$= $4200 + $639.27$
$= $4839.27$

Federal withholding tax
$304.17 \times 3 = $912.51
$4839.27 - $912.51 = $3926.76
$72.50 + .15($3926.76 - $2038) = $355.81

| | |
|---|---|
| FICA tax $($4839.27 \times 6.2\%)$ | $300.03 |
| Medicare $($4839.27 \times 1.45\%)$ | $70.17 |
| Federal withholding tax | $355.81 |
| SDI $($4839.27 \times 1\%)$ | $48.39 |
| Credit union savings | $150.00 |
| Charitable contributions | $25.00 |
| Savings bond | $50.00 |
| Total deductions | $999.40 |

$4839.27 - $999.40 = $3839.87
Beaton's net pay is $3839.87.

## Case Study

1. $42,536 \div 52 = \$818$ weekly

2. $\$818 \div 40 = \$20.45$ per hour
   Overtime rate: $1.5 \times \$20.45 = \$30.675$
   Overtime hours: $52 - 40 = 12$

   12 O.T. hours $\times \$30.675 = \$368.10$

3. Salary $= \$818.00$
   Overtime $= +\ 368.10$
   Gross Earnings $\overline{\$1186.10}$

4. FICA
   $= \$1186.10 \times 6.2\%$
   $= \$1186.10 \times .062$
   $= \$73.54$

5. Medicare
   $= \$1186.10 \times 1.45\%$
   $= \$1186.10 \times .0145$
   $= \$17.20$

6. Federal withholding tax
   $\$70.19 \times 1 = \$70.19$
   $\$1186.10 - \$70.19 = \$1115.91$
   $\$80.60 + .25(\$1115.91 - \$696) = \$185.58$

7. State disability
   $= \$1186.10 \times 1\%$
   $= \$1186.10 \times .01$
   $= \$11.86$

8. State withholding
   $= \$1186.10 \times 4.4\%$
   $= \$1186.10 \times .044$
   $= \$52.19$

10. 
| | |
|---|---|
| FICA tax | $73.54 |
| Medicare | $17.20 |
| Federal withholding | $185.58 |
| SDI | $11.86 |
| State withholding | $52.19 |
| Credit union payments | $125.00 |
| Retirement deductions | $75.00 |
| Association dues | $12.00 |
| Charitable contribution | $25.00 |
| Total deductions | $577.37 |

   $\$1186.10 - \$577.37 = \$608.73$ net pay

## Case in Point Summary Exercise

1. Betinez
   Total Pay
   $\$8.75 \times 28 = \$245$

   Federal withholding tax
   $\$70.19 \times 1 = \$70.19$
   $\$245 - \$70.19 = \$174.81$
   $\$174.81 - \$138 = \$36.81$
   $10\% \times \$36.81 = \$3.68$

| | |
|---|---|
| FICA tax $(\$245 \times 6.2\%)$ | $15.19 |
| Medicare $(\$245 \times 1.45\%)$ | $3.55 |
| Federal withholding tax | $3.68 |
| State tax $(\$245 \times 3.07\%)$ | $7.52 |
| SDI $(\$245 \times 1\%)$ | $2.45 |
| Total deductions | $32.39 |

   $\$245 - \$32.39 = \$212.61$ net pay

   Parton
   Overtime rate: $1\frac{1}{2} \times \$12.25 = \$18.38$

   40 hours $\times \$12.25 \qquad = \$490.00$
   5 O.T. hours $\times \$18.38 = +\ 91.90$
   Total Pay $\qquad\qquad \overline{\$581.90}$

   Federal withholding tax
   $\$70.19 \times 2 = \$140.38$
   $\$581.90 - \$140.38 = \$441.52$
   $\$441.52 - \$303 = \$138.52$
   $10\% \times \$138.52 = \$13.85$

| | |
|---|---|
| FICA tax $(\$581.90 \times 6.2\%)$ | $36.08 |
| Medicare $(\$581.90 \times 1.45\%)$ | $8.44 |
| Federal withholding tax | $13.85 |
| State tax $(\$581.90 \times 3.07\%)$ | $17.86 |
| SDI $(\$581.90 \times 1\%)$ | $5.82 |
| Other | $25.00 |
| Total deductions | $107.05 |

   $\$581.90 - \$107.05 = \$474.85$ net pay

**1. (continued)**
Dickens
Total Pay
$9.35 \times 30 = \$280.50$

Federal withholding tax
$70.19 \times 0 = \$0$
$\$280.50 - \$0 = \$280.50$
$\$280.50 - \$200 = \$80.50$
$\$6.20 + (10\% \times \$80.50) = \$14.25$

| | |
|---|---|
| FICA tax $(\$280.50 \times 6.2\%)$ | $17.39 |
| Medicare $(\$280.50 \times 1.45\%)$ | $4.07 |
| Federal withholding tax | $14.25 |
| State tax $(\$280.50 \times 3.07\%)$ | $8.61 |
| SDI $(\$280.50 \times 1\%)$ | $2.81 |
| Other | $10.00 |
| Total deductions | $57.13 |

$\$280.50 - \$57.13 = \$223.37$  net pay

**2.** Salary
$= \$450 + 6\% (\$8432 - \$5000)$
$= \$450 + .06(\$3432)$
$= \$450 + \$205.92$
$= \$655.92$

Federal withholding tax
$70.19 \times 2 = \$140.38$
$\$655.92 - \$140.38 = \$515.54$
$\$515.54 - \$470 = \$45.54$
$\$16.70 + (15\% \times \$45.54) = \$23.53$

| | |
|---|---|
| FICA tax $(\$655.92 \times 6.2\%)$ | $40.67 |
| Medicare $(\$655.92 \times 1.45\%)$ | $9.51 |
| Federal withholding tax | $23.53 |
| State tax $(\$655.92 \times 3.07\%)$ | $20.14 |
| SDI $(\$655.92 \times 1\%)$ | $6.56 |
| Other | $65.00 |
| Total deductions | $165.41 |

$\$655.92 - \$165.41 = \$490.51$  net pay

**3.** FICA
$(\$15.19 + \$36.08 + \$17.39 + \$40.67) \times 2$
$= \$218.66$

Medicare
$(\$3.55 + \$8.44 + \$4.07 + \$9.51) \times 2$
$= \$51.14$

Federal taxes
$\$3.68 + \$13.85 + \$14.25 + \$23.53$
$= \$55.31$

$\$218.66 + \$51.14 + \$55.31 = \$325.11$

The total amount Brynski must send to the Internal Revenue Service is $325.11.

**4.** State income tax
$\$7.52 + \$17.86 + \$8.61 + \$20.14$
$= \$54.13$

State disability insurance
$\$2.45 + \$5.82 + \$2.81 + \$6.56$
$= \$17.64$

$\$54.13 + \$17.64 = \$71.77$

The total amount Brynski must send to the sate including income tax and disability insurance is $71.77.

## Chapter 6 Test

**1.** Overtime rate: $1.5 \times \$10.80 = \$16.20$
| 40 hours $\times \$10.80$ | $= \$432.00$ |
| 6.5 O.T. hours $\times \$16.20$ | $= +\$105.30$ |
| Gross Earnings | $\$537.30$ |

**2.** Overtime rate: $1.5 \times \$8.60 = \$12.90$
| 40 hours $\times \$8.60$ | $= \$344.00$ |
| 7.5 O.T. hours $\times \$12.90$ | $= +\$96.75$ |
| Gross Earnings | $\$440.75$ |

**3.** **(a)** $\$34,060 \div 52 = \$655$ weekly

**(b)** $\$34,060 \div 26 = \$1310$ biweekly

**(c)** $\$34,060 \div 24 = \$1419.17$ semimonthly

**(d)** $\$34,060 \div 12 = \$2838.33$ monthly

**4.**
| (Total units) | 70 | |
| (First 20 units) | $-20$ at $\$4.50 =$ | $\$90$ |
| | 50 | |
| (Next 10 units) | $-10$ at $\$5.50 =$ | $\$55$ |
| (Over 30 units) | 40 at $\$7.00 =$ | $\$280$ |
| Total commissions | | $\$425$ |

**5.** $\$235,500 \times .06 \times .5 \times .5 = \$3532.50$
Winston receives $\$3532.50$.

**6.** **(a)** FICA $= \$9300 \times 6.2\% = \$576.60$

**(b)** Medicare $= \$9300 \times 1.45\% = \$134.85$

**7.** **(a)** $\$9300 \times 11 = \$102,300$
| $\$110,000$ |
| $-\$102,300$ |
| $\$7,700$ |

FICA $= \$7700 \times 6.2\% = \$477.40$

**(b)** Medicare $= \$9300 \times 1.45\% = \$134.85$

**8.** $\$17$

**9.** $\$26$

**10.** $\$113$

**11.** $\$25$

**12.** $\$3$

**13.** Federal withholding tax
$\$304.17 \times 1 = \$304.17$
$\$1852.75 - \$304.17 = \$1548.58$
$\$26.90 + .15(\$1548.58 - \$867) = \$129.14$

| FICA tax $(\$1852.75 \times 6.2\%)$ | $\$114.87$ |
| Medicare $(\$1852.75 \times 1.45\%)$ | $\$26.86$ |
| Federal withholding tax | $\$129.14$ |
| SDI $(\$1852.75 \times 1\%)$ | $\$18.53$ |
| Other deductions | $\$37.80$ |
| Total deductions | $\$327.20$ |

$\$1852.75 - \$327.20 = \$1525.55$ net pay

**14.** Federal withholding tax
$\$70.19 \times 3 = \$210.57$
$\$1028 - \$210.57 = \$817.43$
$\$16.70 + .15(\$817.43 - \$470) = \$68.81$

| FICA tax $(\$1028 \times 6.2\%)$ | $\$63.74$ |
| Medicare $(\$1028 \times 1.45\%)$ | $\$14.91$ |
| Federal withholding tax | $\$68.81$ |
| SDI $(\$1028 \times 1\%)$ | $\$10.28$ |
| State withholding | $\$50.50$ |
| Credit union savings | $\$50.00$ |
| Contribution | $\$20.00$ |
| Total deductions | $\$278.24$ |

$\$1028 - \$278.24 = \$749.76$ net pay

**15.** Federal withholding tax
$\$70.19 \times 6 = \$421.14$
$\$677.92 - \$421.14 = \$256.78$
Since the amount is not over $\$303$, $\$0$ are owed in federal income tax.

| FICA tax $(\$677.92 \times 6.2\%)$ | $\$42.03$ |
| Medicare $(\$677.92 \times 1.45\%)$ | $\$9.83$ |
| Federal withholding tax | $\$0.00$ |
| SDI $(\$677.92 \times 1\%)$ | $\$6.78$ |
| State withholding | $\$22.18$ |
| Union dues | $\$14.00$ |
| Charitable contribution | $\$15.00$ |
| Total deductions$ | $\$109.82$ |

$\$677.92 - \$109.82 = \$568.10$ net pay

16. Commission Sales = Sales − Returns
    $= (\$712 + \$523 + \$1002 + \$391 + \$609) - \$114$
    $= \$3237 - \$114 = \$3123$
    Wages = Salary + Commission
    $= \$452 + (\$3123 \times 2\%)$
    $= \$452 + \$62.46 = \$514.46$

    (a)  $\$514.46 \times 6.2\% = \$31.90$
         The employee's Social Security tax is \$31.90.

    (b)  $\$514.46 \times 1.45\% = \$7.46$
         The employee's Medicare tax is \$7.46.

    (c)  $\$514.46 \times 1\% = \$5.14$
         The employee's state disability insurance is
         \$5.14.

17. (a)      \$105,000.00
          $\underline{-\$102,375.60}$
             \$2,624.40

         FICA $= \$2624.40 \times 6.2\% = \$162.71$

    (b)  Medicare $= \$2649.78 \times 1.45\% = \$38.42$

18. (a)  Social Security tax
         $= \$36,714.12 \times 12.4\%$
         $= \$36,714.12 \times .124$
         $= \$4552.55$

    (b)  Medicare tax
         $= \$36,714.12 \times 2.9\%$
         $= \$36,714.12 \times .029$
         $= \$1064.71$

19. (a)  Social Security tax
         $= \$42,380.62 \times 12.4\%$
         $= \$42,380.62 \times .124$
         $= \$5255.20$

    (b)  Medicare tax
         $= \$42,380.62 \times 2.9\%$
         $= \$42,380.62 \times .029$
         $= \$1229.04$

20.  \$418.12
      418.12
       96.48
       96.48
     $\underline{1217.34}$
     \$2246.54

    The total amount owed to the Internal Revenue
    Service is \$2246.54.

## 7.1 Invoices and Trade Discounts

**1-7**
$$6 \text{ doz.} \times \$37.80 \text{ doz.} = \$ \phantom{0}226.80$$
$$3 \text{ gro.} \times \$12.60 \text{ gro.} = \$ \phantom{00}37.80$$
$$9 \text{ doz.} \times \$14.04 \text{ doz.} = \$ \phantom{0}126.36$$
$$8 \times \$106.12 \text{ ea.} = \$ \phantom{0}848.96$$
$$53 \text{ pr.} \times \$68.12 \text{ pr.} = \$3610.36$$
$$\text{Invoice Total} = \$4850.28$$
$$\text{Shipping \& Insurance} = \$ \phantom{00}85.60$$
$$\text{Total Amount Due} = \$4935.88$$

**8-14**
$$24 \times \$2.25 \text{ ea.} = \$ \phantom{0}54.00$$
$$12 \text{ pr.} \times \$4.75 \text{ pr.} = \$ \phantom{0}57.00$$
$$6 \text{ pr.} \times \$10.80 \text{ pr.} = \$ \phantom{0}64.80$$
$$2 \text{ gr.} \times \$14.20 \text{ gr.} = \$ \phantom{0}28.40$$
$$18 \times \$16.50 \text{ ea.} = \$297.00$$
$$\text{Invoice Total} = \$501.20$$
$$\text{Shipping \& Insurance} = \$139.40$$
$$\text{Total Amount Due} = \$640.60$$

**15.** foot

**17.** pair

**19.** kilogram

**21.** case

**23.** drum

**25.** liter

**27.** gallon

**29.** cash on delivery

**31.** Answers will vary.

**33.** $10/20$
$$.9 \times .8 = .72$$

**35.** $10/10/10$
$$.9 \times .9 \times .9 = .729$$

**37.** $25/5$
$$.75 \times .95 = .7125$$

**39.** $40/30/20$
$$.6 \times .7 \times .8 = .336$$

**41.** $50/10/20/5$
$$.5 \times .9 \times .8 \times .95 = .342$$

**43.** $20/20$
$$.8 \times .8 = .64$$
$$.64 \times \$418 = \$267.52$$

**45.** $5/10$
$$.95 \times .9 = .855$$
$$.855 \times \$16.40 = \$14.02$$

**47.** $15/25/10$
$$.85 \times .75 \times .9 = .57375$$
$$.57375 \times \$1260 = \$722.93$$

**49.** $20/10/20$
$$.8 \times .9 \times .8 = .576$$
$$.576 \times \$380 = \$218.88$$

**51.** $10/15$
$$.9 \times .85 = .765$$
$$.765 \times \$22 = \$16.83$$

**53.** $10/10/10$
$$.9 \times .9 \times .9 = .729$$
$$.729 \times \$980 = \$714.42$$

**55.** $10/40/10$
$$.9 \times .6 \times .9 = .486$$
$$.486 \times \$2000 = \$972$$

**57.** $20/20/20$
$$.8 \times .8 \times .8 = .512$$
$$.512 \times \$1250 = \$640$$

**59.** Answers will vary.

**61.** Answers will vary.

**63.** 10/10/25
$.9 \times .9 \times .75 = .6075$

$\$299.99 \times .6075 = \$182.24$
The net cost after trade discounts is $182.24.

**65. (a)** 10/15/10
$.9 \times .85 \times .9 = .6885$
$\$480 \times .6885 = \$330.48$

20/15
$.8 \times .85 = .68$
$\$480 \times .68 = \$326.40$

The 20/15 discount gives the lower price.

**(b)** $\$330.48 - \$326.40 = \$4.08$
The difference in net cost is $4.08.

**67. (a)** 15/10/10
$.85 \times .9 \times .9 = .6885$
$\$65 \times .6885 = \$44.75$

15/20
$.85 \times .8 = .68$
$\$65 \times .68 = \$44.20$

The 15/20 discount gives the lower price.

**(b)** $\$44.75 - \$44.20 = \$.55$
The difference is $.55.

**69.** 10/5/20
$.9 \times .95 \times .8 = .684$

$\$468 \times 4 \times .684 = \$1280.45$
The net cost is $1280.45.

**71.** 5/20/5
$.95 \times .8 \times .95 = .722$

$\$78,500 \times .722 = \$56,677$
The net cost after trade discounts is $56,677.

**73.** 30/20
$.7 \times .8 = .56$
$\$5440 \times .56 = \$3046.40$
Robert should have charged $3046.40.

$\$5440 \times .5 = \$2720$
Robert charged $2720.

$\$3046.40 - \$2720 = \$326.40$
$326.40 was undercharged.

## 7.2 Series Discounts and Single Discount Equivalents

**1.** 10/20
$.9 \times .8 = .72$

$1.00 - .72 = .28 = 28\%$

**3.** 20/15
$.8 \times .85 = .68$

$1.00 - .68 = .32 = 32\%$

**5.** 10/30/20
$.9 \times .7 \times .8 = .504$

$1.000 - .504 = .496 = 49.6\%$

**7.** 20/10/10/20
$.8 \times .9 \times .9 \times .8 = .5184$

$1.0000 - .5184 = .4816 = 48.16\%$

**9.** Answers will vary.

**11.** 20/10
$.8 \times .9 = .72$

$B = \dfrac{P}{R} = \dfrac{\$518.40}{.72} = \$720$

**13.** 5/10/20
$.95 \times .9 \times .8 = .684$

$B = \dfrac{P}{R} = \dfrac{\$1559.52}{.684} = \$2280$

**15.** 10/20/5
$.9 \times .8 \times .95 = .684$

$B = \dfrac{P}{R} = \dfrac{\$265.39}{.684} = \$388.00$

**17.** 5/10/15
$.95 \times .9 \times .85 = .72675$

$B = \dfrac{P}{R} = \dfrac{\$4312.40}{.72675} = \$5933.81$

**19.** 10/10/5
$.9 \times .9 \times .95 = .7695$

$B = \dfrac{P}{R} = \dfrac{\$68.72}{.7695} = \$89.30$

**21.** 20/20

$.8 \times .8 = .64$

$$B = \frac{P}{R} = \frac{\$132.54}{.64} = \$207.09$$

**23. (a)** 20/10/10

$.8 \times .9 \times .9 = .648$

$\$39.95 \times .648 = \$25.89$

The wholesaler's price is $25.89.

**(b)** 20/10

$.8 \times .9 = .72$

$\$39.95 \times .72 = \$28.76$

The retailer's price is $28.76.

**(c)** $\$28.76 - \$25.89 = \$2.87$

The difference between the prices is $2.87.

## 7.3 Cash Discounts: Ordinary Dating Methods

**1.** Final discount date is May 14

May 4 + 10 days

Net payment date is June 3

27 days in May + 3 days in June

**3.** Final discount date is July 25

July 10 + 15 days

Net payment date is Sept. 8

21 days in July + 31 days in Aug.

+ 8 days in Sept.

**5.** Final discount date is Oct. 1

Sept. 11 + 20 days

Net payment date is Oct. 11

19 days in Sept + 11 days in Oct.

**7.** $\$85.18 \times .02 = \$1.70$

The amount of discount is $1.70.

$\$85.18 - \$1.70 = \$83.48$

$\$83.48 + \$8.72 = \$92.20$

The total amount due is $92.20.

**9.** There is no discount.

$\$78.07 + \$3.18 = \$81.25$

The total amount due is $81.25.

**11.** $\$1080 \times .02 = \$21.60$

The amount of discount is $21.60.

$\$1080 - \$21.60 = \$1058.40$

$\$1058.40 + \$62.15 = \$1120.55$

The total amount due is $1120.55.

**13.** Answers will vary.

**15.** $\$4635.40 \times .02 = \$92.71$

The amount of discount is $92.71.

$\$4635.40 - \$92.71 = \$4542.69$

The amount needed to pay the invoice is $4542.69.

**17.** 10/20/5

$.9 \times .8 \times .95 = .684$

$\$2630 \times .684 = \$1798.92$

The customer's price is $1798.92.

**19. (a)** First discount date is Jan. 28

Jan. 18 + 10 days

Second discount date is Feb. 7

13 days in Jan. + 7 days in Feb.

Third discount date is Feb. 17

13 days in Jan. + 17 days in Feb.

**(b)** Net payment date is Mar. 9

13 days in Jan. + 28 days in Feb.

+ 9 days in Mar.

**21. (a)** Final discount date is Apr. 25

Apr. 5 + 20 days

**(b)** Net payment date is May 5

25 days in Apr. + 5 days in May

**23.** Answers will vary.

## 7.4  Cash Discounts:  Other Dating Methods

**1.** Final discount date is Mar. 10
  10 days after the end of Feb.

  Net payment date is Mar. 30
    20 days after final discount date

**3.** Final discount date is Dec. 22
    $10 + 20 = 30$ days after Nov. 22
    (8 days in Nov. + 22 days in Dec.)

  Net payment date is Jan. 11
    20 days after final discount date
    (9 days in Dec. + 11 days in Jan.)

**5.** Final discount date is June 16
    $15 + 50 = 65$ days after April 12
    (18 days in April + 31 days in May
    +16 days in June)

  Net payment date is July 6
    20 days after final discount date
    (14 days in June + 6 days in July)

**7.** $\$682.28 \times .03 = \$20.47$
  The amount of discount is $20.47.

  $\$682.28 - \$20.47 = \$661.81$
  The amount due is $661.81.

**9.** There is no discount.

  The amount due is $785.64.

**11.** $\$11,480 \times .02 = \$229.60$
  The amount of discount is $229.60.

  $\$11,480 - \$229.60 = \$11,250.40$
  The amount due is $11,250.40.

**13.** $\$23.95 \times .03 = \$.72$
  The amount of discount is $.72.

  $\$23.95 - \$.72 = \$23.23$
  The amount due is $23.23.

**15.** Answers will vary.

**17. (a)** Final discount date is Dec. 13
      $10 + 30 = 40$ days after Nov. 3
      (27 days in Nov. + 13 days in Dec.)

**17. (b)** $\$2382.58 \times .02 = \$47.65$
      The amount of discount is $47.65.

      $\$2382.58 - \$47.65 = \$2334.93$
      The amount paid was $2334.93.

**19.** $\$6720.50 \times .02 = \$134.41$
  The amount of discount is $134.41.

  $\$6720.50 - \$134.41 = \$6586.09$
  The amount due is $6586.09.

**21.** $25/10/10$
  $.75 \times .9 \times .9 = .6075$
  $.6075 \times \$2538 = \$1541.84$

  $\$1541.84 \times .03 = \$46.26$
  The amount of discount is $46.26.

  $\$1541.84 - \$46.26 = \$1495.58$
  The amount necessary to pay in full is
  $1495.58.

**23. (a)** $100\% - 8\% = 92\% = .92$

  $$B = \frac{P}{R} = \frac{\$1350}{.92} = \$1467.39$$
  The credit given for the partial
  payment is $1467.39.

**(b)** $\$2016.90 - \$1467.39 = \$549.51$
      The balance due is $549.51.

**25.** Final discount date is June 10
    10 days after the end of May

  Net payment date is June 30
    20 days after final discount date

**27.** $\$1525 \times .01 = \$15.25$
  The amount of discount is $15.25.

  $\$1525 - \$15.25 = \$1509.75$
  The amount due is $1509.75.

**29. (a)** $100\% - 3\% = 97\% = .97$

  $$B = \frac{P}{R} = \frac{\$3250}{.97} = \$3350.52$$
  The credit given for the partial
  payment is $3350.52.

**(b)** $\$4402.58 - \$3350.52 = \$1052.06$
      The balance due is $1052.06.

**31.** Answers will vary.

## Case Study

1. 20 / 20
   $.8 \times .8 = .64$

   $\$469.99 \times 12 \times .64 = \$1151.92$
   The cost of one dozen grilling machines is
   $\$1151.92$.

2. 25 / 10
   $.75 \times .9 = .675$

   $\$119.99 \times .675 \times .97 = \$78.56$
   The cost to Kitchen Crafters is $\$78.56$.

3. $\$16.95 - \$13.95 = \$3.00$
   The markdown is $\$3.00$.

   $\dfrac{\$3.00}{\$16.95} \approx .177 = 17.7\%$
   The percent of markdown is $17.7\%$.

## Case in Point Summary Exercise

1. 20/10/10
   $.8 \times .9 \times .9 = .648$

   $\$27,393 \times .648 = \$17,750.66$
   The total amount of the invoice excluding
   shipping is $\$17,750.66$.

2. Final discount date is Oct. 15
   15 days after the end of Sept.

3. Net payment date is Nov. 4
   20 days after final discount date
   (16 days in Oct. + 4 days in Nov.)

4. $\$17,750.66 \times .03 = \$532.52$
   The amount of discount is $\$532.52$.

   $\$17,750.66 - \$532.52 + \$748.38$
   $= \$17,966.52$

   The amount necessary to pay the invoice in full
   on October 11 is $\$17,966.52$.

5. $100\% - 3\% = 97\% = .97$

   $B = \dfrac{P}{R} = \dfrac{\$10,000}{.97} = \$10,309.28$
   The credit given for the partial payment is
   $\$10,309.28$.

   Balance due
   $= \$17,750.66 - \$10,309.28 + \$748.38$
   $= \$8189.76$

## Chapter 7 Test

1. 10 / 20 / 10
   $.9 \times .8 \times .9 = .648$

   $\$348.22 \times .648 = \$225.65$

2. 20 / 25
   $.8 \times .75 = .6$

   $\$1308 \times .6 = \$784.80$

3. (a) 30 / 10
   $.7 \times .9 = .63$

   (b) $1.00 - .63 = .37 = 37\%$

4. (a) 20 / 10 / 20
   $.8 \times .9 \times .8 = .576$

   (b) $1.000 - .576 = .424 = 42.4\%$

5. Final discount date is Mar. 15
   15 days after the end of Feb.

6. Final discount date is May 30
   10 days from receipt of goods
   (on May 20)

7. Final discount date is Jan. 15
   the 15th day of the next month

8. Final discount date is Dec. 19
   $20 + 40 = 60$ days from Oct. 20
   (11 days in Oct. + 30 days in Nov.
   + 19 days in Dec.)

9.
   | | |
   |---|---|
   | $16 \times \$35.00$ ea. $=$ | $\$560.00$ |
   | $8 \times \$6.50$ ea. $=$ | $\$\ 52.00$ |
   | $4 \times \$25.30$ ea. $=$ | $\$101.20$ |
   | $12 \times \$6.30$ ea. $=$ | $\$\ 75.60$ |
   | (a) Invoice Total $=$ | $\$788.80$ |
   | Cash Discount (2%) $=$ | $\$\ 15.78$ |
   | (b) Due after Cash Discount $=$ | $\$773.02$ |
   | Shipping & Insurance $=$ | $\$\ 38.75$ |
   | (c) Total Amount Due $=$ | $\$811.77$ |

10. 20 / 20 / 20
    $.8 \times .8 \times .8 = .512$

    $B = \dfrac{P}{R} = \dfrac{\$46,746}{.512} = \$91,300.78$
    The list price is $\$91,300.78$.

**11. (a)**   Discount date is July 20
    20 days after the end of June

 **(b)**   $\$3168 \times .04 = \$126.72$
  The amount of discount is \$126.72.

  $\$3168 - \$126.72 = \$3041.28$
  The amount necessary to pay the invoice in full is \$3041.28.

**12.**   10/20/10
 $.9 \times .8 \times .9 = .648$
 $\$696 \times .648 = \$451.01$

 $\$451.01 \times .03 = \$13.53$
 $\$451.01 - \$13.53 = \$437.48$
 The amount paid was \$437.48.

**13. (a)**   Fireside shop:
  $25/10 \rightarrow .75 \times .9 = .675$
  $\$120 \times .675 = \$81$

  Builders Supply:
  $25/5 \rightarrow .75 \times .95 = .7125$
  $\$111 \times .7125 = \$79.09$

  Builders Supply offers the lower price.

 **(b)**   $\$81 - \$79.09 = \$1.91$
  The difference in price is \$1.91.

**14. (a)**   $\$1780 \cdot .99 + \$120.39 = \$1882.59$
  \$1882.59 should be paid on March 20.

 **(b)**   $\$1780 + \$120.39 = \$1900.39$
  The full amount of \$1900.39 should be paid on April 3.

**15.**   $\$2514 \times .03 = \$75.42$
 The amount of the discount is \$75.42.

 $\$2514 - \$75.42 + \$88.50 = \$2527.08$
 The amount necessary to pay the invoice in full is \$2527.08.

**16. (a)**   $100\% - 3\% = 97\% = .97$

$$B = \frac{P}{R} = \frac{\$1666}{.97} = \$1717.53$$

  The credit given for the partial payment is \$1717.53.

 **(b)**   Balance due $= \$2916 - \$1717.53$
        $= \$1198.47$

## 8.1   Markup on Cost

1.  | 100% | $C$ | $12.40 |
    |------|-----|--------|
    | 40%  | $M$ | $ 4.96 |
    | 140% | $S$ | $17.36 |

3.  | 100% | $C$ | $27.17 |
    |------|-----|--------|
    | 20%  | $M$ | $ 5.43 |
    | 120% | $S$ | $32.60 |

5.  | 100% | $C$ | $168.00 |
    |------|-----|---------|
    | 30%  | $M$ | $ 50.40 |
    | 130% | $S$ | $218.40 |

7.  Markup

    $P = B \times R = \$9 \times .3 = \$2.70$

    Selling Price

    $\$9 + \$2.70 = \$11.70$

9.  % Markup on Cost

    $R = \dfrac{P}{B} = \dfrac{\$7.20}{\$12} = .6 = 60\%$

    Selling Price

    $\$12 + \$7.20 = \$19.20$

11. Markup

    $\$215.04 - \$153.60 = \$61.44$

    % Markup on Cost

    $R = \dfrac{P}{B} = \dfrac{\$61.44}{\$153.60} = .4 = 40\%$

13. Cost Price
    $\$42.25 - \$8.45 = \$33.80$

    % Markup on Cost

    $R = \dfrac{P}{B} = \dfrac{\$8.45}{\$33.80} = .25 = 25\%$

15. Answers will vary.

17. | 100% | $C$ | $330.30 |
    |------|-----|---------|
    | 45%  | $M$ | $       |
    | 145% | $S$ | $       |

    $P = B \times R = \$330.30 \times .45 = \$148.64$
    The markup is $148.64.

19. | 100% | $C$ | $10.36 |
    |------|-----|--------|
    | 25%  | $M$ | $      |
    | 125% | $S$ | $      |

    $P = B \times R = \$10.36 \times 1.25 = \$12.95$
    The selling price is $12.95.

21. $16\% + 7\% = 23\%$
    The percent of markup is 23%.

    $P = B \times R = \$180 \times .23 = \$41.40$
    The markup is $41.40.

    $\$180 + \$41.40 = \$221.40$
    The selling price is $221.40.

23. (a)  $\$119.95 - \$23.99 = \$95.96$
         The cost is $95.96.
    (b)  $R = \dfrac{P}{B} = \dfrac{\$23.99}{\$95.96} = .25 = 25\%$
         The markup percent on cost is 25%.
    (c)  $100\% + 25\% = 125\%$
         The selling price is 125% of the cost.

25. (a)  $100\% + 26\% = 126\%$
         The selling price is 126% of the cost.
    (b)  $P = B \times R = \$4.50 \times 1.26 = \$5.67$
         The selling price is $5.67.
    (c)  $\$5.67 - \$4.50 = \$1.17$
         The markup is $1.17.

## 8.2 Markup on Selling Price

1. 
| 75% | C | $21 |
|---|---|---|
| 25% | M | $ 7 |
| 100% | S | $28 |

3. 
| 58% | C | $145 |
|---|---|---|
| 42% | M | $105 |
| 100% | S | $250 |

5. 
| 50% | C | $2025 |
|---|---|---|
| 50% | M | $2025 |
| 100% | S | $4050 |

7. Cost

$$B = \frac{P}{R} = \frac{\$480}{.25} = \$1920$$

Selling Price

$1920 + $480 = $2400

9. $100\% - 38\% = 62\%$

The cost as a percent of selling price is 62%.

Selling Price

$$B = \frac{P}{R} = \frac{\$13.80}{.62} = \$22.26$$

Markup

$22.26 - $13.80 = $8.46

% Markup on Cost

$$R = \frac{P}{B} = \frac{\$8.46}{\$13.80} \approx .613 = 61.3\%$$

11. Cost

$$B = \frac{P}{R} = \frac{\$300}{.4} = \$750$$

Selling Price

$750 + $300 = $1050

% Markup on Selling Price

$$R = \frac{P}{B} = \frac{\$300}{\$1050} \approx .286 = 28.6\%$$

13. 
$$\frac{100\%}{100\% + 100\%} = \frac{100\%}{200\%}$$
$$= \frac{1}{2} = .5 = 50\%$$

15. 
$$\frac{18\%}{100\% + 18\%} = \frac{18\%}{118\%}$$
$$= \frac{.18}{1.18} \approx .153 = 15.3\%$$

17. Answers will vary.

19. (a) $B = \dfrac{P}{R} = \dfrac{\$437.50}{.35} = \$1250$

The selling price is $1250.

(b) $1250 - $437.50 = $812.50
The cost is $812.50.

(c) $100\% - 35\% = 65\%$
The cost is 65% of the selling price.

21. (a) $20 - (12 + 5) = 20 - 17 = 3$

$(12 \times \$85) + (5 \times \$68) + (3 \times \$49)$
$= \$1020 + \$340 + \$147$
$= \$1507$

(b) $1507 - $930 = $577
The total markup was $577.

(c) $R = \dfrac{P}{B} = \dfrac{\$577}{\$1507} \approx .383 = 38.3\%$

The markup percent on selling price is 38.3%.

(d) $R = \dfrac{P}{B} = \dfrac{\$577}{\$930} \approx .620 = 62.0\%$

The equivalent markup percent on cost is 62.0%.

23. $500 \times \$0.46 = \$280$
The cost is $280.

$100\% - 45\% = 55\%$
The cost as a percent of selling price is 55%.

$$B = \frac{P}{R} = \frac{\$280}{.55} = \$509.09$$

The total selling price is $509.09.

$90\% \times 500 = .9 \times 500 = 450$
450 pounds of the bananas will be sold.

$$\frac{\$509.09}{450} = \$1.13$$

The selling price per pound of bananas is $1.13.

## Supplementary Application Exercises on Markup

**1.**

| 100% | C | $1040 |
|------|---|-------|
| 53.8% | M | $ |
| 153.8% | S | $ |

$P = B \times R = \$1040 \times .538 = \$559.52$
The markup is $559.52.

**3.** $\$399 - \$335 = \$64$
The markup is $64.

$R = \dfrac{P}{B} = \dfrac{\$64}{\$335} \approx .191 = 19.1\%$

The percent of markup on cost is 19.1%.

**5.** $B = \dfrac{P}{R} = \dfrac{\$41.88}{.5} = \$83.76$

The total selling price is $83.76.

$\dfrac{\$83.76}{12} = \$6.98$

The selling price per can is $6.98.

**7.** $100\% - 22\% = 78\%$
The cost as a percent of selling price is 78%.

$B = \dfrac{P}{R} = \dfrac{\$92.82}{.78} = \$119$

The selling price is $119.

**9. (a)** $100\% - 24\% = 76\%$
The cost as a percent of selling price is 76%.

**(b)** $B = \dfrac{P}{R} = \dfrac{\$112.40}{.76} = \$147.89$

The selling price is $147.89.

**(c)** $\$147.89 - \$112.40 = \$35.49$
The markup is $35.49.

**11. (a)** Markup is $20\% + 15\% = 35\%$ of cost.
$.35 \times \$288 = \$100.80$

$\$288 + \$100.80 = \$388.80$
The total selling price is $388.80.

$\dfrac{\$388.80}{12} = \$32.40$

The selling price is $32.40.

**(b)** $R = \dfrac{P}{B} = \dfrac{\$100.80}{\$388.80} \approx .259 = 25.9\%$

The percent of markup on selling price is 25.9%.

**13. (a)** $\dfrac{\$2100}{12} = \$175$

The cost per bicycle is $175.

$\$199.90 - \$175 = \$24.90$
The markup per bicycle is $24.90.

**(b)** $R = \dfrac{P}{B} = \dfrac{\$24.90}{\$199.90} \approx .125 = 12.5\%$

The percent of markup on selling price is 12.5%.

**(c)** $R = \dfrac{P}{B} = \dfrac{\$24.90}{\$175} \approx .142 = 14.2\%$

The percent of markup on cost is 14.2%.

**15.** $P = B \times R = \$1890 \times 200\% = \$1890 \times 2 = \$3780$
The total selling price is $3780.

12 gross $= 144$ dozen
$.75 \times 144$ dozen $= 108$ dozen

$\dfrac{\$3780}{108} = \$35$

The selling price per dozen roses is $35.

## 8.3   Markdown

**1.** % Markdown
$R = \dfrac{P}{B} = \dfrac{\$215}{\$860} = .25 = 25\%$

Reduced Price
$\$860 - \$215 = \$645$

**3.** Markdown
$\$61.60 - \$43.12 = \$18.48$

% Markdown
$R = \dfrac{P}{B} = \dfrac{\$18.48}{\$61.60} = .3 = 30\%$

**5.** % Markdown
$R = \dfrac{P}{B} = \dfrac{\$1.30}{\$6.50} = .2 = 20\%$

Reduced Price
$\$6.50 - \$1.30 = \$5.20$

**7.** Break-even Point
$\$96 + \$24 = \$120$

Operating Loss
$\$120 - \$100 = \$20$

Absolute Loss
None, since cost is less than reduced price.

**9.** Operating Expense
$$\$66 - \$50 = \$16$$

Operating Loss
$$\$66 - \$44 = \$22$$

Absolute Loss
$$\$50 - \$44 = \$6$$

**11.** Break-even Point
$$\$310 + \$75 = \$385$$

Reduced Price
$$\$385 - \$135 = \$250$$

Absolute Loss
$$\$310 - \$250 = \$60$$

Absolute Loss
$$\$156 - \$140 = \$16$$

**13.** Answers will vary.

**15.** $\$226,284 - \$133,509 = \$92,775$
The markdown is $92,775.

$$R = \frac{P}{B} = \frac{\$92,775}{\$226,284} \approx .41 = 41\%$$

The percent of markdown on the original price is 41%.

**17.** $\$360 + \left(33\frac{1}{3}\% \times \$360\right) = \$360 + \$120 = \$480$

Total costs were $480.

$$\$480 - \$449.99 = \$30.01$$
There is a loss of $30.01.

**19. (a)** Markdown
$$P = B \times R = \$291.90 \times .35 = \$102.17$$

Reduced Price
$$\$291.90 - \$102.17 = \$189.73$$

Break-even Point
$$\$208.50 + (.28 \times \$208.50)$$
$$= \$208.50 + \$58.38 = \$266.88$$

Operating Loss
$$\$266.88 - \$189.73 = \$77.15$$

**(b)** Absolute Loss
$$\$208.50 - \$189.73 = \$18.77$$

## 8.4  Turnover and Valuation of Inventory

**1.** Total Inventory
$$\$18,300 + \$26,580 + \$23,139 = \$68,019$$

Average Inventory
$$\$68,019 \div 3 = \$22,673$$

**3.** Total Inventory
$$\$65,430 + \$58,710 + \$53,410$$
$$+ \$78,950 + \$46,340 = \$302,840$$

Average Inventory
$$\$302,840 \div 5 = \$60,568$$

**5.** Turnover at Cost
$$\$50,394 \div \$17,830 = 2.83$$

Turnover at Retail
$$\$99,450 \div \$35,390 = 2.81$$

**7.** Turnover at Cost
$$\$259,123 \div \$72,120 = 3.59$$

Turnover at Retail
$$\$487,379 \div \$138,460 = 3.52$$

**9.** Turnover at Cost
$$\$846,336 \div \$180,600 = 4.69$$

Turnover at Retail
$$\$1,196,222 \div \$256,700 = 4.66$$

**11. (a)** Weighted-Average Method

| | | |
|---|---|---|
| $10 \times \$\ 8$ | $= \$\ 80$ | |
| $25 \times \$\ 9$ | $= \$225$ | |
| $15 \times \$10$ | $= \$150$ | |
| $50$ | $= \$445$ | |

$$(\$455 \div 50) = \$9.10$$
$$\$9.10 \times 20 = \$182$$

**(b)** FIFO Method

| | |
|---|---|
| $15 \times \$10$ | $= \$150$ |
| $5 \times \$\ 9$ | $= \$\ 45$ |
| $20$ | $= \$195$ |

**(c)** LIFO Method

| | |
|---|---|
| $10 \times \$8$ | $= \$\ 80$ |
| $10 \times \$9$ | $= \$\ 90$ |
| $20$ | $= \$170$ |

13. (a) Weighted-Average Method

$50 \times \$30.50 = \$1525.00$

$70 \times \$31.50 = \$2205.00$

$30 \times \$33.25 = \$\ 997.50$

$\underline{40 \times \$30.75 = \$1230.00}$

$\overline{190 \qquad = \$5957.50}$

$(\$5957.50 \div 190) = \$31.36$

$\$31.36 \times 75 = \$2352$

(b) FIFO Method

$40 \times \$30.75 = \$1230.00$

$30 \times \$33.25 = \$\ 997.50$

$\underline{5 \times \$31.50 = \$\ 157.50}$

$\overline{75 \qquad = \$2385.00}$

(c) LIFO Method

$50 \times \$30.50 = \$1525.00$

$\underline{25 \times \$31.50 = \$\ 787.50}$

$\overline{75 \qquad = \$2312.50}$

15. Answers will vary.

17. $\$85,412 \div \$15,730 = \$5.43$

The stock turnover at cost is $5.43.

19. (a) Weighted-Average Method

$200 \times \$1.10 = \$\ 220$

$400 \times \$1.20 = \$\ 480$

$700 \times \$1.00 = \$\ 700$

$500 \times \$1.15 = \$\ 575$

$\underline{300 \times \$1.30 = \$\ 390}$

$\overline{2100 \qquad = \$2365}$

$(\$2365 \div 2100) = \$1.13$

$\$1.13 \times 450 = \$508.50$

(b) FIFO Method

$300 \times \$1.30 = \$390.00$

$\underline{150 \times \$1.15 = \$172.50}$

$\overline{450 \qquad = \$562.50}$

(c) LIFO Method

$200 \times \$1.10 = \$220$

$\underline{250 \times \$1.20 = \$300}$

$\overline{450 \qquad = \$520}$

21. (a) Weighted-Average Method

$200 \times \$3.10 = \$\ 620$

$250 \times \$3.50 = \$\ 875$

$300 \times \$4.25 = \$1275$

$\underline{280 \times \$4.50 = \$1260}$

$\overline{1030 \qquad = \$4030}$

$(\$4030 \div 1030) = \$3.91$

$\$3.91 \times 320 = \$1251.20$

(b) FIFO Method

$280 \times \$4.50 = \$1260$

$\underline{40 \times \$4.25 = \$\ 170}$

$\overline{320 \qquad = \$1430}$

(c) LIFO Method

$200 \times \$3.10 = \$\ 620$

$\underline{120 \times \$3.50 = \$\ 420}$

$\overline{320 \qquad = \$1040}$

23. 

| At Cost | At retail |
|---|---|
| $43,750 | $62,500 |
| + 51,600 | + 73,800 |
| $95,350 | $136,300 |
| | − 92,500 |
| | $43,800 |

$\dfrac{\$95,350}{\$136,300} \approx .7 = 70\%$

$\$43,800 \times .7 = \$30,660$

25. Answers will vary.

## Case Study

1. $\$1950 \div 24 = \$81.25$

   The cost per pair of skates is $81.25.

   $100\% - 35\% = 65\%$

   The cost as a percent of selling price is 65%.

   $B = \dfrac{P}{R} = \dfrac{\$81.25}{.65} = \$125$

   The original selling price of each pair of skates is $125.

2. $6 \times \$125 = \$750$

   $6 \times (\$125 - .25 \times \$125)$

   $= 6 \times \$93.75 = \$562.50$

   $12 \times (\$125 - .5 \times \$125)$

   $= 12 \times \$62.50 = \$750$

   $\$750 + \$562.50 + \$750 = \$2062.50$

   The total of the selling prices of all the skates is $2062.50.

**3.** $1950 + (.25 \times \$1950) = \$2437.50$

The break-even point is $2437.50.

$2437.50 - \$2062.50 = \$375$
The operating loss is $375.

**4.** Since the selling price is greater than the cost, there is no absolute loss.

## Case in Point Summary Exercise

**1.** $\dfrac{\$4395}{15} = \$293$

The cost per pair of Steep Alpine skis is $293.

$\dfrac{\$7194}{22} = \$327$

The cost per pair of Cliff Hoppers skis is $327.

**2.** $293 \cdot 1.38 = \$404.34$

The list price for a pair of Steep Alpine skis is $404.34.

$327 \cdot 1.38 = \$451.26$

The list price for a pair of Cliff Hoppers skis is $451.26.

**3.** Inventory on January 1
$4395 + \$7194 = \$11,589$

Inventory on January 31
$293 \cdot 7 + \$327 \cdot 14 = \$6629$

Average Inventory
$\dfrac{\$11,589 + \$6629}{2} = \$9109$

**4.** Cost of Goods Sold
$(15 - 7) \cdot \$293 + (22 - 14) \cdot \$327$
$= 8 \cdot \$293 + 8 \cdot \$327 = \$4960$

Turnover at Cost
$\dfrac{\$4960}{\$9109} = .54$

**5.** $404.34(100\% - 40\%) = \$404.34(60\%)$
$= \$404.34 \cdot .6 = \$242.60$

The price per pair of Steep Alpine skis is $242.60.

$451.26(100\% - 40\%) = \$451.26(60\%)$
$= \$451.26 \cdot .6 = \$270.76$

The price per pair of Cliff Hoppers skis is $270.76.

**6.** Total Revenue
$404.34 \cdot 8 + \$451.26 \cdot 8$
$+ \$242.60 \cdot 7 + \$270.76 \cdot 14 = \$12,333.64$

Total Cost
$4395 + \$7194 = \$11,589$

Break-even Point
$11,589 \cdot 1.22 = \$14,138.58$

The firm had an operating loss since total revenue was more than total cost but less than the break-even point.

Operating Loss
$14,138.58 - \$12,333.64 = \$1804.94$

**7.** Discussion may vary, but either is acceptable.

## Chapter 8  Test

**1.** 
| 100% | $C$ | $64.00 |
|---|---|---|
| 20% | $M$ | $12.80 |
| 120% | $S$ | $76.80 |

**2.** 
| 100% | $C$ | $138.89 |
|---|---|---|
| 38% | $M$ | $365.50 |
| 138% | $S$ | $504.39 |

**3.** 
| 80% | $C$ | $134.40 |
|---|---|---|
| 20% | $M$ | $ 33.60 |
| 100% | $S$ | $168.00 |

**4.** 
| 75% | $C$ | $18.45 |
|---|---|---|
| 25% | $M$ | $ 6.15 |
| 100% | $S$ | $24.60 |

**5.** $\dfrac{25\%}{100\% + 25\%} = \dfrac{25\%}{125\%}$
$= \dfrac{.25}{1.25} = \dfrac{1}{5} = .2 = 20\%$

**6.** $\dfrac{100\%}{100\% + 100\%} = \dfrac{100\%}{200\%}$
$= \dfrac{1}{2} = .5 = 50\%$

7.  Break-even Point
    $160 + $40 = $200

    Operating Loss
    $200 − $186 = $14

    Absolute Loss
    None, since cost is less than reduced price.

8.  Operating Expense
    $297 − $225 = $72

    Operating Loss
    $297 − $198 = $99

    Absolute Loss
    $225 − $198 = $27

9.  Turnover at Cost
    $81,312 ÷ $14,120 = 5.76

    Turnover at Retail
    $146,528 ÷ $25,572 = 5.73

10. 100% − 35% = 65%
    The cost as a percent of selling price is 65%.

    $$B = \frac{P}{R} = \frac{\$195}{.65} = \$300$$
    The total selling price is $300 per dozen pair.

    $$\frac{\$300}{12} = \$25$$
    The selling price per pair is $25.

11. $$B = \frac{P}{R} = \frac{\$5250}{1.25} = \$4200$$
    The cost is $4200.

12. $37.50 − $22.50 = $15
    The markup is $15.

    $$R = \frac{P}{B} = \frac{\$15}{\$37.50} = .4 = 40\%$$
    The markup is 40% of the selling price.

13. (a) $$\frac{\$1943.52}{12} = \$161.96$$
    The cost per boat is $161.96.

    $199.95 − $161.96 = $37.99
    The markup is $37.99.

13. (b) $$R = \frac{P}{B} = \frac{\$37.99}{\$199.95} \approx .190 = 19.0\%$$
    The percent of markup on selling price is 19.0%.

    (c) $$R = \frac{P}{B} = \frac{\$37.99}{\$161.96} \approx .235 = 23.5\%$$
    The percent of markup on cost is 23.5%.

14. $13,875 − $9990 = $3885
    The markdown is $3885.

    $$R = \frac{P}{B} = \frac{\$3885}{\$13,875} = .28 = 28\%$$
    The markdown is 28% of the original price.

15. (a) Reduced Price
    $399 − (.4 × $399) = $239.40

    Break-even Point
    $285 + (.3 × $285) = $370.50

    Operating Loss
    $370.50 − $239.40 = $131.10

    (b) Absolute Loss
    $285 − $239.40 = $45.60

16. Total Inventory
    $117,328 + $147,630 + $125,876
    = $390,834

    Average Inventory
    $390,834 ÷ 3 = $130,278

17. Weighted-Average Method
    25 × $270 = $  6,750
    40 × $330 = $13,200
    15 × $217 = $  3,255
    30 × $284 = $  8,520
    ─────────────────────
    110        = $31,725

    ($31,725 ÷ 110) = $288.41
    $288.41 × 45 = $12,978.45 ≈ $12,978

18. (a) FIFO Method
    30 × $284 = $ 8,520
    15 × $217 = $ 3,255
    ──────────────────
    45        = $11,775

    (b) LIFO Method
    25 × $270 = $ 6,750
    20 × $330 = $ 6,600
    ──────────────────
    45        = $13,350

1. $428.80 + \$316.25 + \$68.95 + \$733.18$
   $+ \$38.00 + \$188.36 + \$22.51 + \$162.15$
   $= \$1958.20$

   The total amount of the sales slips is $1958.20.

2. $76.15 + \$118.44 + \$13.86 = \$208.45$
   The total amount of the credit slips is $208.45.

3. Gross deposit $=$ Sales $-$ Credits
   $= \$1958.20 - \$208.45$
   $= \$1749.75$

   The total amount of the deposit is $1749.75.

4. $1749.75 \times .0125 \approx \$21.87$
   The discount charge at the statement date is $21.87.

5. Credit $=$ Sales $-$ Fee
   $= \$1749.75 - \$21.87$
   $= \$1727.88$

   The amount of credit given is $1727.88.

6. $7 + 8 + 8 + 8 + 8 = 39$ regular hours
   $2 + 1 + 2 = 5$ overtime hours
   Overtime rate: $1.5 \times \$12.80 = \$19.20$

   | | |
   |---|---|
   | 39 hours $\times \$12.80$ | $= \$499.20$ |
   | 5 O.T. hours $\times \$19.20$ | $= + 96.00$ |
   | Gross Earnings | $\$595.20$ |

7. $968.50
     968.50
     223.50
     223.50
    1975.38
   $4359.38

   The total amount owed to the Internal Revenue Service is $4359.38.

8. 20/20
   $.8 \times .8 = .64$

   $.64 \times \$475.50 = \$304.32$

9. 25/10/5
   $.75 \times .9 \times .95 = .64125$

   $.64125 \times \$375 = \$240.47$

10. 10/20
    $.9 \times .8 = .72$

    $1.00 - .72 = .28 = 28\%$

11. 30/40/10
    $.7 \times .6 \times .9 = .378$

    $1.00 - .378 = .622 = 62.2\%$

12. Discount date is June 15
    10 days after June 5.

    Net payment date is July 5
    20 days after discount date
    (15 days in June + 5 days in July)

13. Discount date is Nov. 15
    15 days after the end of Oct.

    Net payment date is Dec. 5
    20 days after discount date
    (15 days in Nov. + 5 days in Dec.)

14. Discount date is Aug. 3
    $10 + 30 = 40$ days after June 24
    (6 days in June + 31 days in July
    +3 days in Aug.)

    Net payment date is Aug. 23
    20 days after discount date

15. Break-even Point
    $312 + \$88 = \$400$

    Reduced Price
    $400 - \$120 = \$280$

    Absolute Loss
    $312 - \$280 = \$32$

16. Cost
    $220 + \$32 = \$252$

    Break-even Point
    $220 + \$112 = \$332$

    Operating Expense
    $332 - \$252 = \$80$

**17.** 20 / 20

$.8 \times .8 = .64$

$149.99 \times .64 = \$95.99$

$95.99 \times .03 = \$2.88$

$95.99 - \$2.88 = \$93.11$

The list price is \$93.11.

**18.** $100\% - 52\% = 48\%$

The cost as a percent of selling price is 48%.

$$B = \frac{P}{R} = \frac{\$43.20}{.48} = \$90$$

The total selling price is \$90.

$$\frac{\$90}{36} = \$2.50$$

The selling price per mouse pad is \$2.50.

**19.** $\$241,938 \div \$18,784 = 12.88$

The stock turnover at cost is 12.88.

**20.** $\$53,820 + \$49,510 + \$60,820 + \$56,380$
$= \$220,530$

The total inventory is \$220,530.

$\$220,530 \div 4 = \$55,132.50$

The average inventory is \$55,132.50.

$\$252,077 \div \$55,132.50 = 4.57$

The stock turnover at retail is 4.57.

**21.**

$\begin{aligned}
25 \times \$135.00 &= \$\ \ 3,375.00 \\
40 \times \$165.00 &= \$\ \ 6,600.00 \\
15 \times \$108.50 &= \$\ \ 1,627.50 \\
30 \times \$142.00 &= \$\ \ 4,260.00 \\
\hline
110 \qquad\quad &= \$15,862.50
\end{aligned}$

$(\$15,862.50 \div 110) = \$144.20$

$\$144.20 \times 45 = \$6489$

**22. (a)** FIFO Method

$\begin{aligned}
30 \times \$142.00 &= \$4260.00 \\
15 \times \$108.50 &= \$1627.50 \\
\hline
45 \qquad\quad &= \$5887.50
\end{aligned}$

**(b)** LIFO Method

$\begin{aligned}
25 \times \$135 &= \$3375 \\
20 \times \$165 &= \$3300 \\
\hline
45 \qquad &= \$6675
\end{aligned}$

# Chapter 9 | Simple Interest

## 9.1  Basics of Simple Interest

**1.** Interest
$$I = PRT$$
$$I = \$3800 \times .11 \times \frac{6}{12}$$
$$I = \$209$$

Maturity Value
$$M = P + I$$
$$M = \$3800 + \$209$$
$$M = \$4009$$

**3.** Interest
$$I = PRT$$
$$I = \$5500 \times .08 \times 1$$
$$I = \$440$$

Maturity Value
$$M = P + I$$
$$M = \$5500 + \$440$$
$$M = \$5940$$

**5.** April 24 is day              114
February 15 is day        $\underline{-46}$
                                          68  days

**7.** Last day of the year is number    365
December 1 is day                $\underline{-335}$
                                                  30  days

December 1 to end of year      30
January 1 to March 10          $\underline{+69}$
                                                99  days

**9. (a)** Exact Interest
$$I = PRT$$
$$I = \$52,000 \times .0875 \times \frac{200}{365}$$
$$I = \$2493.15$$

**(b)** Ordinary Interest
$$I = PRT$$
$$I = \$52,000 \times .0875 \times \frac{200}{360}$$
$$I = \$2527.78$$

**(c)** Difference
$$\$2527.78 - \$2493.15 = \$34.63$$

**11. (a)** Exact Interest
$$I = PRT$$
$$I = \$29,500 \times .1125 \times \frac{120}{365}$$
$$I = \$1091.10$$

**(b)** Ordinary Interest
$$I = PRT$$
$$I = \$29,500 \times .1125 \times \frac{120}{360}$$
$$I = \$1106.25$$

**(c)** Difference
$$\$1106.25 - \$1091.10 = \$15.15$$

**13.** Helen Spence

**15.** Donna Sharp

**17.** 90 days

**19.** January 25

**21.** Due Date
March 12 is day              71
                                    $\underline{+220}$
                                        291
Day 291 is October 18, the due date.

Interest
$$I = PRT$$
$$I = \$4800 \times .09 \times \frac{220}{360}$$
$$I = \$264$$

Maturity Value
$$M = P + I$$
$$M = \$4800 + \$264$$
$$M = \$5064$$

**23.** Due Date
November 10 is day     314
                                  $\underline{+180}$
                                      494

494
$\underline{-365}$
129    Day 129 is May 9, the due date.

**23. (continued)**

Interest
$$I = PRT$$
$$I = \$6300 \times .0925 \times \frac{180}{360}$$
$$I = \$291.38$$

Maturity Value
$$M = P + I$$
$$M = \$6300 + \$291.38$$
$$M = \$6591.38$$

**25. (a)** $I = PRT$
$$I = \$2,000,000 \times .0925 \times \frac{9}{12}$$
$$I = \$138,750$$
The interest is \$138,750.

**(b)** $M = P + I$
$$M = \$2,000,000 + \$138,750$$
$$M = \$2,138,750$$
The maturity value is \$2,138,750.

**27.** Present:
$$I = PRT$$
$$I = \$280,000 \times .10 \times \frac{180}{360}$$
$$I = \$14,000$$

1980:
$$I = PRT$$
$$I = \$280,000 \times .22 \times \frac{180}{360}$$
$$I = \$30,800$$

$\$30,800 - \$14,000 = \$16,800$
The difference in the interest charges is \$16,800.

**29. (a)** July 5 is day $\quad$ 186
$$\frac{+90}{276}$$
Day 276 is October 3, the due date.

**(b)** $I = PRT$
$$I = \$6850 \times .0925 \times \frac{90}{360}$$
$$I = \$158.41$$
The interest is $=\$158.41$.

$$M = P + I$$
$$M = \$6850 + \$158.41$$
$$M = \$7008.41$$
The maturity value is \$7008.41.

**31. (a)** March 10 is day $\quad$ 69
$$\frac{+180}{249}$$
Day 249 is September 6, the due date.

**(b)** $I = PRT$
$$I = \$80,000 \times .105 \times \frac{180}{360}$$
$$I = \$4200$$
The interest is \$4200.

$$M = P + I$$
$$M = \$80,000 + \$4200$$
$$M = \$84,200$$
The maturity value is \$84,200.

**33.** July 23 is day $\quad$ 204
April 15 is day $\quad \frac{-105}{99}$ days

$$I = PRT$$
$$I = \$3416.05 \times .093 \times \frac{99}{365}$$
$$I = \$86.17$$
The penalty is \$86.17.

**35. (a)** Due Date
8 months from January 31 is
September 30.

**(b)** $I = PRT$
$$I = \$128,000 \times .095 \times \frac{8}{12}$$
$$I = \$8106.67$$
The interest is \$8106.67.

$$M = P + I$$
$$M = \$128,000 + \$8106.67$$
$$M = \$136,106.67$$
The maturity value is \$136,106.67.

**37.** Answers will vary.

## 9.2 Finding Principal, Rate, and Time

**1.** $P = \dfrac{I}{RT}$

$P = \dfrac{\$271.25}{.0775 \times \frac{90}{360}}$

$P = \$14,000$

**3.** $P = \dfrac{I}{RT}$

$P = \dfrac{\$112}{.10 \times \frac{80}{360}}$

$P = \$5040$

**5.** $P = \dfrac{I}{RT}$

$P = \dfrac{\$306}{.085 \times \frac{120}{360}}$

$P = \$10,800$

**7.** $R = \dfrac{I}{PT}$

$R = \dfrac{\$498.22}{\$7600 \times \frac{200}{360}}$

$R \approx .118 = 11.8\%$

**9.** $R = \dfrac{I}{PT}$

$R = \dfrac{\$677.67}{\$42,800 \times \frac{60}{360}}$

$R \approx .095 = 9.5\%$

**11.** $R = \dfrac{I}{PT}$

$R = \dfrac{\$200}{\$8000 \times \frac{4}{12}}$

$R = .075 = 7.5\%$

**13.** $T = \dfrac{I}{PR} \times 360$

$T = \dfrac{\$2343.33}{\$74,000 \times .095} \times 360$

$T = \dfrac{\$2343.33}{\$7030} \times 360$

$T \approx 120$ days

**15.** $T = \dfrac{I}{PR} \times 360$

$T = \dfrac{\$454.70}{\$24,000 \times .11} \times 360$

$T = \dfrac{\$454.70}{\$2640} \times 360$

$T \approx 62$ days

**17.** $T = \dfrac{I}{PR} \times 360$

$T = \dfrac{\$143.50}{\$3500 \times .1025} \times 12$

$T = \dfrac{\$143.50}{\$358.75} \times 12$

$T = 4.8$ months $\approx 5$ months

**19.** $P = \dfrac{I}{RT}$

$P = \dfrac{\$244.80}{.032 \times \frac{9}{12}}$

$P = \dfrac{\$244.80}{.024}$

$P = \$10,200$

The amount initially invested was \$10,200.

**21.** $R = \dfrac{I}{PT}$

$R = \dfrac{\$237.50}{\$3600 \times \frac{250}{360}}$

$R = \dfrac{\$237.50}{\$2500}$

$R = .095 = 9.5\%$

The rate is 9.5%.

**23.** $R = \dfrac{I}{PT}$

$R = \dfrac{\$1881.25}{\$45,000 \times \frac{140}{360}}$

$R = \dfrac{\$1881.25}{\$17,500}$

$R = .1075 = 10.75\%$

The rate is 10.75%.

**25.** **(a)** $P = \dfrac{I}{RT}$

$P = \dfrac{\$450}{.05 \times \frac{300}{360}}$

$P = \$10,800$

The principal is \$10,800.

**25. (b)** $M = P + I$

$M = \$10,800 + \$450$

$M = \$11,250$

$\$11,250$ is in the account at the end of 300 days.

**27.** $T = \dfrac{I}{PR} \times 360$

$T = \dfrac{\$69.46}{\$9400 \times .035} \times 360$

$T = \dfrac{\$69.46}{\$329} \times 360$

$T \approx 76$ days

**29.** $R = \dfrac{I}{PT}$

$R = \dfrac{\$223.03}{\$6272.73 \times \frac{320}{360}}$

$R = \dfrac{\$223.03}{\$5575.76}$

$R \approx .040 = 4\%$

The interest rate is 4%.

**31. (a)** $P = \dfrac{I}{RT}$

$P = \dfrac{\$150}{.10 \times \frac{45}{360}}$

$P = \dfrac{\$150}{.0125}$

$P = \$12,000$

The cost of the 10 computers is $12,000.

**(b)** $\dfrac{\$12,000}{10} = \$1200$

The cost per computer is $1200.

**33.** $T = \dfrac{I}{PR} \times 360$

$T = \dfrac{\$42.52}{\$640 \times .115} \times 360$

$T = \dfrac{\$42.52}{\$73.60} \times 360$

$T \approx 208$ days

The term of the note is approximately 208 days.

**35. (a)** Bank One

$R = \dfrac{I}{PT}$

$R = \dfrac{\$23,650}{\$220,000 \times 1}$

$R = .1075 = 10.75\%$

The interest rate is 10.75% from Bank One.

**(b)** First National Bank

$R = \dfrac{I}{PT}$

$R = \dfrac{\$25,000}{\$220,000 \times 1}$

$R \approx .114 = 11.4\%$

The interest rate is 11.4% from First National Bank.

**37.** Answers will vary.

## 9.3   Simple Discount Notes

**1.** Discount

$B = MDT$

$B = \$7800 \times .09 \times \dfrac{120}{360}$

$B = \$234$

Proceeds or Loan Amount

$P = M - B$

$P = \$7800 - \$234$

$P = \$7566$

**3.** Discount

$B = MDT$

$B = \$19,000 \times .10 \times \dfrac{180}{360}$

$B = \$950$

Proceeds or Loan Amount

$P = M - B$

$P = \$19,000 - \$950$

$P = \$18,050$

**5.** Discount

$B = MDT$

$B = \$22,400 \times .0875 \times \dfrac{75}{360}$

$B = \$408.33$

Proceeds or Loan Amount

$P = M - B$

$P = \$22,400 - \$408.33$

$P = \$21,991.67$

7. March 22 is day $\qquad$ 81
$$\begin{array}{r} 81 \\ +90 \\ \hline 171 \end{array}$$
Day 171 is June 20, the maturity date.

Proceeds or Loan Amount
$P = M - MDT$
$P = \$6400 - \left( \$6400 \times .095 \times \dfrac{90}{360} \right)$
$P = \$6248$

9. July 12 is day $\qquad$ 193
$$\begin{array}{r} 193 \\ +150 \\ \hline 343 \end{array}$$
Day 343 is December 9, the maturity date.

Proceeds or Loan Amount
$P = M - MDT$
$P = \$10,000 - \left( \$10,000 \times .1025 \times \dfrac{150}{360} \right)$
$P = \$9572.92$

11. December 10 is day $\qquad$ 344
$$\begin{array}{r} 344 \\ +60 \\ \hline 404 \end{array}$$
$$\begin{array}{r} 404 \\ -365 \\ \hline 39 \end{array}$$ Day 39 is February 8, the maturity date.

Proceeds or Loan Amount
$P = M - MDT$
$P = \$24,000 - \left( \$24,000 \times .10 \times \dfrac{60}{360} \right)$
$P = \$23,600$

13. (a) $B = MDT$
$B = \$6000 \times .11 \times \dfrac{120}{360}$
$B = \$220$
The discount is \$220.

(b) $P = M - B$
$P = \$6000 - \$220$
$P = \$5780$
The proceeds are \$5780.

15. $T = \dfrac{B}{MD} \times 360$
$T = \dfrac{\$1527.78}{\$25,000 \times .11} \times 360$
$T = \dfrac{\$1527.78}{\$2750} \times 360$
$T \approx 200$ days

17. $B = M - P$
$B = \$170 - \$157.25$
$B = \$12.75$ million
The bank discount is \$12.75 million.

$D = \dfrac{B}{MT}$
$D = \dfrac{\$12.75}{\$170 \times \frac{270}{360}}$
$D = .1 = 10\%$
The discount rate is 10%.

19. $M = \dfrac{P}{1 - DT}$
$M = \dfrac{\$7260}{1 - \left( .12 \times \frac{240}{360} \right)}$
$M = \$7891.30$
The face value of the loan is \$7891.30.

21. (a) $B = MDT$
$B = \$4200 \times .12 \times \dfrac{10}{12}$
$B = \$420$
The discount is \$420.

$P = M - B$
$P = \$4200 - \$420$
$P = \$3780$
The proceeds are \$3780.

(b) $R = \dfrac{I}{PT}$
$R = \dfrac{\$420}{\$3780 \times \frac{10}{12}}$
$R \approx .133 = 13.3\%$
The effective interest rate is 13.3%.

23. $B = M - P$
$B = 40,000 - 38,833.33$
$B = 1166.67$
The discount is 1166.67 English pounds.

$T = \dfrac{B}{MD} \times 360$
$T = \dfrac{\$1166.67}{\$40,000 \times .10} \times 360$
$T = \dfrac{\$1166.67}{\$4000} \times 360$
$T \approx 105$ days

**25. (a)** $M = \dfrac{P}{1 - DT}$

$M = \dfrac{165,000,000}{1 - \left(.08 \times \frac{30}{360}\right)}$

$M = 166,107,382.6$

Face value of the loan is 166,107,382.6 yen.

**(b)** $B = M - P$

$B = 166,107,382.6 - 165,000,000$

$B = 1,107,382.6$

The discount (or interest) is 1,107,382.6 yen.

$R = \dfrac{I}{PT}$

$R = \dfrac{\$1,107,382.6}{\$165,000,000 \times \frac{30}{360}}$

$R \approx .081 = 8.1\%$

The effective rate is 8.1%.

**27. (a)** $B = M - P$

$B = \$265,000 - \$253,737.50$

$B = \$11,262.50$

The interest is \$11,262.50.

**(b)** $R = \dfrac{I}{PT}$

$R = \dfrac{\$11,262.50}{\$253,737.50 \times \frac{180}{360}}$

$R \approx .089 = 8.9\%$

The true rate is 8.9%.

**29. (a)** $B = MDT$

$B = \$25,000,000 \times .06 \times \dfrac{13}{52}$

$B = \$375,000$

The discount is \$375,000.

$P = M - B$

$P = \$25,000,000 - \$375,000$

$P = \$24,625,000$

The purchase price is \$24,625,000.

**(b)** The maturity value is \$25,000,000.

**(c)** The interest earned is \$375,000.

**(d)** $R = \dfrac{I}{PT}$

$R = \dfrac{\$375,000}{\$24,625,000 \times \frac{13}{52}}$

$R \approx .0609 = 6.09\%$

The effective rate is 6.09%.

**31.** Answers will vary.

## 9.4   Discounting a Note before Maturity

**1.** July 31 is day          212

April 29 is day          $\underline{-119}$

                                      93

Length of Loan is                          200

Loan is discounted on day          $\underline{-93}$

Discount Period is 107 days.     107

**3.** June 18 is day          169

May 28 is day          $\underline{-148}$

                                21

Length of Loan is                        74

Loan is discounted on day          $\underline{-21}$

Discount Period is 53 days.        53

**5.** Discount

$B = MDT$

$B = \$10,400 \times .085 \times \dfrac{90}{360}$

$B = \$221$

Proceeds

$P = M - B$

$P = \$10,400 - \$221$

$P = \$10,179$

**7.** Discount

$B = MDT$

$B = \$25,000 \times .09 \times \dfrac{30}{360}$

$B = \$187.50$

Proceeds

$P = M - B$

$P = \$25,000 - \$187.50$

$P = \$24,812.50$

**9.** Interest

$I = PRT$

$I = \$6200 \times .105 \times \dfrac{90}{360}$

$I = \$162.75$

Maturity Value

$M = P + I$

$M = \$6200 + \$162.75$

$M = \$6362.75$

April 1 is day          91

February 7 is day          $\underline{-38}$

                                    53

**9. (continued)**

| Length of Loan is | 90 |
|---|---|
| Loan is discounted on day | $-53$ |
| Discount Period is 37 days. | 37 |

Discount
$B = MDT$

$$B = \$6362.75 \times .12 \times \frac{37}{360}$$

$$B = \$78.47$$

Proceeds
$P = M - B$
$P = \$6362.75 - \$78.47$
$P = \$6284.28$

**11.** Interest
$I = PRT$

$$I = \$2000 \times .11 \times \frac{72}{360}$$

$$I = \$44$$

Maturity Value
$M = P + I$
$M = \$2000 + \$44$
$M = \$2044$

| August 2 is day | 214 |
|---|---|
| July 10 is day | $-191$ |
| | 23 |

| Length of Loan is | 72 |
|---|---|
| Loan is discounted on day | $-23$ |
| Discount Period is 49 days. | 49 |

Discount
$B = MDT$

$$B = \$2044 \times .12 \times \frac{49}{360}$$

$$B = \$33.39$$

Proceeds
$P = M - B$
$P = \$2044 - \$33.39$
$P = \$2010.61$

**13.** Discount of the Original Note
$B = MDT$

$$B = \$17,800 \times .10 \times \frac{90}{360}$$

$$B = \$445$$

Proceeds from the Original Note
$P = M - B$
$P = \$17,800 - \$445$
$P = \$17,355$

**13. (continue)**

| March 1 is day | 60 |
|---|---|
| January 12 is day | $-12$ |
| | 48 |

| Length of Loan is | 90 |
|---|---|
| Loan is discounted on day | $-48$ |
| Discount Period is 42 days. | 42 |

Discount
$B = MDT$

$$B = \$17,800 \times .11 \times \frac{42}{360}$$

$$B = \$228.43$$

Proceeds after Discounting
$P = M - B$
$P = \$17,800 - \$228.43$
$P = \$17,571.57$

**15.** Discount of the Original Note
$B = MDT$

$$B = \$32,100 \times .095 \times \frac{150}{360}$$

$$B = \$1270.63$$

Proceeds from the Original Note
$P = M - B$
$P = \$32,100 - \$1270.63$
$P = \$30,829.37$

| July 10 is day | 191 |
|---|---|
| May 4 is day | $-124$ |
| | 67 |

| Length of Loan is | 150 |
|---|---|
| Loan is discounted on day | $-67$ |
| Discount Period is 83 days. | 83 |

Discount
$B = MDT$

$$B = \$32,100 \times .11 \times \frac{83}{360}$$

$$B = \$814.09$$

Proceeds after Discounting
$P = M - B$
$P = \$32,100 - \$814.09$
$P = \$31,285.91$

**17. (a)**   $M = P + PRT$

$$M = \$360,000 + \left(\$360,000 \times .07 \times \frac{180}{360}\right)$$

$M = \$360,000 + \$12,600$

$M = \$372,600$

The maturity value is $372,600.

$$\begin{array}{r} 180 \\ -120 \\ \hline 60 \end{array}$$   Discount Period is 60 days.

$B = MDT$

$$B = \$372,600 \times .08 \times \frac{60}{360}$$

$B = \$4968$

The bank discount is $4968.

**(b)**   $P = M - B$

$P = \$372,600 - \$4968$

$P = \$367,632$

The proceeds are $367,632.

**19. (a)**   $P = M - MDT$

$$P = \$250,000 - \left(\$250,000 \times .09 \times \frac{180}{360}\right)$$

$P = \$250,000 - \$11,250$

$P = \$238,750$

The proceeds of the original note to the dealership are $238,750.

**(b)**   
$$\begin{array}{lr} \text{June 14 is day} & 165 \\ \text{March 19 is day} & -78 \\ \hline & 87 \end{array}$$

$$\begin{array}{lr} \text{Length of Loan is} & 180 \\ \text{Loan is discounted on day} & -87 \\ \hline \text{Discount Period is 93 days.} & 93 \end{array}$$

**(c)**   $B = MDT$

$$B = \$250,000 \times .08 \times \frac{93}{360}$$

$B = \$5166.67$

The discount is $5166.67.

**(d)**   $P = M - B$

$P = \$250,000 - \$5166.67$

$P = \$244,833.33$

The proceeds at the sale of the note on June 14 are $244,833.33.

**21. (a)**   $M = P + PRT$

$$M = \$300,000 + \left(\$300,000 \times .09 \times \frac{150}{360}\right)$$

$M = \$300,000 + \$11,250$

$M = \$311,250$

The maturity value is $311,250.

**(b)**   
$$\begin{array}{lr} \text{Last day of the year is number} & 365 \\ \text{November 20 is day} & -324 \\ \hline & 41 \text{ days} \end{array}$$

$$\begin{array}{lr} \text{November 20 to end of year} & 41 \\ \text{January 1 to February 6} & +37 \\ \hline & 78 \text{ days} \end{array}$$

$$\begin{array}{lr} \text{Length of Loan is} & 150 \\ \text{Loan is discounted on day} & -78 \\ \hline \text{Discount Period is 72 days.} & 72 \end{array}$$

$P = M - MDT$

$$P = \$311,250 - \left(\$311,250 \times .105 \times \frac{72}{360}\right)$$

$P = \$311,250 - \$6536.25$

$P = \$304,713.75$

The proceeds to National Bank are $304,713.75.

**23. (a)**   $P = M - MDT$

$$P = \$25,000 - \left(\$25,000 \times .068 \times \frac{26}{52}\right)$$

$P = \$25,000 - \$850$

$P = \$24,150$

Barton's purchase price is $24,150.

**(b)**   26 weeks $-$ 10 weeks $=$ 16 weeks

$B = MDT$

$$B = \$25,000 \times .07 \times \frac{16}{52}$$

$B = \$538.46$

The discount 10 weeks later is $538.46.

**(c)**   $P = M - B$

$P = \$25,000 - \$538.46$

$P = \$24,461.54$

The proceeds to Barton are $24,461.54.

**(d)**   $\$24,461.54 - \$24,150 = \$311.54$

Barton received $311.54 in interest.

$$R = \frac{I}{PT}$$

$$R = \frac{\$311.54}{\$24,150 \times \frac{10}{52}}$$

$R \approx .0671 = 6.71\%$

The effective interest rate is 6.71%.

**25.** Answers will vary.

## Supplementary Application Exercises on Simple Interest and Simple Discount

**1. (a)** $I = PRT$

$$I = \$18,000 \times .11 \times \frac{120}{360}$$

$$I = \$660$$

The interest is $660.

**(b)** $M = P + I$

$$M = \$18,000 + \$660$$

$$M = \$18,660$$

The maturity value is $18,660.

**3.** $P = \dfrac{I}{RT}$

$$P = \frac{\$4800}{.10 \times \frac{180}{360}}$$

$$P = \frac{\$4800}{.05}$$

$$P = \$96,000$$

The principal is $96,000.

**5.** $T = \dfrac{B}{MD} \times 360$

$$T = \frac{\$8750}{\$150,000 \times .105} \times 360$$

$$T = \frac{\$8750}{\$15,750} \times 360$$

$$T = 200 \text{ days}$$

**7. (a)** $I = PRT$

$$I = \$20,000 \times .09 \times \frac{150}{360}$$

$$I = \$750$$

The interest is $750.

**(b)** $M = P + I$

$$M = \$20,000 + \$750$$

$$M = \$20,750$$

The maturity value is $20,750.

**9.** $B = MDT$

$$B = \$145,000 \times .115 \times \frac{5}{12}$$

$$B = \$6947.92$$

The discount is $6947.92.

$$P = M - B$$

$$P = \$145,000 - \$6947.92$$

$$P = \$138,052.08$$

The proceeds are $138,052.08.

$$R = \frac{I}{PT}$$

$$R = \frac{\$6947.92}{\$138,052.08 \times \frac{5}{12}}$$

$$R \approx 0.121 = 12.1\%$$

The effective rate of interest is 12.1%.

**11.** October 14 is day

$$\begin{array}{r} 287 \\ +180 \\ \hline 467 \end{array}$$

$$\begin{array}{r} 467 \\ -365 \\ \hline 102 \end{array} \quad \text{Day 102 is April 12, the due date.}$$

$$P = M - MDT$$

$$P = \$10,000,000 - \left(\$10,000,000 \times .105 \times \frac{180}{360}\right)$$

$$P = \$10,000,000 - \$525,000$$

$$P = \$9,475,000$$

The proceeds are $9,475,000.

**13.** $P = \dfrac{I}{RT}$

$$P = \frac{\$670.83}{.115 \times \frac{140}{360}}$$

$$P \approx \$15,000$$

The principal to the nearest dollar is $15,000.

**15.** $M = P + PRT$

$$M = \$18,000 + \left(\$18,000 \times .09 \times \frac{150}{360}\right)$$

$$M = \$18,000 + \$675$$

$$M = \$18,675$$

The maturity value is $18,675.

Last day of the year is number 365
November 19 is day $\begin{array}{r} -323 \\ \hline 42 \text{ days} \end{array}$

November 19 to end of year 42
January 1 to February 2 $\begin{array}{r} +33 \\ \hline 75 \text{ days} \end{array}$

Length of Loan is 150
Loan is discounted on day $\begin{array}{r} -75 \\ \hline 75 \end{array}$
Discount Period is 75 days.

$$P = M - MDT$$

$$P = \$18,675 - \left(\$18,675 \times .12 \times \frac{75}{360}\right)$$

$$P = \$18,675 - \$466.88$$

$$P = \$18,208.12$$

The proceeds are $18,208.12.

**17. (a)**  $I = PRT$

$$I = \$28,000 \times .10 \times \frac{220}{360}$$

$$I = \$1711.11$$

The interest is $1711.11.

**(b)**  $M = P + I$

$M = \$28,000 + \$1711.11$

$M = \$29,711.11$

The maturity value is $29,711.11.

**(c)**  $\begin{array}{r} 220 \\ -90 \\ \hline 130 \end{array}$    Discount period is 130 days.

**(d)**  $B = MDT$

$$B = \$29,711.11 \times .11 \times \frac{130}{360}$$

$$B = \$1180.19$$

The discount is $1180.19.

**(e)**  $P = M - B$

$P = \$29,711.11 - \$1180.19$

$P = \$28,530.92$

The proceeds to the bank are $28,530.92.

**19. (a)**  Bank One
$I = PRT$

$$I = \$68,000 \times .0925 \times \frac{220}{360}$$

$$I = \$3843.89$$

The interest for the simple interest note is $3843.89.

**(b)**  $M = \dfrac{P}{1 - DT}$

$$M = \frac{\$68,000}{1 - \left(.095 \times \frac{220}{360}\right)}$$

$$M = \$72,191.09$$

**(c)**  Union Bank
$B = MDT$

$$B = \$72,191.09 \times .095 \times \frac{220}{360}$$

$$B = \$4191.09$$

The interest for the discount note is $4191.09.

**(d)**  $\$4191.09 - \$3843.89 = \$347.20$

The savings in interest charges of the simple interest note over the discount note.

**21.** Answers will vary.

**23.** Answers will vary.

## Case Study

**1.** Interest paid to Japanese investment house:
$I = PRT$

$$I = \$80,000,000 \times .05 \times \frac{180}{360}$$

$$I = \$2,000,000$$

Interest received from Canadian firm:
$I = PRT$

$$I = \$38,000,000 \times .07 \times \frac{180}{360}$$

$$I = \$1,330,000$$

Interest received from European contractor:
$I = PRT$

$$I = \$27,500,000 \times .082 \times \frac{180}{360}$$

$$I = \$1,127,500$$

Interest received from Louisiana company:
$I = PRT$

$$I = \$14,500,000 \times .08 \times \frac{180}{360}$$

$$I = \$580,000$$

$\$1,330,000 + \$1,127,500 + \$580,000$
$= \$3,037,500$

Total interest received is $3,037,500.

$\$3,037,500 - \$2,000,000 = \$1,037,500$

The difference between interest received and interest paid by the bank is $1,037,500.

**2.** Amount loaned to Canadian firm:
$38,000,000

Amount loaned to European contractor:
$\$27,500,000 - \$1,127,500 = \$26,372,500$

Amount loaned to Louisiana company:
$\$14,500,000 - \$580,000 = \$13,920,000$

$$\begin{array}{r} \$38,000,000 \\ \$26,372,500 \\ + \ \$13,920,000 \\ \hline \$78,292,500 \end{array} \quad \text{was actually loaned out.}$$

**3.**  $R = \dfrac{I}{PT}$

$$R = \frac{\$1,037,500}{\$78,292,500 \times \frac{180}{360}}$$

$$R \approx 0.0265 = 2.65\%$$

The effective rate of interest is 2.65%.

## Case in Point Summary Exercise

**1.** $M = \dfrac{P}{1 - DT}$

$M = \dfrac{\$85,000}{1 - \left(.10 \times \frac{10}{12}\right)}$

$M = \$92,727.27$

The maturity value is $92,727.27.

$B = M - P$
$B = \$92,727.27 - \$85,000$
$B = \$7727.27$

The discount is $7727.27.

**2.** $I = PRT$

$I = \$85,000 \times .105 \times \dfrac{10}{12}$

$I = \$7437.50$

The interest is $7437.50.

$M = P + I$
$M = \$85,000 + \$7437.50$
$M = \$92,437.50$

The maturity value is $92,437.50.

**3.** The simple interest loan from Union Bank has the lower interest.

$\$7727.27 - \$7437.50 = \$289.77$
The difference in interest is $289.77.

**4.** Bank One

$R = \dfrac{I}{PT}$

$R = \dfrac{\$7727.27}{\$85,000 \times \frac{10}{12}}$

$R \approx .1091 = 10.91\%$

The effective interest rate is 10.91%.

Union Bank

$R = \dfrac{I}{PT}$

$R = \dfrac{\$7437.50}{\$85,000 \times \frac{10}{12}}$

$R = .1050 = 10.50\%$

The effective interest rate is 10.50%.

## Chapter 9    Test

**1.** $I = PRT$

$I = \$12,500 \times .105 \times \dfrac{280}{360}$

$I = \$1020.83$

**2.** $I = PRT$

$I = \$8250 \times .0925 \times \dfrac{8}{12}$

$I = \$508.75$

**3.** August 22 is day     234
    June 8 is day     $\underline{-159}$
              75  days

$I = PRT$

$I = \$6000 \times .11 \times \dfrac{75}{360}$

$I = \$137.50$

**4.** Last day of the year is number    365
    November 13 is day    $\underline{-317}$
              48 days

November 13 to end of year    48
January 1 to March 8    $\underline{+67}$
              115 days

$I = PRT$

$I = \$4500 \times .103 \times \dfrac{115}{360}$

$I = \$148.06$

**5.** $M = P + PRT$

$M = \$12,500 + \left(\$12,500 \times .107 \times \dfrac{140}{365}\right)$

$M = \$12,500 + \$513.01$
$M = \$13,013.01$

The maturity value is $13,013.01.

**6.** $M = P + PRT$

$M = \$24,300 + \left(\$24,300 \times .105 \times \dfrac{6}{12}\right)$

$M = \$24,300 + \$1275.75$
$M = \$25,575.75$

The amount of the repayment is $25,575.75.

**7.** First Lender
$I = PRT$

$$I = \$14,000 \times .105 \times \frac{200}{360}$$

$$I = \$816.67$$

Second Lender
$I = PRT$

$$I = \$14,000 \times .105 \times \frac{200}{365}$$

$$I = \$805.48$$

$\$816.67 - \$805.48 = \$11.19$
Pierce will save $11.19 interest.

**8.** $\$7247.50 - \$6500 = \$747.50$
Interest earned is $747.50.

$$R = \frac{I}{PT}$$

$$R = \frac{\$747.50}{\$6500 \times \frac{15}{12}}$$

$R = 0.092 = 9.2\%$
The interest rate required is 9.2%.

**9.** $T = \dfrac{I}{PR} \times 360$

$$T = \frac{\$100}{\$1200 \times .09} \times 360$$

$$T = \frac{\$100}{\$108} \times 360$$

$T \approx 333$ days

**10.** $P = \dfrac{I}{RT}$

$$P = \frac{\$1254.17}{.05 \times \frac{7}{12}}$$

$P \approx \$43,000$
She invested $43,000.

**11.** $M = \dfrac{P}{1 - DT}$

$$M = \frac{\$25,000}{1 - \left(.09 \times \frac{240}{360}\right)}$$

$M = \$26,595.74$
The face value is $26,595.74.

**12.** Discount
$B = MDT$

$$B = \$9800 \times .11 \times \frac{120}{360}$$

$$B = \$359.33$$

Proceeds
$P = M - B$
$P = \$9800 - \$359.33$
$P = \$9440.67$

**13.** Discount
$B = MDT$

$$B = \$10,250 \times .095 \times \frac{60}{360}$$

$$B = \$162.29$$

Proceeds
$P = M - B$
$P = \$10,250 - \$162.29$
$P = \$10,087.71$

**14. (a)** $P = M - MDT$

$$P = \$15,000 - \left(\$15,000 \times .09 \times \frac{120}{360}\right)$$

$P = \$15,000 - \$450$
$P = \$14,550$
The proceeds are $14,550.

**(b)** $R = \dfrac{I}{PT}$

$$R = \frac{\$450}{\$14,550 \times \frac{120}{360}}$$

$$R = \frac{\$450}{\$4850}$$

$R \approx .093 = 9.3\%$
The effective interest rate is 9.3%.

**15.** $M = P + PRT$

$$M = \$28,400 + \left(\$28,400 \times .085 \times \frac{150}{360}\right)$$

$M = \$28,400 + \$1005.83$

$M = \$29,405.83$

The maturity value is $29,405.83.

| August 20 is day | 232 |
|---|---|
| July 7 is day | $-188$ |
| | 44 days |

| Length of Loan is | 150 |
|---|---|
| Loan is discounted on day | $-44$ |
| Discount Period is 106 days. | 106 |

$P = M - MDT$

$$P = \$29,405.83 - \left(\$29,405.83 \times .09 \times \frac{106}{360}\right)$$

$P = \$29,405.83 - \$779.25$

$P = \$28,626.58$

The proceeds to the bank are $28,626.58.

**16.**
| March 2 is day | 61 |
|---|---|
| January 25 is day | $-25$ |
| | 36 |

| Length of Loan is | 90 |
|---|---|
| Loan is discounted on day | $-36$ |
| Discount Period is 54 days. | 54 |

$P = M - MDT$

$$P = \$9200 - \left(\$9200 \times .12 \times \frac{54}{360}\right)$$

$P = \$9200 - \$165.60$

$P = \$9034.40$

Proceeds at the time of the sale are $9034.40.

**17. (a)** $P = M - MDT$

$$P = \$20,000 - \left(\$20,000 \times .0375 \times \frac{13}{52}\right)$$

$P = \$20,000 - \$187.50$

$P = \$19,812.50$

The purchase price of the T-bill is $19,812.50.

**(b)** The maturity value is $20,000.

**(c)** $20,000 - \$19,812.50 = \$187.50$

The interest earned is $187.50.

**(d)** $R = \dfrac{I}{PT}$

$$R = \frac{\$187.50}{\$19,812.50 \times \frac{13}{52}}$$

$R \approx .0379 = 3.79\%$

The effective interest rate is 3.79%.

**18.** $M = P + PRT$

$$M = \$9200 + \left(\$9200 \times .10 \times \frac{90}{360}\right)$$

$M = \$9200 + \$230$

$M = \$9430$

The maturity value is $9430.

| March 12 is day | 71 |
|---|---|
| January 25 is day | $-25$ |
| | 46 |

| Length of Loan is | 90 |
|---|---|
| Loan is discounted on day | $-46$ |
| Discount Period is 44 days. | 44 |

$B = MDT$

$$B = \$9430 \times .125 \times \frac{44}{360}$$

$B = \$144.07$

The discount is $144.07.

$P = M - B$

$P = \$9430 - \$144.07$

$P = \$9285.93$

The proceeds are $9285.93.

**19.** $M = P + I$

$M = \$9000 + \$450$

$M = \$9450$

The maturity value is $9450.

| Last day of the year is number | 365 |
|---|---|
| October 30 is day | $-303$ |
| | 62 days |

| October 30 to end of year | 62 |
|---|---|
| January 1 to January 3 | $+3$ |
| | 65 days |

| Length of Loan is | 180 |
|---|---|
| Loan is discounted on day | $-65$ |
| Discount Period is 115 days. | 115 |

**(a)** $B = MDT$

$$B = \$9450 \times .15 \times \frac{115}{360}$$

$B = \$452.81$

The discount is $452.81.

**(b)** $P = M - B$

$P = \$9450 - \$452.81$

$P = \$8997.19$

The proceeds are $8997.19.

**(c)** $9000 - \$8997.19 = \$2.81$

Guerra loses $2.81.

# Chapter 10 | Compound Interest and Inflation

## 10.1 Compound Interest

**1.** $i = 8\%$; $n = 4 \times 1 = 4$

Compound Amount
$$M = P(1+i)^n$$
$$= \$12,000(1+.08)^4$$
$$= \$12,000(1.08)^4$$
$$= \$16,325.87$$

Interest
$$I = M - P$$
$$= \$16,325.87 - \$12,000$$
$$= \$4325.87$$

**3.** $i = \frac{10\%}{4} = 2\frac{1}{2}\%$; $n = 1 \times 4 = 4$

Compound Amount
$$M = P(1+i)^n$$
$$= \$28,000(1+.025)^4$$
$$= \$28,000(1.025)^4$$
$$= \$30,906.76$$

Interest
$$I = M - P$$
$$= \$30,906.76 - \$28,000$$
$$= \$2906.76$$

**5.** $i = 6\%$; $n = 4 \times 1 = 4$

Compound Amount
$$M = \$32,350 \times 1.26248 = \$40,841.23$$

Interest
$$I = \$40,841.23 - \$32,350 = \$8491.23$$

**7.** $i = \frac{10\%}{4} = 2\frac{1}{2}\%$; $n = 7 \times 4 = 28$

Compound Amount
$$M = \$14,500 \times 1.99650 = \$28,949.25$$

Interest
$$I = \$28,949.25 - \$14,500 = \$14,449.25$$

**9.** $i = \frac{6\%}{2} = 3\%$; $n = 5 \times 2 = 10$

Compound Amount
$$M = \$45,000 \times 1.34392 = \$60,476.40$$

Interest
$$I = \$60,476.40 - \$45,000 = \$15,476.40$$

**11.** $i = 6\%$; $n = 4 \times 1 = 4$

Simple Interest
$$I = PRT = \$5400 \times .06 \times 4 = \$1296$$

Compound Amount
$$M = \$5400 \times 1.26248 = \$6817.39$$

Compound Interest
$$I = \$6817.39 - \$5400 = \$1417.39$$

Difference
$$\$1417.39 - \$1296 = \$121.39$$

**13.** $i = 8\%$; $n = 15 \times 1 = 15$

Simple Interest
$$I = PRT = \$1200 \times .08 \times 15 = \$1440$$

Compound Amount
$$M = \$1200 \times 3.17217 = \$3806.60$$

Compound Interest
$$I = \$3806.60 - \$1200 = \$2606.60$$

Difference
$$\$2606.60 - \$1440 = \$1166.60$$

**15.** **(a)** $i = \frac{5\%}{2} = 2\frac{1}{2}\%$; $n = 6 \times 2 = 12$

$$M = \$8500 \times 1.34489 = \$11,431.57$$
The compound amount is $11,431.57.

**(b)** $I = \$11,431.57 - \$8500 = \$2931.57$
The interest in 6 years is $2931.57.

**17.** **(a)** $i = \frac{8\%}{4} = 2\%$; $n = 3 \times 4 = 12$

$$M = \$4500 \times 1.26824 = \$5707.08$$
The compound amount is $5707.08.

**(b)** $I = \$5707.08 - \$4500 = \$1207.08$
The interest is $1207.08.

**19.** **(a)** $i = \frac{6\%}{2} = 3\%$; $n = 4 \times 2 = 8$

$$M = 25,000 \text{ yuan} \times 1.26677$$
$$= 31,669.25 \text{ yuan}$$

The compound amount is $31,669.25 yuan.

**(b)** $I = 31,669.25 \text{ yuan} - 25,000 \text{ yuan}$
$$= 6669.25 \text{ yuan}$$
The interest is $6669.25 yuan.

**21.** $I = PRT = \$25{,}000 \times .10 \times 1 = \$2500$
The simple interest is \$2500.

$i = \frac{6\%}{4} = 1\frac{1}{2}\%; \quad n = 1 \times 4 = 4$

$M = \$25{,}000 \times 1.06136 = \$26{,}534$
The compound amount is \$26,534.

$I = \$26{,}534 - \$25{,}000 = \$1534$
The compound interest is \$1534.

$\$2500 - \$1534 = \$966$
The simple interest loan to his sister would generate \$966 additional interest.

**23.** **(a)** $i = \frac{12\%}{12} = 1\%; \quad n = 2 \times 12 = 24$

$M = \$1{,}400{,}000 \times 1.26973 = \$1{,}777{,}622$
The future value is \$1,777,622.

**(b)** $I = \$1{,}777{,}622 - \$1{,}400{,}000 = \$377{,}622$
The interest is \$377,622.

**25.** **(a)** Investment for 2 years:
$i = \frac{6\%}{2} = 3\%; \quad n = 2 \times 2 = 4$

$M = \$25{,}000 \times 1.12551 = \$28{,}137.75$
The compound amount is \$28,137.75.

**(b)** Investment for 12 years:
$i = \frac{6\%}{2} = 3\%; \quad n = 12 \times 2 = 24$

$M = \$25{,}000 \times 2.03279 = \$50{,}819.75$
The compound amount is \$50,819.75.

**(c)** $\$50{,}819.75 - \$28{,}137.75 = \$22{,}682$
An additional \$22,682 is earned.

**27.** **(a)** 8% compounded quarterly for 2 years:
$i = \frac{8\%}{4} = 2\%; \quad n = 2 \times 4 = 8$

$M = \$7500 \times 1.17166 = \$8787.45$
The compound amount is \$8787.45.

**(b)** 6% compounded semiannually for 5 years:
$i = \frac{6\%}{2} = 3\%; \quad n = 5 \times 2 = 10$

$M = \$7500 \times 1.34392 = \$10{,}079.40$
The compound amount is \$10,079.40.

**(c)** The second is larger.

**29.** Answers will vary.

**31.** Answers will vary.

## 10.2 Interest-Bearing Bank Accounts and Inflation

**1.** September 30 is day $\qquad$ 273
July 6 is day $\qquad$ $-187$
Number of days is $\qquad$ 86

Compound Amount
$\$4800 \times 1.008280273 = \$4839.75$

Interest Earned
$\$4839.75 - \$4800 = \$39.75$

**3.** December 7 is day $\qquad$ 341
October 4 is day $\qquad$ $-277$
Number of days is $\qquad$ 64

Compound Amount
$\$8200 \times 1.006155560 = \$8250.48$

Interest Earned
$\$8250.48 - \$8200 = \$50.48$

**5.** November 7 is day $\qquad$ 311
September 9 is day $\qquad$ $-252$
Number of days is $\qquad$ 59

Compound Amount
$\$17{,}958 \times 1.005673296 = \$18{,}059.88$

Interest Earned
$\$18{,}059.88 - \$17{,}958 = \$101.88$

**7.** Compound Amount
$\$3900 \times 1.22138603 = \$4763.41$

**9.** Compound Amount
$\$12{,}900 \times 1.34984217 = \$17{,}412.96$

**11.** Answers will vary.

**13.** **(a)** June 30 is day $\qquad$ 181
April 1 is day $\qquad$ $-91$
Number of days is $\qquad$ 90

$\$2530 \times 1.008667067 = \$2551.93$

June 30 is day $\qquad$ 181
May 8 is day $\qquad$ $-128$
Number of days is $\qquad$ 53

$\$150 \times 1.005094883 = \$150.76$

**13. (a) (continued)**

|  |  |
|---|---|
| June 30 is day | 181 |
| May 24 is day | $-144$ |
| Number of days is | 37 |

$580 \times 1.003554076 = \$582.06$

$\$2551.93 + \$150.76 + \$582.06 = \$3284.75$
The balance on June 30 is $3284.75.

**(b)** $\$3284.75 - (\$2530 + \$150 + \$580)$
$= \$24.75$
The interest earned is $24.75.

**15. (a)**

|  |  |
|---|---|
| July 1 is day | 182 |
| April 1 is day | $-91$ |
| Number of days is | 91 |

$\$17,500 - \$5000 - \$980 = \$11,520$
$11,520 was on deposit for 91 days.
$\$11,520 \times \$1.008763788 = \$11,620.96$

$5000 was on deposit for 21 days.
$\$5000 \times 1.002015631 = \$5010.08$
$\$5010.08 - \$5000 = \$10.08$
Interest is $10.08.

$980 was on deposit for 79 $(91-12)$ days.
$\$980 \times 1.007603742 = \$987.45$
$\$987.45 - \$980 = \$7.45$
Interest is $7.45.

$\$11,620.96 + \$10.08 + \$7.45$
$= \$11,638.49$

The balance on July 1 is $11,638.49.

**(b)** $(\$11,620.96 - \$11,520) + \$10.08 + \$7.45$
$= \$118.49$
The interest earned is $118.49.

**17.** Invested for 2 years:
$\$4000 \times 1.10516335 = \$4420.65$
The compound amount is $4420.65.

Invested for 3 years:
$\$4000 \times 1.16182231 = \$4647.29$
The compound amount is $4647.29.

**19. (a)** $\$800,000 \times 1.12748573$
$= \$901,988.58$
The compound amount is $901,988.58.

**(b)** $\$901,988.58 - \$800,000$
$= \$101,988.58$
The interest earned is $101,988.58.

**21.** $\$235,000 \times .06 = \$14,100$
Annual interest at 6% is $14,100.

$\$235,000 \times .04 = \$9400$
Annual interest at 4% is $9400.

$\$14,100 - \$9400 = \$4700$
The difference in their annual income is
$4700.

**23.** $\$26,500 \times 1.03 = \$27,295$
Net wages after increase in wages are
$27,295.

$\$26,500 \times 1.045 = \$27,692.50$
Budget after effects of inflation is
$27,692.50.

$\$27,692.50 - \$27,295 = \$397.50$
The net loss in purchasing power is
$397.50.

**25. (a)** $\$180,000 \times 1.04080849 = \$187,345.53$
The future value at 4% per year
compounded daily is $187,345.53.

**(b)** $\$180,000 \times 1.06183131 = \$191,129.64$
The future value at 6% per year
compounded daily is $191,129.64.

**(c)** $\$191,129.64 - \$187,345.53 = \$3784.11$
The difference is $3784.11.

**27.** Answers will vary.

**29.** Answers will vary.

## 10.3 Present Value and Future Value

**1.** Present Value
$\$12,300 \times .83962 = \$10,327.33$

Interest Earned
$\$12,300 - \$10,327.33 = \$1972.67$

**3.** Present Value
$\$9350 \times .82075 = \$7674.01$

Interest Earned
$\$9350 - \$7674.01 = \$1675.99$

**5.** Present Value
$\$18,853 \times .51939 = \$9792.06$

Interest Earned
$\$18,853 - \$9792.06 = \$9060.94$

**7. (a)** $\$40,000 \times .66112 = \$26,444.80$

A lump sum of $\$26,444.80$ must be invested.

**(b)** $\$40,000 - \$26,444.80 = \$13,555.20$

The interest earned is $\$13,555.20$.

**9.** $\$10,000 \times .35034 = \$3503.40$

She must give each child $\$3503.40$.

**11. (a)** $i = 12\%; \ n = 5 \times 1 = 5$

$$M = P(1+i)^n$$
$$= \$450,000(1+.12)^5$$
$$= \$450,000(1.12)^5$$
$$\approx \$793,054$$

The future value is $\$793,054$.

**(b)** $\$793,054 \times .74726 \approx \$592,618$

The present value is $\$592,618$.

**13. (a)** $\$20,000 \times 1.33100 = \$26,620$

The future value is $\$26,620$.

**(b)** $\$26,620 \times .78849 = \$20,989.60$

The present value is $\$20,989.60$.

**15.** Answers will vary.

## Case Study

**1.** $i = 12\%; \ n = 5 \times 1 = 5$

$$M = P(1+i)^n$$
$$= \$2,300,000(1+.12)^5$$
$$= \$2,300,000(1.12)^5$$
$$\approx \$4,053,386$$

The future value is $\$4,053,386$.
$\$4,053,386 \times .74409 \approx \$3,016,084$
They should sell the chain for $\$3,016,084$.

**2.** $\$2,300,000 \times 1.10408 = \$2,539,384$

The future value is $\$2,539,384$.

$\$2,539,384 \times .74409 = \$1,889,530$
They should ask for $\$1,889,530$.

**3.** $\$2,300,000 \times 1.21665 = \$2,798,295$

The future value of the chain is $\$2,798,295$.

$\$2,798,295 \times .74409 \approx \$2,082,183$
They should ask $\$2,082,183$ for the chain.

**4.**

| Growth Rate | Future Value | Value Today |
|---|---|---|
| 2% | $\$2,539,386$ | $\$1,889,542$ |
| 4% | $\$2,798,302$ | $\$2,082,199$ |
| 12% | $\$4,053,386$ | $\$3,016,100$ |

## Case in Point Summary Exercise

**1.** Year 2006:
$\$92,080,000 \times .046 = \$4,235,680$

Year 2007:
$\$64,160,000 \times (-.123) = -\$7,891,680$

Year 2008:
$\$28,034,000 \times (-.305) = -\$8,550,370$

Year 2009:
$\$15,509,000 \times (-.114) = -\$1,768,026$

Year 2010:
$\$24,000,000 \times .02 = \$480,000$

**2.** $2007 - 1995 = 12$ years
$\$2,500,000 \times 2.01220 = \$5,030,500$
This was not enough to offset the loss of $\$7,891,680$ in 2007.

**3. (a)** $\$7,891,680 + \$8,550,370 + \$1,768,026$
$= \$18,210,076$

**(b)** $2008 - 1995 = 13$ years
$\$18,210,076 \times .46884 \approx \$8,537,612$

**4.** Answers will vary.

## Chapter 10   Test

1. $i = 10\%$; $n = 8 \times 1 = 8$

   Compound Amount
   $M = \$8700 \times 2.14359 = \$18,649.23$

   Interest Earned
   $I = \$18,649.23 - \$8700 = \$9949.23$

2. $i = \frac{6\%}{2} = 3\%$; $n = 5 \times 2 = 10$

   Compound Amount
   $M = \$12,000 \times 1.34392 = \$16,127.04$

   Interest Earned
   $I = \$16,127.04 - \$12,000 = \$4127.04$

3. $i = \frac{6\%}{2} = 3\%$; $n = 5 \times 2 = 10$

   Compound Amount
   $M = \$9800 \times 1.34392 = \$13,170.42$

   Interest Earned
   $I = \$13,170.42 - \$9800 = \$3370.42$

4. $i = \frac{10\%}{4} = 2\frac{1}{2}\%$; $n = 4 \times 4 = 16$

   Compound Amount
   $M = \$12,500 \times 1.48451 = \$18,556.38$

   Interest Earned
   $I = \$18,556.38 - \$12,500 = \$6056.38$

5. December 15 is day    349
   September 24 is day  $-267$
   Number of days is     82

   Compound Amount
   $\$6400 \times 1.007893628 = \$6450.52$

   Interest Earned
   $\$6450.52 - \$6400 = \$50.52$

6. Last day of the year is number   365
   December 5 is day           $-339$
                         26  days

   December 5 to end of year    26
   January 1 to March 2      $+61$
                         87  days

   Compound Amount
   $\$63,340 \times 1.008376958 = \$63,870.60$

   Interest Earned
   $\$63,870.60 - \$63,340 = \$530.60$

7. Last day of the year is number   365
   December 12 is day           $-346$
                         19  days

   December 12 to end of year    19
   January 1 to February 29    $+60$
                         79  days

   Compound Amount
   $\$37,650 \times 1.007603742 = \$37,936.28$

   Interest Earned
   $\$37,936.28 - \$37,650 = \$286.28$

8. Present Value
   $\$35,000 \times .21455 = \$7509.25$

9. Present Value
   $\$15,750 \times .65910 = \$10,380.83$

10. Present Value
    $\$56,900 \times .67297 = \$38,291.99$

11. October 1 is day     274
    July 3 is day      $-184$
    Number of days is    90

    $\$12,500 \times 1.008667067 = \$12,608.34$

    October 1 is day     274
    August 5 is day    $-217$
    Number of days is    57

    $\$3450 \times 1.005480454 = \$3468.91$

    $\$12,608.34 + \$3468.91 = \$16,077.25$
    The balance on October 1 is $16,077.25.

12. April 1 is day     91
    January 1 is day   $-1$
    Number of days is  90

    $\$1800 \times 1.008667067 = \$1815.60$

    April 1 is day     91
    March 12 is day  $-71$
    Number of days is  20

    $\$2300 \times 1.001919556 = \$2304.41$

    $\$1815.60 + \$2304.41 = \$4120.01$
    The balance on April 1 is $4120.01.

13. $\$4000 \times 1.34982553 = \$5399.30$
    The compound amount is $5399.30.

14. $\$35,000 \times 1.10516335 = \$38,680.72$
    The compound amount is $38,680.72.

**15.** $3.8\% - 2.5\% = 1.3\%$

$\$52,000 \times .013 = \$676$

The net loss in her purchasing power is $676.

**16.** $4\% - 1.5\% = 2.5\%$

$\$65,000 \times .025 = \$1625$

The net loss in his purchasing power is $1625.

**17. (a)** $\$3500 \times 1.25971 = \$4408.99$

The maturity value is $4408.99.

**(b)** $\$4408.99 \times .86230 = \$3801.87$

The present value is $3801.87.

**18. (a)** $\$12,540 \times 1.21000 = \$15,173.40$

The maturity value is $15,173.40.

**(b)** $\$15,173.40 \times .88849 = \$13,481.41$

The present value is $13,481.41.

**19. (a)** $i = 12\%;\ n = 4 \times 1 = 4$

$$M = P(1+i)^n$$
$$= \$180,000(1+.12)^4$$
$$= \$180,000(1.12)^4$$
$$= \$283,233.48$$

The expected future value is $283,233.48.

**(b)** $\$283,233.48 \times .73069 = \$206,955.87$

The minimum acceptable price is
$206,955.87.

**20. (a)** $\$40$ million $\times 1.46933 \approx \$59$ million

The future value is $59 million.

**(b)** $i = 12\%;\ n = 4 \times 1 = 4$

$$M = P(1+i)^n$$
$$= \$59 \text{ million}(1+.12)^4$$
$$= \$59 \text{ million}(1.12)^4$$
$$\approx \$93 \text{ million}$$

The expected future value is $93
million.

**1.** Interest
$$I = PRT$$
$$I = \$6800 \times .08 \times \frac{6}{12}$$
$$I = \$272$$

**2.** Interest
$$I = PRT$$
$$I = \$6200 \times .097 \times \frac{250}{360}$$
$$I = \$417.64$$

**3.** Principal
$$P = \frac{I}{RT}$$
$$P = \frac{\$165.28}{.07 \times \frac{100}{360}}$$
$$P = \$8500.11$$

**4.** Principal
$$P = \frac{I}{RT}$$
$$P = \frac{\$475}{.095 \times \frac{180}{360}}$$
$$P = \frac{\$475}{.0475}$$
$$P = \$10,000$$

**5.** Rate
$$R = \frac{I}{PT}$$
$$R = \frac{\$249.38}{\$10,500 \times \frac{90}{360}}$$
$$R = \frac{\$249.38}{\$2625}$$
$$R \approx .095 = 9.5\%$$

**6.** Rate
$$R = \frac{I}{PT}$$
$$R = \frac{\$733.33}{\$12,000 \times \frac{200}{360}}$$
$$R \approx .110 = 11.0\%$$

**7.** Time
$$T = \frac{I}{PR} \times 360$$
$$T = \frac{\$202.22}{\$9100 \times .10} \times 360$$
$$T = \frac{\$202.22}{\$910} \times 360$$
$$T \approx 80 \text{ days}$$

**8.** Time
$$T = \frac{I}{PR} \times 360$$
$$T = \frac{\$915}{\$18,300 \times .12} \times 360$$
$$T = \frac{\$915}{\$2196} \times 360$$
$$T = 150 \text{ days}$$

**9.** Discount
$$B = MDT$$
$$B = \$9000 \times .12 \times \frac{90}{360}$$
$$B = \$270$$

Proceeds
$$P = M - B$$
$$P = \$9000 - \$270$$
$$P = \$8730$$

**10.** Discount
$$B = MDT$$
$$B = \$875 \times .065 \times \frac{210}{360}$$
$$B = \$33.18$$

Proceeds
$$P = M - B$$
$$P = \$875 - \$33.18$$
$$P = \$841.82$$

**11.** Discount
$B = MDT$

$B = \$5000 \times .10 \times \dfrac{90}{360}$

$B = \$125$

Net Proceeds
$P = M - B$
$P = \$5000 - \$125$
$P = \$4875$

**12.** Discount
$B = MDT$

$B = \$12,000 \times .12 \times \dfrac{150}{360}$

$B = \$600$

Net Proceeds
$P = M - B$
$P = \$12,000 - \$600$
$P = \$11,400$

**13.** Compound Amount
$M = \$1000 \times 1.94790 = \$1947.90$

**14.** Compound Amount
$M = \$3520 \times 2.15892 = \$7599.40$

**15.**  
| | |
|---|---|
| June 3 is day | 154 |
| March 24 is day | $-83$ |
| Number of days is | 71 |

Compound Amount
$\$12,600 \times 1.006831119 = \$12,686.07$

Interest Earned
$\$12,686.07 - \$12,600 = \$86.07$

**16.**  
| | |
|---|---|
| Last day of the year is number | 365 |
| November 20 is day | $-324$ |
| | 41 days |

| | |
|---|---|
| November 20 to end of year | 41 |
| January 1 to February 14 | $+45$ |
| | 86 days |

Compound Amount
$\$7500 \times 1.008280273 = \$7562.10$

Interest Earned
$\$7562.10 - \$7500 = \$62.10$

**17.** Present Value
$\$1000 \times .58349 = \$583.49$

Interest Earned
$\$1000 - \$583.49 = \$416.51$

**18.** Present Value
$\$19,000 \times .64117 = \$12,182.23$

Interest Earned
$\$19,000 - \$12,182.23 = \$6817.77$

**19.** $B = MDT$

$B = \$25,000 \times .10 \times \dfrac{180}{360}$

$B = \$1250$
The interest is $1250.

$P = M - B$
$P = \$25,000 - \$1250$
$P = \$23,750$
The proceeds are $23,750.

**20.** $\$18,000 \times 1.34686 = \$24,243.48$
The future value is $24,243.48.

**21.** $\$12,000 \times .90595 = \$10,871.40$
$10,871.40 must be invested today.

**22.** $M = P + PRT$

$M = \$7850 + \left( \$7850 \times .06 \times \dfrac{5}{12} \right)$

$M = \$7850 + \$196.25$
$M = \$8046.25$
The maturity value is $8046.25.

$P = M - MDT$

$P = \$8046.25 - \left( \$8046.25 \times .0792 \times \dfrac{1}{12} \right)$

$P = \$7993.14$
The relative receives $7993.14.

**23.** $\$3200 \times 1.006252041 = \$3220.01$
$\$3220.01 - \$3200 = \$20.01$
The interest is $20.01.

# Chapter 11 | Annuities, Stocks, and Bonds

## 11.1 Annuities and Retirement Accounts

**1.** $i = 5\%$; $n = 18 \times 1 = 18$

Amount of Annuity
$900 \times 28.13238 = \$25,319.14$

Interest Earned
$\$25,319.14 - (18 \times \$900) = \$9119.14$

**3.** $i = \frac{6\%}{2} = 3\%$; $n = 10 \times 2 = 20$

Amount of Annuity
$7500 \times 26.87037 = \$201,527.78$

Interest Earned
$\$201,527.78 - (20 \times \$7500) = \$51,527.78$

**5.** $i = \frac{10\%}{4} = 2\frac{1}{2}\%$; $n = 7 \times 4 = 28$

Amount of Annuity
$3500 \times 39.85980 = \$139,509.30$

Interest Earned
$\$139,509.30 - (28 \times \$3500) = \$41,509.30$

**7.** $i = 8\%$; $n = 5 \times 1 + 1 = 6$

Amount of Annuity Due
$1200 \times 7.33593 - \$1200 = \$7603.12$

Interest Earned
$\$7603.12 - (5 \times \$1200) = \$1603.12$

**9.** $i = \frac{4\%}{2} = 2\%$; $n = 9 \times 2 + 1 = 19$

Amount of Annuity Due
$9500 \times 22.84056 - \$9500 = \$207,485.32$

Interest Earned
$\$207,485.32 - (18 \times \$9500) = \$36,485.32$

**11.** $i = \frac{8\%}{4} = 2\%$; $n = 3 \times 4 + 1 = 13$

Amount of Annuity Due
$3800 \times 14.68033 - \$3800 = \$51,985.25$

Interest Earned
$\$51,985.25 - (12 \times \$3800) = \$6385.25$

**13.** Answers will vary.

**15. (a)** $i = 6\%$; $n = 35 \times 1 = 35$

$3800 \times 111.43478 = \$423,452.16$
The amount of the annuity is
$423,452.16.

**(b)** $\$423,452.16 - (35 \times \$3800)$
$= \$290,452.16$
The interest earned is $290,452.16.

**17. (a)** $i = \frac{8\%}{4} = 2\%$; $n = 8 \times 4 + 1 = 33$

$250 \times 46.11157 - \$250$
$= \$11,277.89$
The amount of the annuity is
$11,277.89.

**(b)** $\$11,277.89 - (32 \times \$250) = \$3277.89$
The interest earned is $3277.89.

**19.** $i = \frac{10\%}{2} = 5\%$; $n = 12 \times 2 = 24$

$1000 \times 44.50200 = \$44,502$
The future value is $44,502.

## 11.2 Present Value of an Ordinary Annuity

**1.** $i = 10\%$; $n = 18 \times 1 = 18$
Present Value
$1800 \times 8.20141 = \$14,762.54$

**3.** $i = \frac{8\%}{2} = 4\%$; $n = 12 \times 2 = 24$
Present Value
$2000 \times 15.24696 = \$30,493.92$

**5.** $i = \frac{4\%}{4} = 1\%$; $n = 6 \times 4 = 24$
Present Value
$894 \times 21.24339 = \$18,991.59$

**7.** Answers will vary.

**9.** $i = 5\%$; $n = 20 \times 1 = 20$

$\$65,000 \times 12.46221 = \$810,043.65$

The company must set aside $810,043.65.

**11. (a)** $i = \frac{5\%}{2} = 2\frac{1}{2}\%$; $n = 5 \times 2 = 10$

$\$8000 \times 8.75206 = \$70,016.48$

$70,016.48 must be deposited.

**(b)** $\left(10 \times \$8000\right) - \$70,016.48 = \$9983.52$

The interest earned is $9983.52.

**13. (a)** $i = \frac{8\%}{4} = 2\%$; $n = 4 \times 4 = 16$

$\$3600 \times 13.57771 = \$48,879.76$

The total amount needed is $48,879.76.

**(b)** Find the future value using the amount of an Annuity Table in section 11.1.

$i = \frac{8\%}{4} = 2\%$; $n = 8 \times 4 = 32$

$\$700 \times 44.22703 = \$30,958.92$

No, since this amount is less than $48,879.76, he will not have enough money available.

**15. (a)** $i = \frac{8\%}{4} = 2\%$; $n = 5 \times 4 = 20$

$\$25,000 + \$3500 \times 16.35143 = \$82,230.01$

The first offer of a cash payment of $85,000 is better.

**(b)** $\$85,000 - \$82,230.01 = \$2769.99$

The difference in the present values is $2769.99.

**17.** $i = 8\%$; $n = 14 \times 1 = 14$

$\$18,400 \times 8.24424 = \$151,694.02$

The present value of the annuity is $151,694.02.

## 11.3 Sinking Funds (Finding Annuity Payments)

**1.** $i = 5\%$; $n = 4 \times 1 = 4$

Payment

$\$12,000 \times .23201 = \$2784.12$

**3.** $i = \frac{6\%}{2} = 3\%$; $n = 5 \times 2 = 10$

Payment

$\$8200 \times .08723 = \$715.29$

**5.** $i = \frac{4\%}{4} = 1\%$; $n = 5 \times 4 = 20$

Payment

$\$50,000 \times .04542 = \$2271$

**7.** $i = \frac{12\%}{12} = 1\%$; $n = 3 \times 12 = 36$

Payment

$\$7894 \times .02321 = \$183.22$

**9.** Answers will vary.

**11. (a)** $i = \frac{5\%}{2} = 2\frac{1}{2}\%$; $n = 3 \times 2 = 6$

$\$920,000 \times .15655 = \$144,026$

Each payment is $144,026.

**(b)** $\$920,000 - \left(6 \times \$144,026\right) = \$55,844$

The total interest earned is $55,844.

**13. (a)** $i = 8\%$; $n = 60 - 20 = 40$

$\$1,000,000 \times .00386 = \$3860$

Each annual payment is $3860.

**(b)** $\$1,000,000 - \left(40 \times \$3860\right) = \$845,600$

The total interest earned is $845,600.

**15.** $i = 10\%$; $n = 7 \times 1 = 7$

$\$120,000 \times .10541 = \$12,649.20$

The payment is $12,649.20.

**17. (a)** $i = \frac{12\%}{12} = 1\%$; $n = 3 \times 12 = 36$

$\$2,300,000 \times .02321 = \$53,383$

$53,383 should be deposited each month for 3 years.

**(b)** $i = \frac{12\%}{12} = 1\%$; $n = 4 \times 12 = 48$

$\$2,300,000 \times .01633 = \$37,559$

$37,559 should be deposited each month for 4 years.

**19. (a)** $I = PRT$

$$= \$60,000 \times .08 \times \frac{1}{4}$$

$$= \$1200$$

Each quarterly interest payment is $1200.

**(b)** $i = \frac{8\%}{2} = 4\%$; $n = 4 \times 2 = 8$

$\$60,000 \times .10853 = \$6511.80$

Each payment is $6511.80.

**(c)**

| Payment Number | Amount of Deposit | Interest Earned | Total in Account |
|---|---|---|---|
| 1 | $6511.80 | $0 | $6511.80 |
| 2 | $6511.80 | $260.47 | $13,284.07 |
| 3 | $6511.80 | $531.36 | $20,327.23 |
| 4 | $6511.80 | $813.09 | $27,652.12 |
| 5 | $6511.80 | $1106.08 | $35,270.00 |
| 6 | $6511.80 | $1410.80 | $43,192.60 |
| 7 | $6511.80 | $1727.70 | $51,432.10 |
| 8 | $6510.62 | $2057.28 | $60,000.00 |

**21.**

| Payment Number | Amount of Deposit | Interest Earned | Total in Account |
|---|---|---|---|
| 1 | $713,625 | $0 | $713,625.00 |
| 2 | $713,625 | $10,704.38 | $1,437,954.38 |
| 3 | $713,625 | $21,569.32 | $2,173,148.70 |
| 4 | $713,625 | $32,597.23 | $2,919,370.93 |

**23.** Use the compound interest table from section 10.1.

$i = 8\%$; $n = 4$

$\$22,500 \times 1.36049 = \$30,611$

In 4 years, tuition will be $30,611.

$i = \frac{6\%}{4} = 1\frac{1}{2}\%$; $n = 4 \times 4 = 16$

$\$30,611 \times .05577 = \$1707$

The end-of-quarter payments are $1707.

**25.** Use the compound interest table from section 10.1.

$i = 8\%$; $n = 5$

$\$52,000 \times 1.46933 = \$76,405.16$

In 5 years, the cost will be $76,405.16.

$i = \frac{5\%}{2} = 2\frac{1}{2}\%$; $n = 5 \times 2 = 10$

$\$76,405.16 \times .08926 = \$6819.92$

The semiannual payments are $6819.92.

## Supplementary Application Exercises on Annuities and Sinking Funds

**1.** $i = \frac{8\%}{4} = 2\%$; $n = 6 \times 4 = 24$

**(a)** $\$500 \times 30.42186 = \$15,210.93$

The future value is $15,210.93.

**(b)** $\$15,210.93 - (24 \times \$500) = \$3210.93$

The interest is $3210.93.

**3.** $i = 6\%$; $n = 20 \times 1 = 20$

**(a)** $\$2000 \times 39.99273 - \$2000 = \$77,985.46$

The future value is $77,985.46.

**(b)** $\$77,985.46 - (20 \times \$2000) = \$37,985.46$

The interest is $37,985.46.

**5.** $i = \frac{10\%}{4} = 2\frac{1}{2}\%$; $n = 3 \times 4 = 12$

$\$135,000 \times 10.25776 = \$1,384,797.60$

A lump sum of $1,384,797.60 could be deposited today.

**7.** $i = \frac{4\%}{4} = 1\%$; $n = 6 \times 4 = 24$

$\$5000 \times 21.24339 = \$106,216.95$

A lump sum of $106,216.95 must be deposited.

**9.** $i = 8\%$; $n = 3 \times 1 = 3$

$\$870,000 \times .30803 = \$267,986.10$

The firm must make an annual payment of $267,986.10.

| Payment Number | Amount of Deposit | Interest Earned | Total in Account |
|---|---|---|---|
| 1 | $267,986.10 | $0 | $267,986.10 |
| 2 | $267,986.10 | $21,438.89 | $557,411.09 |
| 3 | $267,996.02 | $44,592.89 | $870,000.00 |

**11. (a)** $i = 6\%$; $n = 20 \times 1 = 20$

$\$25,000 \times 11.46992 = \$286,748$

The amount needed at 65 to fund Ben's retirement is $286,748.

**(b)** $i = 8\%$; $n = 20 \times 1 = 20$

$\$286,748 \times .02185 = \$6265.44$

The end-of-the-year payment is $6265.44.

## 11.4 Stocks

**1.** $4.00

**3.** $0

**5.** 178,700

**7.** 47

**9.** $1.90

**11.** 6.3%

**13.** $.40

**15.** −$.17

**17.** $51.04

**19.** Cost
$800 \times \$15.48 = \$12,384$

Dividend
$800 \times (4 \times \$.04) = \$128$

**21.** Cost
$100 \times \$39.50 = \$3950$

Dividend
$100 \times (4 \times \$.14) = \$56$

**23.** Cost
$600 \times \$4.59 = \$2754$

Dividend
$600 \times (4 \times \$0) = \$0$

**25.** Answers will vary.

**27.** Current Yield
$\dfrac{\$1.24}{\$50.06} \approx .025 = 2.5\%$

**29.** Current Yield
$\dfrac{\$2.20}{\$63.36} \approx .035 = 3.5\%$

**31.** Current Yield
$\dfrac{\$1.08}{\$65.44} \approx .017 = 1.7\%$

**33.** PE Ratio
$\dfrac{\$37.51}{\$1.16} \approx 32$

**35.** PE Ratio
$\dfrac{\$15.41}{\$1.09} \approx 14$

**37.** PE Ratio
$\dfrac{\$22.29}{\$.54} \approx 41$

**39.** Increase
$\$35.20 - \$34.35 = .85$

Percent Increase
$\dfrac{.85}{34.35} \approx .025 = 2.5\%$

**41.** $200 \times \$56.30 + 100 \times \$38.60$
$\$11,260 + \$3860 = \$15,120$
The total cost is $15,120.

**43. (a)** $i = \frac{5\%}{2} = 2\frac{1}{2}\%$; $n = 10 \times 2 = 20$
$\$600 \times 25.54466 = \$15,326.80$
The future value of the CDs is $15,326.80.

**(b)** $i = \frac{8\%}{2} = 4\%$; $n = 10 \times 2 = 20$
$\$600 \times 29.77808 = \$17,866.85$
The future value of the mutual fund is $17,866.85.

**(c)** $\$17,866.85 - \$15,326.80 = \$2540.05$
The difference is $2540.05.

## 11.5 Bonds

**1.** $1065.00

**3.** May 15, 2016

**5.** 4.749%

**7.** $(\$1016.50 + \$10) \times 50 = \$51,325$

**9.** $(\$1137.29 + \$10) \times 80 = \$91,783.20$

**11.** $(\$1033.00 + \$10) \times 250 = \$260,750$

**13.** Answers will vary.

**15. (a)** $(1.033 \times \$1000 + \$.80) \times 4000$

$= \$4,135,200$

The total cost of the purchase, including commissions, is $4,135,200.

**(b)** $(.0675 \times \$1000) \times 4000 = \$270,000$

The annual interest is $270,000.

**(c)** $\dfrac{\$270,000}{\$4,135,200} \approx .065 = 6.5\%$

The effective interest rate is 6.5%.

**17. (a)** $(1.23249 \times \$1000 + \$10) \times 15$

$= \$18,637.35$

The total cost of the purchase, including commissions, is $18,637.35.

**(b)** $(.0925 \times \$1000) \times 15 = \$1387.50$

The annual interest is $1387.50.

**(c)** $\dfrac{\$1387.50}{\$18,637.35} \approx .074 = 7.4\%$

The effective interest rate is 7.4%.

**19. (a)** $I = PRT$

$= \$45,000 \times .08 \times 1$

$= \$3600$

The interest for the first year is $3600.

**(b)** $i = 8\%; \ n = 10 \times 1 = 10$  (See Section 10.1.)

$\$45,000 \times 2.15892 = \$97,151.40$

There is $97,151.40 in the account.

## Case Study

**1.** $i = 5\%; \ n = 30$

$\$45,000 \times 4.32194 = \$194,487.30$

The future value of $45,000 net worth is $194,487.30.

$i = 10\%; \ n = 30$

$\dfrac{1}{2} \times \$3500 \times 164.49402 = \$287,864.54$

$i = 6\%; \ n = 30$

$\dfrac{1}{2} \times \$3500 \times 79.05819 = \$138,351.83$

$\$194,487.30 + \$287,864.54 + \$138,351.83$

$= \$620,703.67$

Li's future accumulation is $620,703.67.

**2.** $i = 3\%; \ n = 30$

$\$40,000 \times 2.42726 = \$97,090.40$

He needs an income of $97,090.40.

**3.** $\$97,090.40 - \$30,000 = \$67,090.40$

He needs additional income of $67,090.40.

**4.** $i = 8\%; \ n = 20$

$\$67,090.40 \times 9.81815 = \$658,703.61$

The present value is $658,703.61.

**5.** $\$658,703.61 - \$620,703.67 = \$37,999.94$

No, shortage will be almost $38,000.

**6.** Answers will vary.

## Case in Point Summary Exercise

**1.** $\$42,000(10\% + 8\%)$

$= \$42,000(.10 + .08)$

$= \$42,000(.18)$

$= \$7560$

The total annual contribution is $7560.

**2.** $\$7560 \times 113.28321 = \$856,421.07$

The future value is $856,421.07.

**3.** $422 \times \$48,500 = \$20,467,000$

The annual payroll for the faculty is $856,421.07.

**4.** $\$20,467,000 \times .08 = \$1,637,360$

American River must make annual contributions of $1,637,360.

**5.** $i = 6\%; \ n = 5 \times 1 = 5$

$\$250,000 \times 4.21236 = \$1,053,090$

The present value of these gifts is $1,053,090.

**6.** $i = \dfrac{5\%}{2} = 2\dfrac{1}{2}\%; \ n = 7 \times 2 = 14$

$\$8,250,000 \times .06054 = \$499,455$

The payment is $499,455.

## Chapter 11   Test

**1.** $i = 6\%$;  $n = 8 \times 1 = 8$

Amount of Annuity
$1000 \times 9.89747 = \$9897.47$

**2.** $i = \frac{10\%}{2} = 5\%$;  $n = 9 \times 2 = 18$

Amount of Annuity
$4500 \times 28.13238 = \$126,595.71$

**3.** $i = \frac{8\%}{4} = 2\%$;  $n = 6 \times 4 + 1 = 25$

Amount of Annuity Due
$30,000 \times 32.03030 - \$30,000 = \$930,909$

**4.** $i = \frac{5\%}{2} = 2\frac{1}{2}\%$;  $n = 12 \times 2 + 1 = 25$

Amount of Annuity Due
$2600 \times 34.15776 - \$2600 = \$86,210.18$

**5.** $i = 8\%$;  $n = 15 \times 1 = 15$

$2500 \times 27.15211 = \$67,880.28$
Rivera will have accumulated $67,880.28.

**6.** $i = \frac{8\%}{2} = 3\%$;  $n = 15 \times 2 = 30$

$1000 \times 47.57542 = \$47,575.42$
Rivera will have accumulated $47,575.42.

**7.** $i = 6\%$;  $n = 9 \times 1 = 9$

Present Value
$1000 \times 6.80169 = \$6801.69$

**8.** $i = \frac{10\%}{2} = 5\%$;  $n = 6 \times 2 = 12$

Present Value
$4500 \times 8.86325 = \$39,884.63$

**9.** $i = \frac{12\%}{12} = 1\%$;  $n = 3 \times 12 = 36$

Present Value
$708 \times 30.10751 = \$21,316.12$

**10.** $i = \frac{8\%}{4} = 2\%$;  $n = 6 \times 4 = 24$

Present Value
$14,000 \times 18.91393 = \$264,795.02$

**11.** $i = \frac{8\%}{4} = 2\%$;  $n = 6 \times 4 = 24$

$1200 \times 18.91393 = \$22,696.72$
Betty must set aside $22,696.72.

**12.** $i = \frac{12\%}{12} = 1\%$;  $n = 4 \times 12 = 48$

$650 \times 37.97396 = \$24,683.07$
Mary must set aside $24,683.07.

**13.** $i = 6\%$;  $n = 9 \times 1 = 9$

Amount of Payment
$100,000 \times .08702 = \$8702$

**14.** $i = \frac{8\%}{2} = 4\%$;  $n = 10 \times 2 = 20$

Amount of Payment
$250,000 \times .03358 = \$8395$

**15.** $i = \frac{6\%}{4} = 1\frac{1}{2}\%$;  $n = 11 \times 4 = 44$

Amount of Payment
$360,000 \times .01621 = \$5835.60$

**16.** $i = \frac{10\%}{2} = 5\%$;  $n = 12 \times 2 = 24$

Amount of Payment
$800,000 \times .02247 = \$17,976$

**17.** $i = \frac{6\%}{2} = 3\%$;  $n = 4 \times 2 = 8$

$200,000 \times .11246 = \$22,492$
The required payment is $22,492.

**18.** $i = \frac{10\%}{4} = 2\frac{1}{2}\%$;  $n = 4 \times 4 = 16$

$45,000 \times .05160 = \$2322$
The required payment is $2322.

**19. (a)**   $200 \times \$45.60 = \$9120$
The total cost is $9120.

**(b)**   $200 \times \$1.52 = \$304$
The annual dividend is $304.

**20. (a)**   $(.951 \times \$1000 + \$10) \times 25 = \$24,025$
The total cost is $24,025.

**(b)**   $(.042 \times \$1000) \times 25 = \$1050$
The annual interest is $1050.

**(c)**   $\dfrac{\$1050}{\$24,025} \approx .044 = 4.4\%$

The effective interest rate is 4.4%.

**21.** Highest and lowest prices for the year were $65.90 and $20.10.

Weekly volume was 7,451,500 shares.

Dividend yield is .8% of current price.

PE ratio is 27.

Stock closed at $63.44.

The stock price was up $1.23 for the week.

Earnings were $5.47 last year and are expected to be $2.53 this year and $2.89 next year.

The last quarterly dividend was $.12 per share.

**22.** Annual interest is 7.950% of $1000 or $79.50 per bond.

Bond matures on June 15, 2018.

Bond closed at $1173.89.

Yield to maturity is 5.369%.

Estimated volume for the week is $209,183,000.

## 12.1 Open-End Credit and Charge Cards

**1.** Finance Charge
$6425.40 \times .008 = \$51.40$

**3.** Finance Charge
$1201.43 \times .0125 = \$15.02$

**5.** October:
Finance Charge
$437.18 \times .014 = \$6.12$

Unpaid Balance
$437.18 + \$6.12 + \$128.72 - \$27.85 - \$125$
$= \$419.17$

November:
Finance Charge
$419.17 \times .014 = \$5.87$

Unpaid Balance
$419.17 + \$5.87 + \$291.64 - \$175$
$= \$541.68$

December:
Finance Charge
$541.68 \times .014 = \$7.58$

Unpaid Balance
$541.68 + \$7.58 + \$147.11 - \$17.15 - \$150$
$= \$529.22$

January:
Finance Charge
$529.22 \times .014 = \$7.41$

Unpaid Balance
$529.22 + \$7.41 + \$27.84 - \$127.76 - \$225$
$= \$211.71$

**7.** Answers will vary.

**9.** Finance Charge
$1458.25 \times .014 = \$20.42$

**11.** Finance Charge
$389.95 \times .0125 = \$4.87$

**13.** Finance Charge
$1235.68 \times .014 = \$17.30$

**15. (a)** $6500 \times .016 = \$104$
Interest charges at 1.6% are $104.

**(b)** $6500 \times .01 = \$65$
Interest charges at 1% are $65.

**(c)** $104 - \$65 = \$39$
The savings are $39.

**17.**

| Unpaid Balance | | Days | | Total Balance |
|---|---|---|---|---|
| $2340.52 | $\times$ | 8 | = | $18,724.16 |
| $2340.52 - \$1000 = \$1340.52$ | $\times$ | 1 | = | $ 1,340.52 |
| $1340.52 + \$1440.30 = \$2780.82$ | $\times$ | 9 | = | $25,027.38 |
| $2780.82 + \$65.40 = \$2846.22$ | $\times$ | 12 | = | $34,154.64 |
| | | 30 | | $79,246.70 |

**(a)** $\dfrac{\$79,246.70}{30} = \$2641.56$

The average daily balance is $2641.56.

**(b)** $2641.56 \times .015 = \$39.62$
The finance charge is $39.62.

**(c)** $2340.52 + \$39.62 + (\$1440.30 + \$65.40)$
$-\$1000 = \$2885.84$
The new balance is $2885.84.

**19.**

| Unpaid Balance | | Days | | Total Balance |
|---|---|---|---|---|
| $312.78 | $\times$ | 4 | = | $1251.12 |
| $312.78 - \$106.45 = \$206.33$ | $\times$ | 5 | = | $1031.65 |
| $206.33 + \$115.73 = \$322.06$ | $\times$ | 4 | = | $1288.24 |
| $322.06 + \$74.19 = \$396.25$ | $\times$ | 9 | = | $3566.25 |
| $396.25 - \$115 = \$281.25$ | $\times$ | 8 | = | $2250.00 |
| | | 30 | | $9387.26 |

**(a)** $\dfrac{\$9387.26}{30} = \$312.91$

The average daily balance is $312.91.

**(b)** $312.91 \times .015 = \$4.69$
The finance charge is $4.69.

**(c)** $312.78 + \$4.69 + (\$115.73 + \$74.19)$
$-\$106.45 - \$115 = \$285.94$
The new balance is $285.94.

**21.**

| Unpaid Balance | | Days | | Total Balance |
|---|---|---|---|---|
| $355.72 | × | 2 | = | $711.44 |
| $355.72 − $209.53 = $146.19 | × | 2 | = | $292.38 |
| $146.19 + $28.76 = $174.95 | × | 8 | = | $1399.60 |
| $174.95 + $14.80 = $189.75 | × | 2 | = | $379.50 |
| $189.75 − $63.54 = $126.21 | × | 1 | = | $126.21 |
| $126.21 − $11.71 = $114.50 | × | 7 | = | $801.50 |
| $114.50 − $72.00 = $42.50 | × | 1 | = | $42.50 |
| $42.50 + $29.72 = $72.22 | × | 8 | = | $577.76 |
| | | 31 | | $4330.89 |

(a) $\dfrac{\$4330.89}{31} = \$139.71$

The average daily balance is $139.71.

(b) $\$139.71 \times .015 = \$2.10$
The finance charge is $2.10.

(c) $\$355.72 + \$2.10 + (\$28.76 + \$14.80 + \$29.72)$
$-(\$209.53 + \$63.54 + \$11.71) - \$72 = \$74.32$
The new balance is $74.32.

## 12.2 Installment Loans

**1.** Total Installment Cost
$\$400 + (24 \times \$68.75) = \$2050$

Finance Charge
$\$2050 - \$1800 = \$250$

**3.** Total Installment Cost
$\$0 + (12 \times \$15) = \$180$

Finance Charge
$\$180 - \$150 = \$30$

**5.** Total Installment Cost
$\$375 + (18 \times \$176) = \$3543$

Finance Charge
$\$3543 - \$2900 = \$643$

**7.** Approximate APR
$\dfrac{24 \times \$1200}{\$11,500 \times (1 + 30)}$
$= \dfrac{\$28,800}{\$356,500}$
$\approx .081 = 8.1\%$

**9.** Approximate APR
$\dfrac{24 \times \$1780}{\$7542 \times (1 + 48)}$
$= \dfrac{\$42,720}{\$369,558}$
$\approx .116 = 11.6\%$

**11.** Approximate APR
$\dfrac{24 \times \$11}{\$132 \times (1 + 12)}$
$= \dfrac{\$264}{\$1716}$
$\approx .154 = 15.4\%$

**13.** $\dfrac{\$185.68 \times \$100}{\$1400} = \$13.26$

Look down the left column of table to 24 payments. The number closest to 13.26 is 13.26, which corresponds to 12.25%.

**15.** $\dfrac{\$28.68 \times \$100}{\$442} = \$6.49$

Look down the left column of table to 14 payments. The number closest to 6.49 is 6.52, which corresponds to 10.25%.

**17.** $\dfrac{\$132.50 \times \$100}{\$1450} = \$9.14$

Look down the left column of table to 18 payments. The number closest to 9.14 is 9.14, which corresponds to 11.25%.

**19.** Answers will vary.

**21.** (a) $.20 \times \$74,800 = \$14,960$
The down payment is $14,960.

$\$74,800 - \$14,960 = \$59,840$
The amount financed is $59,840.

(b) $\$14,960 + (36 \times \$1916.85) = \$83,966.60$
The total installment cost is $83,966.60.

(c) $\$83,966.60 - \$74,800 = \$9166.60$
The finance charge is $9166.60.

(d) $\dfrac{24 \times \$9166.60}{\$59,840 \times (1 + 36)}$
$= \dfrac{\$219,998.40}{\$2,214,080}$
$\approx .099 = 9.9\%$
The approximate APR is 9.9%.

**23.** (a)
$$\frac{24\times\$260}{\$3600\times(1+12)}$$
$$=\frac{\$6240}{\$46,800}$$
$$\approx .133 = 13.3\%$$
The approximate APR is 13.3%.

(b)
$$\frac{\$260\times\$100}{\$3600} = \$7.22$$
Look down the left column of table to 12 payments. The number closest to 7.22 is 7.18, which corresponds to 13.00%.

**25.** $(24\times\$3.88\text{ million})-\$84\text{ million}$
$=\$9.12\text{ million}$
The finance charge is $9.12 million.

$$\frac{\$9.12\text{ million}\times\$100}{\$84\text{ million}} = \$10.86$$
Look down the left column of table to 24 payments. The number closest to 10.86 is 10.75, which corresponds to 10.00%.

**27.** (a) $\$20,800-\$2000=\$18,800$
The amount financed is $18,800.

(b) $\$2000+(50\times\$472)=\$25,600$
The total installment cost is $25,600.

(c) $\$25,600-\$20,800=\$4800$
The total interest paid is $4800.

(d)
$$\frac{\$4800\times\$100}{\$18,800} = \$25.53$$
Look down the left column of table to 50 payments. The number closest to 25.53 is 25.72, which corresponds to 11.25%.

**29.** (a) $100,000+(24\times 26,342.18)$
$=732,212.32$ pesos
The total installment cost is 732,212.32 pesos.

(b) $732,212.32-650,000=82,212.32$ pesos
The finance charge is 82,212.32 pesos.

$650,000-100,000=550,000$ pesos
The amount financed is 550,000 pesos.

$$\frac{82,212.32\times100}{550,000} = 14.95 \text{ pesos}$$
Look down the left column of table to 24 payments. The number closest to 14.95 is 14.95, which corresponds to 13.75%.

**31.** (a) $\$20,000+(40\times\$1942.24)$
$=\$97,689.60$
The total installment cost is $97,689.60.

(b) $\$97,689.60-\$85,000=\$12,689.60$
The finance charge is $12,689.60.

$\$85,000-\$20,000=\$65,000$
The amount financed is $65,000.

$$\frac{\$12,689.60\times100}{\$65,000} = 19.52$$
Look down the left column of table to 40 payments. The number closest to 19.52 is 19.43, which corresponds to 10.75%.

**33.** Answers will vary.

## 12.3 Early Payoffs of Loans

**1.** Interest to day 50
$$I = PRT = \$9800\times.085\times\frac{50}{360} = \$115.69$$
Amount of Payment Applied to Principal
$\$1800-\$115.69=\$1684.31$

New Principal
$\$9800-\$1684.31=\$8115.69$

Interest on new principal is charged for
$150-50=100$ days.

$$I = PRT = \$8115.69\times.085\times\frac{100}{360} = \$191.62$$

Balance Due
$\$8115.69+\$191.62=\$8307.31$

Total Interest Paid
$\$115.69+\$191.62=\$307.31$

**3.** Interest to day 100

$$I = PRT = \$15,000 \times .105 \times \frac{100}{360} = \$437.50$$

Amount of Payment Applied to Principal
$6500 − $437.50 = $6062.50

New Principal
$15,000 − $6062.50 = $8937.50

Interest on new principal is charged for
$200 − 100 = 100$  days.

$$I = PRT = \$8937.50 \times .105 \times \frac{100}{360} = \$260.68$$

Balance Due
$8937.50 + $260.68 = $9198.18

Total Interest Paid
$437.50 + $260.68 = $698.18

**5.** Interest to day 34

$$I = PRT = \$18,457 \times .12 \times \frac{34}{360} = \$209.18$$

Amount of 1$^{st}$ Payment Applied to Principal
$5978 − $209.18 = $5768.82

New Principal after 1$^{st}$ Payment
$18,457 − $5768.82 = $12,688.18

Interest on new principal after 1$^{st}$ payment is
charged for $55 − 34 = 21$ days.

$$I = PRT = \$12,688.18 \times .12 \times \frac{21}{360} = \$88.82$$

Amount of 2$^{nd}$ Payment Applied to Principal
$3124 − $88.82 = $3035.18

New Principal after 2$^{nd}$ Payment
$12,688.18 − $3035.18 = $9653

Interest on new principal after 2nd payment is
charged for $120 − 55 = 65$ days.

$$I = PRT = \$9653 \times .12 \times \frac{65}{360} = \$209.15$$

Balance Due
$9653 + $209.15 = $9862.15

Total Interest Paid
$209.18 + $88.82 + $209.15 = $507.15

**7.** Unearned Interest

$$U = F\left(\frac{N}{P}\right)\left(\frac{1+N}{1+P}\right)$$
$$= \$1050 \times \frac{11}{24} \times \left(\frac{1+11}{1+24}\right)$$
$$= \$231$$

**9.** Unearned Interest

$$U = F\left(\frac{N}{P}\right)\left(\frac{1+N}{1+P}\right)$$
$$= \$881 \times \frac{12}{36} \times \left(\frac{1+12}{1+36}\right)$$
$$= \$103.18$$

**11.** Unearned Interest

$$U = F\left(\frac{N}{P}\right)\left(\frac{1+N}{1+P}\right)$$
$$= \$900 \times \frac{6}{36} \times \left(\frac{1+6}{1+36}\right)$$
$$= \$28.38$$

**13.** Answers will vary.

**15. (a)** Interest is paid to day 140.
$$I = PRT$$
$$= \$8900 \times .12 \times \frac{140}{360}$$
$$= \$415.33$$
The interest due is $415.33.

**(b)** $8900 + $415.33 = $9315.33
The total amount due is $9315.33.

**17. (a)**  June 24 is day          175
         May 7 is day          $\underline{-127}$
                          48 days

$$I = PRT = \$92,000 \times .1125 \times \frac{48}{360} = \$1380$$

The interest paid to June 24 is $1380.

$24,350 − $1380 = $22,970
The amount applied to the principal is $22,970.

$92,000 − $22,970 = $69,030
The balance owed is $69,030.

Interest on new principal is charged for
$90 − 48 = 42$  days.

$$I = PRT = \$69,030 \times .1125 \times \frac{42}{360} = \$906.02$$

The interest due is $906.02.

$69,030 + $906.02 = $69,936.02
The amount due on the maturity date is
$69,936.02.

**(b)** $1380 + $906.02 = $2286.02
The interest paid on the note is $2286.02.

**19. (a)**

March 20 is day       79

February 18 is day    $\underline{-49}$

              30 days

$I = PRT$

$\phantom{I} = \$104,500 \times .11 \times \dfrac{30}{360}$

$\phantom{I} = \$957.92$

The interest paid to March 20 is $957.92.

$38,000 - \$957.92 = \$37,042.08$

The amount applied to the principal is
$37,042.08.

$104,500 - \$37,042.08 = \$67,457.92$

The balance owed after the $1^{\text{st}}$ payment is
$67,457.92.

April 16 is day       106

March 20 is day    $\underline{-79}$

              27 days

$I = PRT$

$\phantom{I} = \$67,457.92 \times .11 \times \dfrac{27}{360}$

$\phantom{I} = \$556.53$

The interest paid to April 16 is $556.53.

$27,200 - \$556.53 = \$26,643.47$

The amount applied to the principal is
$26,643.47.

$67,457.92 - \$26,643.47 = \$40,814.45$

The balance owed after the $2^{\text{nd}}$ payment is
$40,814.45.

May 15 is day       135

April 16 is day    $\underline{-106}$

              29 days

$I = PRT$

$\phantom{I} = \$40,814.45 \times .11 \times \dfrac{29}{360}$

$\phantom{I} = \$361.66$

The interest due is $361.66.

$40,814.45 + \$361.66 = \$41,176.11$

The amount due on the maturity date is
$41,176.11.

**(b)** $957.92 + \$556.53 + \$361.66 = \$1876.11$

The interest paid on the note is $1876.11.

**21. (a)** $100 + (12 \times \$95) - \$1150 = \$90$

The finance charge is $90.

$$U = F\left(\frac{N}{P}\right)\left(\frac{1+N}{1+P}\right)$$

$$\phantom{U} = \$90 \times \frac{5}{12} \times \left(\frac{1+5}{1+12}\right)$$

$$\phantom{U} = \$17.31$$

The unearned interest is $17.31.

**(b)** $(5 \times \$95) - \$17.31 = \$457.69$

The amount necessary is $457.69.

**23. (a)** $5000 + (20 \times \$1025) - \$23,800 = \$1700$

The finance charge is $1700.

**(b)** $U = F\left(\dfrac{N}{P}\right)\left(\dfrac{1+N}{1+P}\right)$

$$\phantom{U} = \$1700 \times \frac{6}{20} \times \left(\frac{1+6}{1+20}\right)$$

$$\phantom{U} = \$170$$

The unearned interest is $170.

**(c)** $(6 \times \$1025) - \$170 = \$5980$

The amount necessary is $5980.

**25. (a)** $15,000 + (30 \times \$2423.89) = \$87,716.70$

The total installment cost is $87,716.70.

**(b)** $87,716.70 - \$76,800 = \$10,916.70$

The finance charge is $10,916.70.

**(c)** $U = F\left(\dfrac{N}{P}\right)\left(\dfrac{1+N}{1+P}\right)$

$$\phantom{U} = \$10,916.70 \times \frac{20}{30} \times \left(\frac{1+20}{1+30}\right)$$

$$\phantom{U} = \$4930.12$$

The unearned interest is $4930.12.

**(d)** $(20 \times \$2423.89) - \$4930.12 = \$43,547.68$

The amount needed is $43,547.68.

## 12.4 Personal Property Loans

**1.** $i = 8\%$; $n = 5 \times 1 = 5$

Payment
$6800 \times .25046 = \$1703.13$

**3.** $i = \frac{8\%}{2} = 4\%$; $n = 7\frac{1}{2} \times 2 = 15$

Payment
$4500 \times .08994 = \$404.73$

**5.** $i = \frac{8\%}{4} = 2\%$; $n = 7\frac{3}{4} \times 4 = 31$

Payment
$96,000 \times .04360 = \$4185.60$

**7.** $i = \frac{12\%}{12} = 1\%$; $n = 3 \times 12 = 36$

Payment
$4876 \times .03321 = \$161.93$

**9.** Monthly Payment
$5300 \times .02785 = \$147.61$

Finance Charge
$(42 \times \$147.61) - \$5300 = \$899.62$

**11.** Monthly Payment
$12,000 \times .02683 = \$321.96$

Finance Charge
$(48 \times \$321.96) - \$12,000 = \$3454.08$

**13.** Monthly Payment
$11,750 \times .02174 = \$255.45$

Finance Charge
$(60 \times \$255.45) - \$11,750 = \$3577$

**15.** Answers will vary.

**17. (a)** $i = \frac{12\%}{12} = 1\%$; $n = 40$
$62,400 \times .03046 = \$1900.70$
The monthly payment is \$1900.70.

**(b)** $(40 \times \$1900.70) - \$62,400 = \$13,628$
The total interest paid is \$13,628.

**19.**

| Payment Number | Amount of Payment | Interest for Period | Portion to Principal | Principal at End of Period |
|---|---|---|---|---|
| 0 | — | — | — | $4000.00 |
| 1 | $1207.68 | $320.00 | $887.68 | $3112.32 |
| 2 | $1207.68 | $248.99 | $958.69 | $2153.63 |
| 3 | $1207.68 | $172.29 | $1035.39 | $1118.24 |
| 4 | $1207.70* | $89.46 | $1118.24 | $0 |

*Difference is due to rounding in previous years.

**21.**

| Payment Number | Amount of Payment | Interest for Period | Portion to Principal | Principal at End of Period |
|---|---|---|---|---|
| 0 | — | — | — | $14,500.00 |
| 1 | $374.83 | $132.92 | $241.91 | $14,258.09 |
| 2 | $374.83 | $130.70 | $244.13 | $14,013.96 |
| 3 | $374.83 | $128.46 | $246.37 | $13,767.59 |
| 4 | $374.83 | $126.20 | $248.63 | $13,518.96 |
| 5 | $374.83 | $123.92 | $250.91 | $13,268.05 |

**23.**

| Payment Number | Amount of Payment | Interest for Period | Portion to Principal | Principal at End of Period |
|---|---|---|---|---|
| 0 | — | — | — | $35,000.00 |
| 1 | $1196.30 | $408.33 | $787.97 | $34,212.03 |
| 2 | $1196.30 | $399.14 | $797.16 | $33,414.87 |
| 3 | $1196.30 | $389.84 | $806.46 | $32,608.41 |
| 4 | $1196.30 | $380.43 | $815.87 | $31,792.54 |
| 5 | $1196.30 | $370.91 | $825.39 | $30,967.15 |

## 12.5 Real Estate Loans

**1.** Monthly Payment
$310 \times \$7.31 = \$2266.10$

**3.** Monthly Payment
$112.8 \times \$9.85 = \$1111.08$

**5.** Monthly Payment
$92.4 \times \$6.49 = \$599.68$

**7.** Answers will vary.

**9.** Monthly Payment
$$\left(98 \times \$6.65\right) + \left(\frac{\$1250 + \$560}{12}\right)$$
$$= \$651.70 + \$150.83$$
$$= \$802.53$$

**11.** Monthly Payment
$$\left(275.8 \times \$6.83\right) + \left(\frac{\$6840 + \$758}{12}\right)$$
$$= \$1883.71 + \$633.17$$
$$= \$2516.88$$

**13.** Monthly Payment
$$\left(91.58 \times \$7.89\right) + \left(\frac{\$1326 + \$489}{12}\right)$$
$$= \$722.57 + \$151.25$$
$$= \$873.82$$

**15.** $\$127,000 - \$10,000 = \$117,000$
The loan amount is \$117,000.
$$\left(117 \times \$7.00\right) + \left(\frac{\$720 + \$2300}{12}\right)$$
$$= \$819 + \$251.67$$
$$= \$1070.67$$
The total monthly payment is \$1070.67.
Since this does not exceed \$1200, they are
qualified for the loan.

**17.** $122.5 \times \$9.28 = \$1136.80$
The monthly payment is \$1136.80.

| Payment Number | Total Payment | Interest Payment | Principal Payment | Balance of Principal |
|---|---|---|---|---|
| 0 | – | – | – | \$122,500.00 |
| 1 | \$1136.80 | \$765.63 | \$371.17 | \$122,128.83 |
| 2 | \$1136.80 | \$763.31 | \$373.49 | \$121,755.34 |

## Case Study

Use the loan payoff table from section 12.4 and the
real estate amortization table from section 12.5.

**1.** Honda Accord
$\$18,800 \times .02633 = \$495.00$

Ford truck
$\$14,300 \times .02937 = \$419.99$

Home
$96.5 \times \$9.85 = \$950.53$

$2^{nd}$ mortgage on home
$\$4500 \times .03321 = \$149.45$

$\$495.00 + \$419.99 + \$950.53 + \$149.45$
$= \$2014.97$
The total monthly payment is \$2014.97.

**2.** $\$3350 \div 12 = \$279.17$
Monthly real estate tax costs are \$2791.17.

$\$2014.97 + \$215.00 + \$290.00 + \$279.17$
$= \$2799.14$
The total monthly outlay is \$2799.14.

**3.** Honda Accord
$\$14,900 \times .02633 = \$392.32$

Ford truck
$\$8600 \times .03321 = \$285.61$

Home
$94.8 \times \$7.34 = \$695.83$

$2^{nd}$ mortgage on home
\$149.45 (no change)

Car insurance
$\$215.00 - \$28.00 = \$187.00$

Health insurance
\$290.00 (no change)

Real estate taxes on home
\$279.17 (no change)

$\$392.32 + \$285.61 + \$695.83 + \$149.45$
$+ \$187.00 + \$290.00 + \$279.17 = \$2279.38$
The total monthly outlay is \$2279.38.

**4.** $\$2799.14 - \$2279.38 = \$519.76$
The reduction in the Hernandez's monthly
payments is \$519.76.

## Case #2 Home Financing

1. $1100 + \left(\dfrac{\$6400 + \$980}{12}\right)$

   $= \$1100 + \$615$

   $= \$1715$

   The monthly payment is $1715.

2. $306,500 \times .75 = \$229,875$

   Their house was worth $229,875 in 2011.

   $306,500 - \$229,875 = \$76,625$

   They were underwater by $76,625.

3. $76,625 + \$23,000 \approx \$100,000$

   The Dustons would have to pay approximately $100,000 to sell their home.

4. $285 \times \$6.49 = \$1849.65$

   The new home payment was $1849.65.

5. $1849.65 - \$1100 = \$749.65$

   The increase in the monthly payment is $749.65.

## Chapter 12  Test

1. $214,500 - \$20,000 = \$194,500$

   The amount financed is $194,500.

   $(24 \times \$8975) - \$194,500 = \$20,900$

   The finance charge is $20,900.

2. $680.45 \times .015 = \$10.21$

   The finance charge is $10.21.

   $680.45 + \$10.21 + \$337.32 - \$45.42 - \$50$
   $= \$932.56$

   The balance on December 1 is $932.56.

3. $\dfrac{\$1010.59 \times \$100}{\$5280} = \$19.14$

   Look down the left column of table to 36 payments. The number closest to 19.14 is 19.14, which corresponds to 11.75%.

4. $\dfrac{\$149.84 \times \$100}{\$1130} = \$13.26$

   Look down the left column of table to 24 payments. The number closest to 13.26 is 13.26, which corresponds to 12.25%.

5. $(36 \times \$612.25) - \$18,700 = \$3341$

   The finance charge is $3341.

   $\dfrac{\$3341 \times \$100}{\$18,700} = \$17.87$

   Look down the left column of table to 36 payments. The number closest to 17.87 is 17.86, which corresponds to 11.00%.

6. July 17 is day      198
   June 21 is day    $\underline{-172}$
                 26 days

   $I = PRT = \$7000 \times .13 \times \dfrac{26}{360} = \$65.72$

   The interest paid to July 17 is $65.72.

   $2800 - \$65.72 = \$2734.28$

   The amount applied to the principal is $2734.28.

   $7000 - \$2734.28 = \$4265.72$

   The balance owed is $4265.72.

   Interest on new principal is charged for $90 - 26 = 64$ days.

   $I = PRT = \$4265.72 \times .13 \times \dfrac{64}{360} = \$98.59$

   The interest due is $98.59.

   $4265.72 + \$98.59 = \$4364.31$

   The amount due on the maturity date is $4364.31.

7. (a) $(48 \times \$228.14) - \$7400 = \$3550.72$

   The finance charge is $3550.72.

   $U = F\left(\dfrac{N}{P}\right)\left(\dfrac{1+N}{1+P}\right)$

   $= \$3550.72 \times \dfrac{12}{48} \times \left(\dfrac{1+12}{1+48}\right)$

   $= \$235.51$

   The unearned interest is $235.51.

   (b) $(12 \times \$228.14) - \$235.51 = \$2502.17$

   The amount necessary is $2502.17.

8. $i = \dfrac{10\%}{4} = 2\tfrac{1}{2}\%; \quad n = 2 \times 4 = 8$

   $34,500 \times .13947 = \$4811.72$

   The quarterly payment is $4811.72.

**9.** $i = \frac{10\%}{4} = 2\frac{1}{2}\%;\ n = 5 \times 4 = 20$

$\$36,000 - \$6000 = \$30,000$
The amount financed is $30,000.

$\$30,000 \times .06415 = \$1924.50$
The amount of each payment is $1924.50.

**10.** Monthly Payment
$123.5 \times \$7.00 = \$864.50$

**11.** Monthly Payment
$134.56 \times \$8.99 = \$1209.69$

**12.** $.20 \times \$90,000 = \$18,000$
The down payment is $18,000.

$\$90,000 - \$18,000 = \$72,000$
The loan amount is $72,000.

$(72 \times \$7.34) + \left(\dfrac{\$960 + \$252}{12}\right)$
$= \$528.48 + \$101$
$= \$629.48$
The monthly payment is $629.48.

**13. (a)** $.20 \times \$680,000 = \$136,000$
The down payment is $136,000.

$\$680,000 - \$136,000 = \$544,000$
The loan amount is $544,000.

$(544 \times \$9.13) + \left(\dfrac{\$14,500 + \$3200}{12}\right)$
$= \$4966.72 + \$1475$
$= \$6441.72$
The monthly payment is $6441.72.

**(b)** $\$136,000 + (\$6441.72 \times 12 \times 15)$
$= \$1,295,509.60$
The total cost of owning the building for 15 years is $1,295,509.60.

**14. (a)** $(122.5 \times \$8.37) + \left(\dfrac{\$3200 + \$1275}{12}\right)$
$= \$1025.33 + \$372.92$
$= \$1398.25$
The total monthly payment is $1398.25.

**(b)** $\$25,000 + \$1398.25 \times 12 \times 20$
$= \$360,580$
The total cost of owning the building for 20 years is $360,580.

**1.** $i = 4\%$; $n = 8 \times 1 = 8$

Amount of Annuity
$1000 \times 9.21423 = \$9214.23$

Interest Earned
$\$9214.23 - (8 \times \$1000) = \$1214.23$

**2.** $i = \frac{6\%}{4} = 1\frac{1}{2}\%$; $n = 5 \times 4 = 20$

Amount of Annuity
$\$2000 \times 23.12367 = \$46,247.34$

Interest Earned
$\$46,247.34 - (20 \times \$2000) = \$6247.34$

**3.** $i = 5\%$; $n = 6 \times 1 + 1 = 7$

Amount of Annuity Due
$\$2500 \times 8.14201 - \$2500 = \$17,855.03$

Interest Earned
$\$17,855.03 - (6 \times \$2500) = \$2855.03$

**4.** $i = \frac{8\%}{2} = 4\%$; $n = 5 \times 2 + 1 = 11$

Amount of Annuity Due
$\$1800 \times 13.48635 - \$1800 = \$22,475.43$

Interest Earned
$\$22,475.43 - (10 \times \$1800) = \$4475.43$

**5.** $i = \frac{8\%}{2} = 4\%$; $n = 11 \times 2 = 22$

Present Value
$\$925 \times 14.45112 = \$13,367.29$

**6.** $i = \frac{8\%}{4} = 2\%$; $n = 8 \times 4 = 32$

Present Value
$\$27,235 \times 23.46833 = \$639,159.97$

**7.** $i = 8\%$; $n = 7 \times 1 = 7$

Payment
$\$3600 \times .11207 = \$403.45$

**8.** $i = \frac{10\%}{4} = 2\frac{1}{2}\%$; $n = 7 \times 4 = 28$

Payment
$\$4500 \times .02509 = \$112.91$

**9. (a)** $i = \frac{10\%}{4} = 2\frac{1}{2}\%$; $n = 7 \times 4 = 28$

$\$300 \times 39.85980 = \$11,957.94$
The accumulated amount at age 65 is
$\$11,957.94$.

**(b)** $i = \frac{10\%}{4} = 2\frac{1}{2}\%$; $n = 12 \times 4 = 48$

$\$300 \times 90.85958 = \$27,257.87$
The accumulated amount at age 70 is
$\$27,257.87$.

**10.** $i = 10\%$; $n = 5 \times 1 = 5$

$\$60 \text{ million} \times .16380 = \$9.828 \text{ million}$
They must make an annual payment of
$\$9.828$ million.

**11. (a)** $100 \times \$23.45 = \$2345$
The cost is $\$2345$.

**(b)** $\dfrac{\$23.45}{\$1.56} \approx 15$

The PE ratio is 15.

**(c)** $\dfrac{\$.35}{\$23.45} \approx .015 = 1.5\%$

The dividend yield is $1.5\%$.

**12. (a)** $(1.0438 \times \$1000 + \$1) \times 9000$
$= \$9,403,200$
The cost is $\$9,403,200$.

**(b)** $(.064 \times \$1000) \times 9000 = \$576,000$
The annual interest is $\$576,000$.

**(c)** $\dfrac{\$576,000}{\$9,403,200} \approx .061 = 6.1\%$

The effective interest rate is $6.1\%$.

**13. (a)** $\$500 + (24 \times \$108.27) = \$3098.48$
The total installment cost is $\$3098.48$.

**(b)** $\$3098.48 - \$2800 = \$298.48$
The finance charge is $\$298.48$.

**(c)** $\$2800 - \$500 = \$2300$
The amount financed is $\$2300$.

**(d)** $\dfrac{\$298.48 \times \$100}{\$2300} = \$12.98$

Look down the left column of table to 24
payments. The number closest to 12.98 is
12.98, which corresponds to 12.00%.

**14. (a)** Unpaid Balance Method:

$$\$204.37 \times .016 = \$3.27$$

The finance charge is \$3.27.

$$\$204.37 + \$3.27 + \$34.95 + \$95.12 - \$100$$
$$= \$237.71$$

The balance on August 8 is \$237.71.

**(b)** Average-Daily-Balance Method

| Unpaid Balance | | Days | | Total Balance |
|---|---|---|---|---|
| \$204.37 | × | 6 | = | \$1226.22 |
| \$204.37 − \$100.00 = \$104.37 | × | 2 | = | \$ 208.74 |
| \$104.37 + \$ 34.95 = \$139.32 | × | 14 | = | \$1950.48 |
| \$139.32 + \$95.12 = \$234.44 | × | 9 | = | \$2109.96 |
| | | 31 | | \$5495.40 |

$$\frac{\$5495.40}{31} = \$177.27$$

The average daily balance is \$177.27.

$$\$177.27 \times .016 = \$2.84$$

The finance charge is \$2.84.

$$\$204.37 + \$2.84 + (\$34.95 + \$95.12) - \$100$$
$$= \$237.28$$

The balance on August 8 is \$237.28.

**15. (a)** $i = \frac{8\%}{4} = 2\%$; $n = 3 \times 4 = 12$

$$\$22,400 \times .09456 = \$2118.14$$

The quarterly payment is \$2118.14.

**(b)** $(12 \times \$2118.14) - \$22,400 = \$3017.68$

The total amount of interest paid is \$3017.68.

**16.** $\$195,000 \times .95 = \$185,250$

The loan amount is \$185,250.

$$(185.25 \times \$7.00) + \left(\frac{\$720 + \$4140}{12}\right)$$
$$= \$1296.75 + \$405$$
$$= \$1701.75$$

The monthly payment is \$1701.75.

**17. (a)**   April 15 is day      105
        January 10 is day    $\underline{-10}$
                                  95 days

$$I = PRT = \$24,000 \times .09 \times \frac{95}{360} = \$570$$

The interest paid to April 15 is \$570.

$$\$10,000 - \$570 = \$9430$$

The amount applied to the principal is \$9430.

$$\$24,000 - \$9430 = \$14,570$$

The balance owed is \$14,570.

**(b)** Interest on new principal is charged for $200 - 95 = 105$ days.

$$I = PRT = \$14,570 \times .09 \times \frac{105}{360} = \$382.46$$

The interest due is \$382.46.

$$\$14,570 + \$382.46 = \$14,952.46$$

The amount due at maturity is \$14,952.46.

**18. (a)** $(8 \times \$290.69) - \$2200 = \$125.52$

The finance charge is \$125.52.

$$U = F\left(\frac{N}{P}\right)\left(\frac{1+N}{1+P}\right)$$
$$= \$125.52 \times \frac{5}{8} \times \left(\frac{1+5}{1+8}\right)$$
$$= \$52.30$$

The unearned interest is \$52.30.

**(b)** $(5 \times \$290.69) - \$52.30 = \$1401.15$

The amount needed is \$1401.15.

**19.** $i = \frac{8\%}{4} = 2\%$; $n = 1 \times 4 = 4$

$$\$3500 \times 3.80773 = \$13,327.06$$

The total amount needed is \$13,327.06.

**20.** $i = 8\%$; $n = 3$

$$\$35,000 \times 2.57710 = \$90,198.50$$

The present value of the annuity is \$90,198.50.

$i = 8\%$; $n = 4$

$$\$90,198.50 \times .73503 = \$66,298.60$$

The present value needed to meet this obligation is \$66,298.60.

**21.** Answers will vary.

**22.** Answers will vary.

# Chapter 13 | Taxes and Insurance

## 13.1 Property Tax

1. Assessed Value
$85,000 \times .40 = \$34,000$

3. Assessed Value
$142,300 \times .50 = \$71,150$

5. Assessed Value
$1,300,500 \times .25 = \$325,125$

7. Tax Rate
$\$18,300,000 \div \$60,850,000 \approx .0027 \approx .3\%$

9. Tax Rate
$\$1,580,000 \div \$19,750,000 = .08 = 8\%$

11. Tax Rate
$\$1,224,000 \div \$40,800,000 = .03 = 3\%$

13. 4.84%
    (a) $4.84 per $100

    (b) $48.40 per $1000

    (c) 48.4 mills

15. $70.80 per $1000
    (a) 7.08%

    (b) $7.08 per $100

    (c) 70.8 mills

17. Answers will vary.

19. $86,200 = 862$ hundreds
Tax $= 862 \times \$6.80 = \$5861.60$

21. Tax $= \$128,200 \times .042 = \$5384.40$

23. $\$328,500 \times .35 = \$114,975$
The assessed value is $114,975.

$\$114,975 \times .052 = \$5978.70$
The tax is $5978.70.

25. $\$334,400 \times .25 = \$83,600$
The assessed value is $83,600.

$\$83,600 = 83.6$ thousands

$83.6 \times \$75.30 = \$6295.08$
The tax is $6295.08.

27. $\$18,500,000 \times .65 = \$12,025,000$
The assessed value is $12,025,000.

$\$12,025,000 = \$120,250$ hundreds

$120,250 \times \$2.18 = \$262,145$
The tax is $262,145.

29. (a) $\$95,000 \times .40 = \$38,000$
The assessed value is $38,000.

$\$38,000 \times .0321 = \$1219.80$
The tax is $1219.80.

$\$95,000 \times .24 = \$22,800$
The assessed value is $22,800.

$\$22,800 \times .0502 = \$1144.56$
The tax is $1144.56.

The second parish charges the lower property tax.

(b) $\$1219.80 - \$1144.56 = \$75.24$
The annual amount saved is $75.24.

## 13.2  Personal Income Tax

**1.** Adjusted gross income
$$= \$22,840 + \$234 + \$1209 + \$48 - \$1200$$
$$= \$23,131$$

**3.** Adjusted gross income
$$= \$21,380 + \$625 + \$139 + \$184 - \$618$$
$$= \$21,710$$

**5.** Adjusted gross income
$$= \$38,643 + \$1020 + \$3820 + \$1050 - \$0$$
$$= \$44,533$$

**7.** Adjusted gross income
$$= \$21,370 + \$420 + \$0 + \$0 - \$0$$
$$= \$21,790$$

**9.** Taxable income
$$= \$36,840 - \$5700 - (1 \times \$3650)$$
$$= \$27,490$$

Tax
$$= \$835 + .15(\$27,490 - \$8350)$$
$$= \$3706$$

**11.** Taxable income
$$= \$72,450 - \$11,400 - (2 \times \$3650)$$
$$= \$53,750$$

Tax
$$= \$1670 + .15(\$53,750 - \$16,700)$$
$$= \$7227.50$$

**13.** Taxable income
$$= \$99,500 - \$14,320 - (3 \times \$3650)$$
$$= \$74,230$$

Tax
$$= \$9350 + .25(\$74,230 - \$67,900)$$
$$= \$10,932.50$$

**15.** Taxable income
$$= \$85,332 - \$8170 - (2 \times \$3650)$$
$$= \$69,862$$

Tax
$$= \$13,318.75 + .28(\$69,862 - \$68,525)$$
$$= \$13,693.11$$

**17.** Taxable income
$$= \$82,650 - \$8350 - (2 \times \$3650)$$
$$= \$67,000$$

Tax
$$= \$6227.50 + .25(\$67,000 - \$45,500)$$
$$= \$11,602.50$$

**19.** Tax
$$= \$4675 + .25(\$78,500 - \$33,950)$$
$$= \$15,812.50$$

$$\$1516 \times 12 = \$18,192$$

$$\$18,192 - \$15,812.50$$
$$= \$2379.50 \text{ tax refund}$$

**21.** Tax
$$= \$835 + .15(\$23,552 - \$8350)$$
$$= \$3115.30$$

$$\$72.18 \times 52 = \$3753.36$$

$$\$3753.36 - \$3115.30$$
$$= \$638.06 \text{ tax refund}$$

**23.** Tax
$$= \$26,637.50 + .28(\$202,100 - \$137,050)$$
$$= \$44,851.50$$

$$\$3200 \times 12 = \$38,400$$

$$\$44,851.50 - \$38,400$$
$$= \$6451.50 \text{ tax due}$$

**25.** Answers will vary.

**27.** Total deductions
$$= \$2820 + \$490 + \$4400 + \$5800 + \$1450$$
$$= \$14,960$$
Use the total deductions of \$14,960.

Taxable income
$$= \$98,700 - \$14,960 - (5 \times \$3650)$$
$$= \$65,490$$

Tax
$$= \$1670 + .15(\$65,490 - \$16,700)$$
$$= \$8988.50$$

**29.** Total deductions $= \$7143$
Use the standard deduction of $8350.

Taxable income
$= \$73,200 - \$8350 - (2 \times \$3650)$
$= \$57,550$

Tax
$= \$6227.50 + .25(\$57,550 - \$45,500)$
$= \$9240$

**31.** Adjusted gross income
$= \$73,800 + \$385 + \$1672 - \$1058$
$= \$74,799$

Total deductions
$= \$877 + \$342 + \$4986 + \$5173 + \$1800$
$= \$13,178$
Use the total deductions of $13,178.

Taxable income
$= \$74,799 - \$13,178 - (4 \times \$3650)$
$= \$47,021$

Tax $= \$6227.50 + .25(\$47,021 - \$45,500)$
$\quad\quad = \$6607.75$

**33.** Adjusted gross income
$= \$64,280 + \$5283 + \$324 + \$668 - \$2484$
$= \$68,071$

Total deductions
$= \$7615 + \$2250 + \$3300 + \$1219$
$= \$14,384$
Use the total deductions of $14,384.

Taxable income
$= \$68,071 - \$14,384 - (3 \times \$3650)$
$= \$42,737$

Tax $= \$1670 + .15(\$42,737 - \$16,700)$
$\quad\quad = \$5575.55$

## 13.3 Fire Insurance

**1.** $280,000 = 2800$ hundreds
$2800 \times \$.45 = \$1260$
The premium for the building is $1260.

$80,000 = 800$ hundreds
$800 \times \$.55 = \$440$
The premium for the contents is $440.

$1260 + \$440 = \$1700$
The total annual premium is $1700.

**3.** $285,000 = 2850$ hundreds
$2850 \times \$.45 = \$1282.50$
The premium for the building is $1282.50.

$152,000 = 1520$ hundreds
$1520 \times \$.60 = \$912$
The premium for the contents is $912.

$1282.50 + \$912 = \$2194.50$
The total annual premium is $2194.50.

**5.** $782,600 = 7826$ hundreds
$7826 \times \$.92 = \$7199.92$
The premium for the building is $7199.92.

$212,000 = 2120$ hundreds
$2120 \times \$.99 = \$2098.80$
The premium for the contents is $2098.80.

$7199.92 + \$2098.80 = \$9298.72$
The total annual premium is $9298.72.

**7.** $1,450,000 \times .80 = \$1,160,000$

$\dfrac{\$850,000}{\$1,160,000} \times \$96,000 = \$70,344.83$

The insurance company will pay $70,344.83.

**9.** $287,000 \times .80 = \$229,600$

The face value of the policy is greater than $229,600. The insurance company will pay the entire $19,850 loss.

**11.** $218,500 \times .80 = \$174,800$

The face value of the policy is greater than $174,800. The insurance company will pay the entire $36,500 loss.

**13.** $750,000 + $250,000 = $1,000,000$

Company 1: $\dfrac{\$750,000}{\$1,000,000} \times \$80,000 = \$60,000$

Company 2: $\dfrac{\$250,000}{\$1,000,000} \times \$80,000 = \$20,000$

**15.** $1,350,000 + \$1,200,000 + \$450,000$
$= \$3,000,000$

Company 1:

$\dfrac{\$1,350,000}{\$3,000,000} \times \$650,000 = \$292,500$

Company 2:

$\dfrac{\$1,200,000}{\$3,000,000} \times \$650,000 = \$260,000$

Company 3:

$\dfrac{\$450,000}{\$3,000,000} \times \$650,000 = \$97,500$

**17.** $1,400,000 = 14,000$ hundreds
$14,000 \times \$1.05 = \$14,700$
The premium for the building is \$14,700.

$360,000 = 3600$ hundreds
$3600 \times \$1.14 = \$4104$
The premium for the contents is \$4104.

$14,700 + \$4104 = \$18,804$
The total annual premium is \$18,804.

**19.** $107,500 = 1075$ hundreds
$1075 \times \$.45 = \$483.75$
The premium for the building is \$483.75.

$39,800 = 398$ hundreds
$398 \times \$.55 = \$218.90$
The premium for the contents is \$218.90.

$483.75 + \$218.90 = \$702.65$
The total annual premium is \$702.65.

**21.** Answers will vary.

**23. (a)** $328,500 \times .80 = \$262,800$

$\dfrac{\$200,000}{\$262,800} \times \$180,000 = \$136,986.30$

The insurance company will pay
\$136,986.30.

**(b)** $180,000 - \$136,986.30 = \$43,013.70$
The amount paid by the insured is
\$43,013.70.

**25. (a)** $550,000 \times .80 = \$440,000$

$\dfrac{\$300,000}{\$440,000} \times \$45,000 = \$30,681.82$

The insurance company will pay
\$30,681.82.

**(b)** $45,000 - \$30,681.82 = \$14,318.18$
The amount paid by the insured is
\$14,318.18.

**27.** $600,000 + \$400,000 + \$200,000 = \$1,200,000$

Company A:

$\dfrac{\$600,000}{\$1,200,000} \times \$548,000 = \$274,000$

Company B:

$\dfrac{\$400,000}{\$1,200,000} \times \$548,000 = \$182,666.67$

Company C:

$\dfrac{\$200,000}{\$1,200,000} \times \$548,000 = \$91,333.33$

**29.** $360,000 + \$120,000 + \$240,000 = \$720,000$

Company 1:

$\dfrac{\$360,000}{\$720,000} \times \$250,000 = \$125,000$

Company 2:

$\dfrac{\$120,000}{\$720,000} \times \$250,000 = \$41,666.67$

Company 3:

$\dfrac{\$240,000}{\$720,000} \times \$250,000 = \$83,333.33$

**31. (a)** $1,200,000 \times .80 = \$960,000$
$200,000 + \$300,000 = \$500,000$

$\dfrac{\$500,000}{\$960,000} \times \$420,000 = \$218,750$

The amount of the loss covered is
\$218,750.

**(b)** Company A:
$\dfrac{\$200,000}{\$500,000} \times \$218,750 = \$87,500$

Company B:
$\dfrac{\$300,000}{\$500,000} \times \$218,750 = \$131,250$

## 13.4 Motor-Vehicle Insurance

1. Annual Premium
   $375 + $134 + $66 + $139 + $76 = $790

3. Annual Premium
   $459 + $145 + $90 + $162 + $76 = $932

5. Annual Premium
   $398 + $262 + $42 + $97 + $70 = $869

7. Answers will vary.

9. $445 + $262 + $40 + $94 + $70 = $911
   Bill's annual insurance premium is $911.

11. $253 + $93 + $44 + $116 + $66 = $572

   $572 × 2.10 = $1201.20
   Brandy's annual insurance premium is
   $1201.20.

13. The coverage limit is $25,000.
   (a) The company will pay $25,000.

   (b) You will pay $36,500 − $25,000 = $11,500.

15. (a) The property damage limit is $10,000.
       The company will pay $4300 for
       damages to the automobile.

   (b) The medical expense limit is $1000.
       The company will pay $850 for medical
       expenses.

17. (a) $1878 − $100 = $1778
       The insurance company will pay $1778 to
       repair Silva's car (damages minus the
       deductible).

   (b) Since the property damage limit is $25,000,
       the insurance company will pay the entire
       $6936 to repair the other car.

   (c) The insurance company will pay up to the
       policy limit of $100,000.

   (d) $(\$60,000 + \$55,000) - \$100,000$
       $= \$115,000 - \$100,000 = \$15,000$
       $\$15,000 + \$100 = \$15,100$
       Silva must pay $15,100.

19. Answers will vary.

## 13.5 Life Insurance

1. $100,000 = 100$ thousands

   | | |
   |---|---|
   | $100 × $2.56 = $256 | annual |
   | $256 × .51 = $130.56 | semiannual |
   | $256 × .26 = $66.56 | quarterly |
   | $256 × .0908 = $23.24 | monthly |

3. $35,000 = 35$ thousands

   | | |
   |---|---|
   | $35 × $24.26 = $849.10 | annual |
   | $849.10 × .51 = $433.04 | semiannual |
   | $849.10 × .26 = $220.77 | quarterly |
   | $849.10 × .0908 = $77.10 | monthly |

5. $85,000 = 85$ thousands

   | | |
   |---|---|
   | $85 × $6.08 = $516.80 | annual |
   | $516.80 × .51 = $263.57 | semiannual |
   | $516.80 × .26 = $134.37 | quarterly |
   | $516.80 × .0908 = $46.93 | monthly |

7. $75,000 = 75$ thousands

   | | |
   |---|---|
   | $75 × $4.26 = $319.50 | annual |
   | $319.50 × .51 = $162.95 | semiannual |
   | $319.50 × .26 = $83.07 | quarterly |
   | $319.50 × .0908 = $29.01 | monthly |

9. $65,000 = 65$ thousands

   | | |
   |---|---|
   | $65 × $45.74 = $2973.10 | annual |
   | $2973.10 × .51 = $1516.28 | semiannual |
   | $2973.10 × .26 = $773.01 | quarterly |
   | $2973.10 × .0908 = $269.96 | monthly |

11. Answers will vary.

13. $1.82 × 200 (thousands) = $364
    The annual premium is $364.

15. (a) $2.01 × 50 (thousands) = $100.50
        The annual premium for 10-year level term
        is $100.50.

    (b) $7.68 × 50 (thousands) = $384
        The annual premium for whole life is $384.

17. $5.06 × 20 (thousands) = $101.20
    The annual premium is $101.20.

    $101.20 × 30 = $3036
    The total premium paid over 30 years is $3036.

**19. (a)** Semiannual premium
$$= \$872 \times .51 = \$444.72$$

**(b)** Quarterly premium
$$= \$872 \times .26 = \$226.72$$

**(c)** Monthly premium
$$= \$872 \times .0908 = \$79.18$$

## Case Study

**1.** $\$1,990,000 \times .75 = \$1,492,500$
The assessed value is $1,492,500.

$\$1,492,500 = 1492.5$ thousands

$1492.5 \times \$7.90 = \$11,790.75$
The tax is $11,790.75.

**2.** $\$1,730,000 = 17,300$ hundreds
$17,300 \times \$.75 = \$12,975$
The premium for the building is $12,975.

$\$3,502,000 = 35,020$ hundreds
$35,020 \times \$.77 = \$26,965.40$
The premium for the contents is $26,965.40.

$\$12,975 + \$26,965.40 = \$39,940.40$
The annual fire insurance premium is
$39,940.40.

**3.** $\$3.45 \times 250 \text{(thousands)} = \$862.50$

$\$862.50 \times .51 = \$439.88$
The semiannual premium is $439.88.

**4.** $\$11,790.75 + \$39,940.40 + \$439.88$
$= \$52,171.03$
The total amount needed is $52,171.03.

**5.** $\$53,500 - \$52,171.03 = \$1328.97$
They set aside $1328.97 more than needed.

## Case in Point Summary Exercise

**1.** $\$310,000 \times .30 = \$93,000$
The assessed value is $93,000.

$\$93,000 = 93$ thousands

$93 \times \$64 = \$5952$
The property tax is $5952.

**2.** $\$28,410 + \$212 + \$84 = \$28,706$
Total income is $28,706.

$\$28,706 - \$500 = \$28,206$
Adjusted gross income is $28,206.

$\$28,206 - \$5700 - \$(1 \times \$3650) = \$18,856$
Taxable income is $18,856.

$\$835 + .15(\$18,856 - \$8350)$
$= \$2410.90$
Income tax is $2410.90.

**3.** Use a replacement cost of $420,000.
$\$420,000 = 4200$ hundreds

$\$145,000 = 1450$ hundreds

$4200 \times \$1.05 + 1450 \times \$1.14 = \$6063$
The total annual premium is $6063.

**4.** $\$392 + \$251 + \$40 + \$104 + \$44 = \$831$
The annual premium is $831.

**5.** $\$1.89 \times 500 \text{(thousands)} = \$945$
The annual cost is $945.

**6.** Note that Janet Chino's income taxes in
Question 2 are not paid by Martha Spencer.

$\$5952 + \$6063 + \$831 + \$945 = \$13,791$
The combined costs are $13,791.

## Chapter 13   Test

1. 5.76%
   (a) $5.76 per $100
   
   (b) $57.60 per $1000

2. $93.50 per $1000
   (a) 9.35%
   
   (b) $9.35 per $100

3. Taxable income
   $= \$68,295 - \$5700 - (2 \times \$3650)$
   $= \$55,295$

   Tax
   $= \$4675 + .25(\$55,295 - \$33,950)$
   $= \$10,011.25$

4. Taxable income
   $= \$43,487 - \$11,400 - (4 \times \$3650)$
   $= \$17,487$

   Tax
   $= \$1670 + .15(\$17,487 - \$16,700)$
   $= \$1788.05$

5. $\$209,200 \times .30 = \$62,760$
   The assessed value is $62,760.

   $\$62,760 \times .0365 = \$2290.74$
   The tax is $2290.74.

6. Taxable income
   $= \$98,316 - \$11,400 - (5 \times \$3650)$
   $= \$68,666$

   Tax
   $= \$9350 + .25(\$68,666 - \$67,900)$
   $= \$9541.50$

7. Total deductions
   $= \$1280 + \$3620 + \$3540 + \$343$
   $= \$8783$
   Use the total deductions of $8783.

   Taxable income
   $= \$44,600 - \$8783 - (1 \times \$3650)$
   $= \$32,167$

   Tax
   $= \$835 + .15(\$32,167 - \$8350)$
   $= \$4407.55$

8. $\$780,000 = 7800$ hundreds
   $7800 \times \$.92 = \$7176$
   The premium for the building is $7176.

   $\$128,600 = 1286$ hundreds
   $1286 \times \$.99 = \$1273.14$
   The premium for the contents is $1273.14.

   $\$7176 + \$1273.14 = \$8449.14$
   The total annual premium is $8449.14.

9. $\$220,000 \times .80 = \$176,000$

   $\$50,000 \times \dfrac{\$150,000}{\$176,000} = \$42,613.64$

   The insurance company will pay $42,613.64.

10. $\$250,000 + \$150,000 + \$100,000 = \$500,000$

    Company A: $\dfrac{\$250,000}{\$500,000} \times \$72,000 = \$36,000$

    Company B: $\dfrac{\$150,000}{\$500,000} \times \$72,000 = \$21,600$

    Company C: $\dfrac{\$100,000}{\$500,000} \times \$72,000 = \$14,400$

11. Annual Premium
    $\$310 + \$129 + \$64 + \$122 + \$76 = \$701$
    $\$701 \times 1.55 = \$1086.55$

12. Annual Premium
    $\$253 + \$103 + \$90 + \$184 + \$66 = \$696$

13. $28,000 = 28$ thousands

    | | |
    |---|---|
    | $28 \times \$5.66 = \$158.48$ | annual |
    | $\$158.48 \times .51 = \$80.82$ | semiannual |
    | $\$158.48 \times .26 = \$41.20$ | quarterly |
    | $\$158.48 \times .0908 = \$14.39$ | monthly |

14. $80,000 = 80$ thousands

    | | |
    |---|---|
    | $80 \times \$24.26 = \$1940.80$ | annual |
    | $\$1940.80 \times .51 = \$989.81$ | semiannual |
    | $\$1940.80 \times .26 = \$504.61$ | quarterly |
    | $\$1940.80 \times .0908 = \$176.22$ | monthly |

**15. (a)**   $341 + $192 + $24 + $77 + $44

  $= $678$

  The annual cost of the auto insurance
  is $678.

**(b)**  Jim:   $1.89 \times 100 \text{(thousands)} = $189$

  Betsy:   $4.56 \times 50 \text{(thousands)} = $228$

  $189 + $228 = $417$

  The annual cost of life insurance is $417.

**16.** Hernandez must pay $6400 to repair his truck
  because he has no collision insurance.

  The property damage limit is $10,000. The
  company will pay $8200 for all damages to
  the other vehicle.

  The liability limit is $15,000. The company will
  pay $12,900 for all medical expenses.

# Chapter 14 | Depreciation

## 14.1 Depreciation: Straight-Line Method

**1.** Straight-line rate of depreciation

$$\frac{1}{5} = .20 = 20\%$$

**3.** Straight-line rate of depreciation

$$\frac{1}{8} = .125 = 12.5\%$$

**5.** Straight-line rate of depreciation

$$\frac{1}{20} = .05 = 5\%$$

**7.** Straight-line rate of depreciation

$$\frac{1}{15} = .06\overline{6} = 6\frac{2}{3}\%$$

**9.** Straight-line rate of depreciation

$$\frac{1}{80} = .0125 = 1.25\%$$

**11.** Straight-line rate of depreciation

$$\frac{1}{50} = .02 = 2\%$$

**13.** Annual Depreciation

$$\frac{\$9000 - \$0}{20} = \frac{\$9000}{20} = \$450$$

**15.** Annual Depreciation

$$\frac{\$2700 - \$300}{3} = \frac{\$2400}{3} = \$800$$

**17.** Annual Depreciation

$$\frac{\$4200 - \$0}{5} = \frac{\$4200}{5} = \$840$$

**19.** Annual Depreciation

$$\frac{\$3200 - \$400}{8} = \frac{\$2800}{8} = \$350$$

Book Value at the End of the First Year
$\$3200 - \$350 = \$2850$

**21.** Annual Depreciation

$$\frac{\$5400 - \$600}{12} = \frac{\$4800}{12} = \$400$$

Book Value at the End of the First Year
$\$5400 - \$400 = \$5000$

**23.** Annual Depreciation

$$\frac{\$4800 - \$750}{10} = \frac{\$4050}{10} = \$405$$

Book Value at the End of 5 Years
$\$4800 - \$405 \times 5 = \$2775$

**25.** Annual Depreciation

$$\frac{\$80,000 - \$10,000}{50} = \frac{\$70,000}{50} = \$1400$$

Book Value at the End of 5 Years
$\$80,000 - \$1400 \times 5 = \$73,000$

**27.** Straight-line rate of depreciation
$\$12,000 - \$3000 = \$9000$

$$\frac{1}{3} = .3\overline{3} = 33\frac{1}{3}\%$$

| Year | Computation | Amount of Depreciation | Accumulated Depreciation | Book Value |
|------|-------------|------------------------|--------------------------|------------|
| 0 | — | — | — | $12,000 |
| 1 | $\left(33\frac{1}{3}\% \times \$9000\right)$ | $3000 | $3000 | $ 9,000 |
| 2 | $\left(33\frac{1}{3}\% \times \$9000\right)$ | $3000 | $6000 | $ 6,000 |
| 3 | $\left(33\frac{1}{3}\% \times \$9000\right)$ | $3000 | $9000 | $ 3,000 |

**29.** Straight-line rate of depreciation
$51,200 - $14,000 = $37,200

$$\frac{1}{6} = .16\overline{6} = 16\frac{2}{3}\%$$

| Year | Computation | Amount of Depreciation | Accumulated Depreciation | Book Value |
|---|---|---|---|---|
| 0 | – | – | – | $51,200 |
| 1 | $\left(16\frac{2}{3}\% \times \$37,200\right)$ | $6200 | $ 6,200 | $45,000 |
| 2 | $\left(16\frac{2}{3}\% \times \$37,200\right)$ | $6200 | $12,400 | $38,800 |
| 3 | $\left(16\frac{2}{3}\% \times \$37,200\right)$ | $6200 | $18,600 | $32,600 |
| 4 | $\left(16\frac{2}{3}\% \times \$37,200\right)$ | $6200 | $24,800 | $26,400 |
| 5 | $\left(16\frac{2}{3}\% \times \$37,200\right)$ | $6200 | $31,000 | $20,200 |
| 6 | $\left(16\frac{2}{3}\% \times \$37,200\right)$ | $6200 | $37,200 | $14,000 |

**31.** Answers will vary.

**33. (a)**
$$\frac{\$1,300,000 - \$200,000}{20}$$
$$= \frac{\$1,100,000}{20} = \$55,000$$
The annual depreciation is $55,000.

**(b)** $1,300,000 - $55,000 \times 5 = $1,025,000
The book value at the end of 5 years is
$1,025,000.

**35. (a)** $\frac{1}{8} = .125 = 12.5\%$

The annual rate of depreciation is 12.5%.

**(b)** $\frac{\$88,000 - \$16,000}{8} = \frac{\$72,000}{8} = \$9000$

The annual depreciation is $9000.

**(c)** $88,000 - $9000 = $79,000
The book value at the end of the first year is
$79,000.

## 14.2 Depreciation: Declining-Balance Method

**1.** Double-declining-balance rate of depreciation
$$\frac{1}{5} \times 2 = .20 \times 2 = 20\% \times 2 = 40\%$$

**3.** Double-declining-balance rate of depreciation
$$\frac{1}{8} \times 2 = .125 \times 2 = 12.5\% \times 2 = 25\%$$

**5.** Double-declining-balance rate of depreciation
$$\frac{1}{15} \times 2 = .06\overline{6} \times 2 = 6\frac{2}{3}\% \times 2 = 13\frac{1}{3}\%$$

**7.** Double-declining-balance rate of depreciation
$$\frac{1}{10} \times 2 = .10 \times 2 = 10\% \times 2 = 20\%$$

**9.** Double-declining-balance rate of depreciation
$$\frac{1}{6} \times 2 = .16\overline{6} \times 2 = 16\frac{2}{3}\% \times 2 = 33\frac{1}{3}\%$$

**11.** Double-declining-balance rate of depreciation
$$\frac{1}{50} \times 2 = .02 \times 2 = 2\% \times 2 = 4\%$$

**13.** Double-declining-balance rate of depreciation
$$\frac{1}{10} \times 2 = .10 \times 2 = 10\% \times 2 = 20\%$$

First Year's Depreciation
$20\% \times \$15,000 = \$3000$

**15.** Double-declining-balance rate of depreciation
$$\frac{1}{5} \times 2 = .20 \times 2 = 20\% \times 2 = 40\%$$

First Year's Depreciation
$40\% \times \$22,500 = \$9000$

**17.** Double-declining-balance rate of depreciation
$$\frac{1}{4} \times 2 = .25 \times 2 = 25\% \times 2 = 50\%$$

First Year's Depreciation
$50\% \times \$3800 = \$1900$

**19.** Double-declining-balance rate of depreciation

$$\frac{1}{10} \times 2 = .10 \times 2 = 10\% \times 2 = 20\%$$

First Year's Depreciation
$20\% \times \$4200 = \$840$

Book Value at the End of the First Year
$\$4200 - \$840 = \$3360$

**21.** Double-declining-balance rate of depreciation

$$\frac{1}{8} \times 2 = .125 \times 2 = 12.5\% \times 2 = 25\%$$

First Year's Depreciation
$25\% \times \$1620 = \$405$

Book Value at the End of the First Year
$\$1620 - \$405 = \$1215$

**23.** Double-declining-balance rate of depreciation

$$\frac{1}{8} \times 2 = .125 \times 2 = 12.5\% \times 2 = 25\%$$

| Year | Computation | Amount of Depreciation | Accumulated Depreciation | Book Value |
|---|---|---|---|---|
| 0 | – | – | – | $16,200 |
| 1 | $(25\% \times \$16,200)$ | $4050 | $4050 | $12,150 |
| 2 | $(25\% \times \$12,150)$ | $3038 | $7088 | $ 9,112 |
| 3 | $(25\% \times \$9112)$ | $2278 | $9366 | $ 6,834 |

**25.** Double-declining-balance rate of depreciation

$$\frac{1}{3} \times 2 = .33\overline{3} \times 2 = 33\frac{1}{3}\% \times 2 = 66\frac{2}{3}\%$$

| Year | Computation | Amount of Depreciation | Accumulated Depreciation | Book Value |
|---|---|---|---|---|
| 0 | – | – | – | $6000 |
| 1 | $\left(66\frac{2}{3}\% \times \$6000\right)$ | $4000 | $4000 | $2000 |
| 2 | $\left(66\frac{2}{3}\% \times \$2000\right)$ | $1250* | $5250 | $ 750 |
| 3 | – | – | $5250 | $ 750 |

**27.** Double-declining-balance rate is 50%.

| Year | Computation | Amount of Depreciation | Accumulated Depreciation | Book Value |
|---|---|---|---|---|
| 0 | – | – | – | $14,400 |
| 1 | $(50\% \times \$14,400)$ | $7200 | $ 7,200 | $ 7,200 |
| 2 | $(50\% \times \$7,200)$ | $3600 | $10,800 | $ 3,600 |
| 3 | $(50\% \times \$3,600)$ | $1800 | $12,600 | $ 1,800 |
| 4 | – | $1800* | $14,400 | $0 |

*Since the estimated life is 4 years, we must depreciate to the $0 scrap value in the fourth year.

**29.** Double-declining-balance rate is 40%.

| Year | Computation | Amount of Depreciation | Accumulated Depreciation | Book Value |
|---|---|---|---|---|
| 0 | – | – | – | $14,000 |
| 1 | $(40\% \times \$14,000)$ | $5600 | $ 5,600 | $ 8,400 |
| 2 | $(40\% \times \$8,400)$ | $3360 | $ 8,960 | $ 5,040 |
| 3 | $(40\% \times \$5,040)$ | $2016 | $10,976 | $ 3,024 |
| 4 | – | $ 524* | $11,500 | $ 2,500 |
| 5 | – | $0 | $11,500 | $ 2,500 |

*Only $524 is used so that the book value does not fall below the salvage value of $2500.

**31.** Answers will vary.

**33.** Double-declining-balance rate is 25%.

| Year | Computation | Amount of Depreciation | Accumulated Depreciation | Book Value |
|---|---|---|---|---|
| 0 | – | – | – | $8200 |
| 1 | $(25\% \times \$8200)$ | $2050 | $2050 | $6150 |
| 2 | $(25\% \times \$6150)$ | $1538 | $3588 | $4612 |
| 3 | $(25\% \times \$4612)$ | $1153 | $4741 | $3459 |

The depreciation in the third year was $1153.

**35.** Double-declining balance rate is 40%.

| Year | Computation | Amount of Depreciation | Accumulated Depreciation | Book Value |
|---|---|---|---|---|
| 0 | – | – | – | $39,240 |
| 1 | $(40\% \times \$39,240)$ | $15,696 | $15,696 | $23,544 |
| 2 | $(40\% \times \$23,544)$ | $ 9,418 | $25,114 | $14,126 |
| 3 | $(40\% \times \$14,126)$ | $ 5,650 | $30,764 | $ 8,476 |

The book value at the end of third year is $8476.

**37. (a)** $\frac{1}{8} \times 2 = .125 \times 2 = 12.5\% \times 2 = 25\%$

The annual rate of depreciation is 25%.

**(b)** $25\% \times \$5800 = \$1450$

The amount of depreciation in the first year is $1450.

| Year | Computation | Amount of Depreciation | Accumulated Depreciation | Book Value |
|---|---|---|---|---|
| 0 | – | – | – | $5800 |
| 1 | $(25\% \times \$5800)$ | $1450 | $1450 | $4350 |
| 2 | $(25\% \times \$4350)$ | $1088 | $2538 | $3262 |
| 3 | $(25\% \times \$3262)$ | $ 816 | $3354 | $2446 |
| 4 | $(25\% \times \$2446)$ | $ 612 | $3966 | $1834 |
| 5 | $(25\% \times \$1834)$ | $ 459 | $4425 | $1375 |

**(c)** The accumulated depreciation at the end of the fifth year is $4425.

**(d)** The book value at the end of the fifth year is $1375.

### 14.3 Sum-of-the-Years'-Digits Method

**1.** Sum-of-the-Years'-Digits
Depreciation Fraction
$$\frac{n(n+1)}{2} = \frac{4(4+1)}{2} = \frac{4(5)}{2} = 10; \ r = \frac{4}{10}$$

**3.** Sum-of-the-Years'-Digits
Depreciation Fraction
$$\frac{n(n+1)}{2} = \frac{6(6+1)}{2} = \frac{6(7)}{2} = 21; \ r = \frac{6}{21}$$

**5.** Sum-of-the-Years'-Digits
Depreciation Fraction
$$\frac{n(n+1)}{2} = \frac{7(7+1)}{2} = \frac{7(8)}{2} = 28; \ r = \frac{7}{28}$$

**7.** Sum-of-the-Years'-Digits
Depreciation Fraction
$$\frac{n(n+1)}{2} = \frac{10(10+1)}{2} = \frac{10(11)}{2} = 55$$
$$r = \frac{10}{55}$$

**9.** Sum-of-the-Years'-Digits
Depreciation Fraction
$$\frac{n(n+1)}{2} = \frac{4(4+1)}{2} = \frac{4(5)}{2} = 10; \ r = \frac{4}{10}$$

First Year's Depreciation
$$\frac{4}{10} \times (\$4800 - \$700)$$
$$= \frac{4}{10} \times \$4100$$
$$= \$1640$$

**11.** Sum-of-the-Years'-Digits
Depreciation Fraction
$$\frac{n(n+1)}{2} = \frac{10(10+1)}{2} = \frac{10(11)}{2} = 55; \ r = \frac{10}{55}$$

First Year's Depreciation
$$\frac{10}{55} \times (\$60,000 - \$5000)$$
$$= \frac{10}{55} \times \$55,000$$
$$= \$10,000$$

**13.** Sum-of-the-Years'-Digits
Depreciation Fraction
$$\frac{n(n+1)}{2} = \frac{3(3+1)}{2} = \frac{3(4)}{2} = 6; \ r = \frac{3}{6}$$

First Year's Depreciation
$$\frac{3}{6} \times (\$18,500 - \$3500)$$
$$= \frac{3}{6} \times \$15,000$$
$$= \$7500$$

**15.** Sum-of-the-Years'-Digits
Depreciation Fraction
$$\frac{n(n+1)}{2} = \frac{8(8+1)}{2} = \frac{8(9)}{2} = 36; \ r = \frac{8}{36}$$

Book Value at the end of the first year
$$\$9500 - \frac{8}{36} \times (\$9500 - \$1400)$$
$$= \$9500 - \frac{8}{36} \times \$8100$$
$$= \$9500 - \$1800$$
$$= \$7700$$

**17.** Sum-of-the-Years'-Digits
Depreciation Fraction
$$\frac{n(n+1)}{2} = \frac{5(5+1)}{2} = \frac{5(6)}{2} = 15; \ r = \frac{5}{15}$$

Book Value at the end of the first year
$$\$3800 - \frac{5}{15} \times (\$3800 - \$500)$$
$$= \$3800 - \frac{5}{15} \times \$3300$$
$$= \$3800 - \$1100$$
$$= \$2700$$

**19.**
$$\frac{n(n+1)}{2} = \frac{6(6+1)}{2} = \frac{6(7)}{2} = 21$$
$$\frac{6}{21} + \frac{5}{21} + \frac{4}{21} = \frac{15}{21}$$
$$\$2240 - \$350 = \$1890$$
$$\frac{15}{21} \times \$1890 = \$1350 \text{ depreciation}$$
$$\$2240 - \$1350 = \$890$$
The book value at the end of 3 years is \$890.

**21.** $\dfrac{n(n+1)}{2}=\dfrac{8(8+1)}{2}=\dfrac{8(9)}{2}=36$

$\dfrac{8}{36}+\dfrac{7}{36}+\dfrac{6}{36}=\dfrac{21}{36}$

$\$4500-\$900=\$3600$

$\dfrac{21}{36}\times\$3600=\$2100$ depreciation

$\$4500-\$2100=\$2400$

The book value at the end of 3 years is $2400.

**23.** $\dfrac{n(n+1)}{2}=\dfrac{3(3+1)}{2}=\dfrac{3(4)}{2}=6$

$\$3900-\$480=\$3420$

| Year | Computation | Amount of Depreciation | Accumulated Depreciation | Book Value |
|---|---|---|---|---|
| 0 | – | – | – | $3900 |
| 1 | $\left(\frac{3}{6}\times\$3420\right)$ | $1710 | $1710 | $2190 |
| 2 | $\left(\frac{2}{6}\times\$3420\right)$ | $1140 | $2850 | $1050 |
| 3 | $\left(\frac{1}{6}\times\$3420\right)$ | $ 570 | $3420 | $ 480 |

**25.** $\dfrac{n(n+1)}{2}=\dfrac{6(6+1)}{2}=\dfrac{6(7)}{2}=21$

$\$10,800-\$2400=\$8400$

| Year | Computation | Amount of Depreciation | Accumulated Depreciation | Book Value |
|---|---|---|---|---|
| 0 | – | – | – | $10,800 |
| 1 | $\left(\frac{6}{21}\times\$8400\right)$ | $2400 | $2400 | $ 8,400 |
| 2 | $\left(\frac{5}{21}\times\$8400\right)$ | $2000 | $4400 | $ 6,400 |
| 3 | $\left(\frac{4}{21}\times\$8400\right)$ | $1600 | $6000 | $ 4,800 |
| 4 | $\left(\frac{3}{21}\times\$8400\right)$ | $1200 | $7200 | $ 3,600 |
| 5 | $\left(\frac{2}{21}\times\$8400\right)$ | $ 800 | $8000 | $ 2,800 |
| 6 | $\left(\frac{1}{21}\times\$8400\right)$ | $ 400 | $8400 | $ 2,400 |

**27.** Answers will vary.

**29.** $\dfrac{n(n+1)}{2}=\dfrac{10(10+1)}{2}=\dfrac{10(11)}{2}=55$

$\$3,200,000-\$650,000=\$2,550,000$

The depreciable value is $2,550,000.

$\dfrac{8}{55}\times\$2,550,000\approx\$370,909$

The depreciation for the third year is approximately $370,909.

**31.** $\dfrac{n(n+1)}{2}=\dfrac{10(10+1)}{2}=\dfrac{10(11)}{2}=55$

The depreciable amount is $12,800.

Year 1 Rate: $\dfrac{10}{55}$

Year 2 Rate: $\dfrac{9}{55}$

Year 3 Rate: $\dfrac{8}{55}$

Year 4 Rate: $\dfrac{7}{55}$

$\phantom{\text{Year 4 Rate:}}\dfrac{34}{55}$

$\$12,800-\dfrac{34}{55}\times\$12,800=\$4887$

The book value at the end of the fourth year is $4887.

**33.** $\dfrac{n(n+1)}{2}=\dfrac{6(6+1)}{2}=\dfrac{6(7)}{2}=21$

**(a)** $\dfrac{6}{21}\times\$25,200=\$7200$

The first year's depreciation is $7200.

**(b)** $\dfrac{5}{21}\times\$25,200=\$6000$

The second year's depreciation is $6000.

**35.** $\dfrac{n(n+1)}{2}=\dfrac{8(8+1)}{2}=\dfrac{8(9)}{2}=36$

$\$12,420-\$1800=\$10,620$

**(a)** The first year's depreciation fraction is $\dfrac{8}{36}$.

**(b)** $\dfrac{8}{36}\times\$10,620=\$2360$

The amount of depreciation in the first year is $2360.

**(c)** $\dfrac{36}{36}\times\$10,620=\$10,620$

The accumulated depreciation at the end of the eighth year is $10,620.

**(d)** $\dfrac{8}{36}+\dfrac{7}{36}+\dfrac{6}{36}+\dfrac{5}{36}=\dfrac{26}{36}$

$\dfrac{26}{36}\times\$10,620=\$7670$

$\$12,420-\$7670=\$4750$

The book value at the end of the fourth year is $4750.

## Supplementary Application Exercises on Depreciation

**1.** $\dfrac{\$2,600,000 - \$400,000}{40}$

$= \dfrac{\$2,200,000}{40} = \$55,000$

The annual depreciation is $55,000.

$\$2,600,000 - \$55,000 \times 10 = \$2,050,000$

The book value at the end of 10 years is $2,050,000.

**3.** $\dfrac{1}{5} \times 2 = .20 \times 2 = 20\% \times 2 = 40\%$

The double-declining-balance rate of depreciation is 40%.

$40\% \times \$18,500 = \$7400$

The depreciation in the first year is $7400.

**5.** $\dfrac{n(n+1)}{2} = \dfrac{6(6+1)}{2} = \dfrac{6(7)}{2} = 21$

$\$2850 - \$600 = \$2250$

| Year | Computation | Amount of Depreciation | Accumulated Depreciation | Book Value |
|------|-------------|------------------------|--------------------------|------------|
| 0 | – | – | – | $2850 |
| 1 | $\left(\frac{6}{21} \times \$2250\right)$ | $643 | $ 643 | $2207 |
| 2 | $\left(\frac{5}{21} \times \$2250\right)$ | $536 | $1179 | $1671 |
| 3 | $\left(\frac{4}{21} \times \$2250\right)$ | $429 | $1608 | $1242 |

The book value at the end of the third year is $1242.

**7.** $\dfrac{\$45,600 - \$8000}{10} = \dfrac{\$37,600}{10} = \$3760$

$3760 depreciation should be charged off each year.

**9.** Double-declining-balance rate is 10%.

| Year | Computation | Amount of Depreciation | Accumulated Depreciation | Book Value |
|------|-------------|------------------------|--------------------------|------------|
| 0 | – | – | – | $78,000 |
| 1 | $(10\% \times \$78,000)$ | $7800 | $7800 | $70,200 |
| 2 | $(10\% \times \$70,200)$ | $7020 | $14,820 | $63,180 |

The book value at the end of 2 years is $63,180.

**11.** $\dfrac{n(n+1)}{2} = \dfrac{4(4+1)}{2} = \dfrac{4(5)}{2} = 10$

$\$38,600 - \$4400 = \$34,200$

**11. (continued)**

Year 1:   $\frac{4}{10} \times \$34,200 = \$13,680$

Year 2:   $\frac{3}{10} \times \$34,200 = \$10,260$

Year 3:   $\frac{2}{10} \times \$34,200 = \$6840$

Year 4:   $\frac{1}{10} \times \$34,200 = \$3420$

**13.** $\$14,825 \times 5 = \$74,125$

The total cost is $74,125.

$\dfrac{n(n+1)}{2} = \dfrac{10(10+1)}{2} = \dfrac{10(11)}{2} = 55$

$\$14,825 - \$3000 = \$11,825$

$5 \times \$11,825 = \$59,125$

The depreciable amount is $59,125.

Year 1 Rate:   $\dfrac{10}{55}$

Year 2 Rate:   $\dfrac{9}{55}$

Year 3 Rate:   $\dfrac{8}{55}$

Year 4 Rate:   $\dfrac{7}{55}$

$\dfrac{34}{55}$

$\$74,125 - \frac{34}{55} \times \$59,125 = \$37,575$

The book value at the end of the fourth year is $37,575.

**15.** $\dfrac{n(n+1)}{2} = \dfrac{5(5+1)}{2} = \dfrac{5(6)}{2} = 15$

$\$21,600 - \$2400 = \$19,200$

| Year | Computation | Amount of Depreciation | Accumulated Depreciation | Book Value |
|------|-------------|------------------------|--------------------------|------------|
| 0 | – | – | – | $21,600 |
| 1 | $\left(\frac{5}{15} \times \$19,200\right)$ | $6400 | $ 6,400 | $15,200 |
| 2 | $\left(\frac{4}{15} \times \$19,200\right)$ | $5120 | $11,520 | $10,080 |

The book value at the end of the second year Is $10,080.

**17. (a)** $\dfrac{\$10,800 - \$1500}{10} = \dfrac{\$9300}{10} = \$930$

The annual depreciation is $930.

$6 \times \$930 = \$5580$

The accumulated depreciation at the end of the sixth year is $5580.

**(b)**   $\$10,800 - \$5580 = \$5220$

The book value at the end of the sixth year is $5220.

## 14.4 Depreciation: Units-of-Production Method

**1.** Depreciation per Unit
$$\frac{\$16,800 - \$1800}{20,000} = \frac{\$15,000}{20,000} = \$.75$$

**3.** Depreciation per Unit
$$\frac{\$3750 - \$250}{120,000} = \frac{\$3500}{120,000} = \$.029$$

**5.** Depreciation per Unit
$$\frac{\$37,500 - \$7500}{125,000} = \frac{\$30,000}{125,000} = \$.24$$

**7.** Depreciation per Unit
$$\frac{\$175,000 - \$25,000}{5000} = \frac{\$150,000}{5000} = \$30$$

**9.** Amount of Depreciation
$$55,000 \times \$.46 = \$25,300$$

**11.** Amount of Depreciation
$$32,000 \times \$.54 = \$17,280$$

**13.** Amount of Depreciation
$$15,000 \times \$.185 = \$2775$$

**15.** Amount of Depreciation
$$22,200 \times \$.14 = \$3108$$

**17.** Answers will vary.

**19.** $\dfrac{\$6800 - \$500}{5000} = \dfrac{\$6300}{5000} = \$1.26$

The depreciation per unit is $1.26.

| Year | Computation | Amount of Depreciation | Accumulated Depreciation | Book Value |
|------|-------------|-----------------------|--------------------------|------------|
| 0 | – | – | – | $6800 |
| 1 | $(1350 \times \$1.26)$ | $1701 | $1701 | $5099 |
| 2 | $(1820 \times \$1.26)$ | $2293 | $3994 | $2806 |
| 3 | $(730 \times \$1.26)$ | $ 920 | $4914 | $1886 |
| 4 | $(1100 \times \$1.26)$ | $1386 | $6300 | $ 500 |

## 14.5 Depreciation: Modified Accelerated Cost Recovery System

**1.** 19.2%

**3.** 6.56%

**5.** 20%

**7.** 3.636%

**9.** 5.76%

**11.** 2.564%

**13.** First Year's Depreciation
$$14.29\% \times \$12,250 = \$1751$$

**15.** First Year's Depreciation
$$10.00\% \times \$430,500 = \$43,050$$

**17.** First Year's Depreciation
$$10.00\% \times \$48,000 = \$4800$$

**19.** Book Value at the end of the first year
$$\$9380 - 33.33\% \times 9380 = \$6254$$

**21.** Book Value at the end of the first year
$$\$18,800 - 10.00\% \times 18,800 = \$16,920$$

**23.** Year 1 Rate: 20.00%
Year 2 Rate: 32.00%
Year 3 Rate: <u>19.20%</u>
71.20%

Book Value at the end of 3 years
$$\$9570 - 71.20\% \times \$9570 = \$2756$$

**25.** Year 1 Rate: 3.485%
Year 2 Rate: 3.636%
Year 3 Rate: <u>3.636%</u>
10.757%

Book Value at the end of 3 years
$$\$136,800 - 10.757\% \times \$136,800 = \$122,084$$

**27.** Cost: $10,980, Recovery period: 3 years

| Year | Computation | Amount of Depreciation | Accumulated Depreciation | Book Value |
|------|-------------|------------------------|--------------------------|------------|
| 0 | – | – | – | $10,980 |
| 1 | $(33.33\% \times \$10,980)$ | $3660 | $ 3,660 | $ 7,320 |
| 2 | $(44.45\% \times \$10,980)$ | $4881 | $ 8,541 | $ 2,439 |
| 3 | $(14.81\% \times \$10,980)$ | $1626 | $10,167 | $ 813 |
| 4 | $(7.41\% \times \$10,980)$ | $ 813* | $10,980 | $0 |

*Difference is due to rounding in previous years.

**29.** Cost: $122,700, Recovery period: 10 years

| Year | Computation | Amount of Depreciation | Accumulated Depreciation | Book Value |
|------|-------------|------------------------|--------------------------|------------|
| 0 | – | – | – | $122,700 |
| 1 | $(10.00\% \times \$122,700)$ | $12,270 | $ 12,270 | $110,430 |
| 2 | $(18.00\% \times \$122,700)$ | $22,086 | $ 34,356 | $ 88,344 |
| 3 | $(14.40\% \times \$122,700)$ | $17,669 | $ 52,025 | $ 70,675 |
| 4 | $(11.52\% \times \$122,700)$ | $14,135 | $ 66,160 | $ 56,540 |
| 5 | $(9.22\% \times \$122,700)$ | $11,313 | $ 77,473 | $ 45,227 |
| 6 | $(7.37\% \times \$122,700)$ | $ 9043 | $ 86,516 | $ 36,184 |
| 7 | $(6.55\% \times \$122,700)$ | $ 8037 | $ 94,553 | $ 28,147 |
| 8 | $(6.55\% \times \$122,700)$ | $ 8037 | $102,590 | $ 20,110 |
| 9 | $(6.56\% \times \$122,700)$ | $ 8049 | $110,639 | $ 12,061 |
| 10 | $(6.55\% \times \$122,700)$ | $ 8037 | $118,676 | $ 4,024 |
| 11 | $(3.28\% \times \$122,700)$ | $ 4024* | $122,700 | $0 |

**31.** Answers will vary.

**33.** Cost: $74,125, Recovery period: 10 years

The eighth year of a 10-year recovery period
has a depreciation rate of 6.55%
$6.55\% \times \$74,125 = \$4855$
The depreciation in year 8 is $4855.

**35.** Cost: $1700, Recovery period: 5 years

Year 1 Rate: 　20.00%
Year 2 Rate: 　32.00%
Year 3 Rate: 　19.20%
　　　　　　　71.20%

$\$1700 - 71.20\% \times \$1700 = \$490$
The book value at the end of the third year
is $490.

**37.** Cost: $860,000, Recovery period: 39 years

Year 1: 　$2.461\% \times \$860,000 = \$21,165$
Year 2: 　$2.564\% \times \$860,000 = \$22,050$
Year 3: 　$2.564\% \times \$860,000 = \$22,050$
Year 4: 　$2.564\% \times \$860,000 = \$22,050$
Year 5: 　$2.564\% \times \$860,000 = \$22,050$

## Case Study

**1.** $\dfrac{\$285,000 - \$0}{5} = \dfrac{\$285,000}{5} = \$57,000$

The annual depreciation is $57,000.

$\$285,000 - \$57,000 \times 3 = \$114,000$
The book value at the end of 3 years is
$114,000.

**2.** Double-declining-balance rate is 40%.

| Year | Computation | Amount of Depreciation | Accumulated Depreciation | Book Value |
|------|-------------|------------------------|--------------------------|------------|
| 0 | – | – | – | $285,000 |
| 1 | $(40\% \times \$285,000)$ | $114,000 | $114,000 | $171,000 |
| 2 | $(40\% \times \$171,000)$ | $ 68,400 | $182,400 | $102,600 |
| 3 | $(40\% \times \$102,600)$ | $ 41,040 | $223,440 | $ 61,560 |

The book value at the end of the third year
is $61,650.

**3.** $\dfrac{n(n+1)}{2} = \dfrac{5(5+1)}{2} = \dfrac{5(6)}{2} = 15$

The depreciable amount is $285,000.

Year 1 Rate: $\dfrac{5}{15}$

Year 2 Rate: $\dfrac{4}{15}$

Year 3 Rate: $\dfrac{3}{15}$

　　　　　　$\dfrac{12}{15}$

$\dfrac{12}{15} \times \$285,000 = \$228,000$

The accumulated depreciation at the end of
3 years is $228,000.

**4.** Straight-line depreciation-Year 4
$\dfrac{\$285,000 - \$0}{5} = \dfrac{\$285,000}{5} = \$57,000$

Double-declining-balance depreciation-Year 4
$40\% \times \$61,560 = \$24,624$

Sum-of-the-Years'-Digits Depreciation-Year 4
$\dfrac{2}{15} \times \$285,000 = \$38,000$

## Case in Point Summary Exercise

1. $\dfrac{\$26,500 - \$4500}{5} = \dfrac{\$22,000}{5} = \$4400$

   The annual depreciation is $4400.

   $\$26,500 - \$4400 \times 3 = \$13,300$
   The book value after 3 years is $13,300.

2. $\dfrac{1}{5} \times 2 = .20 \times 2 = 20\% \times 2 = 40\%$

   The double-declining-balance rate of depreciation is 40%.

| Year | Computation | Amount of Depreciation | Accumulated Depreciation | Book Value |
|------|-------------|------------------------|--------------------------|------------|
| 0 | – | – | – | $26,500 |
| 1 | $(40\% \times \$26,500)$ | $10,600 | $10,600 | $15,900 |
| 2 | $(40\% \times \$15,900)$ | $ 6,360 | $16,960 | $ 9,540 |
| 3 | $(40\% \times \$9,540)$ | $ 3,816 | $20,776 | $ 5,724 |

The book value at the end of 3 years is $5724.

3. The company must use the MACRS method of depreciation. A 5-year property recovery class is appropriate.

4. Year 1:  $20.00\% \times \$118,350 = \$23,670$
   Year 2:  $32.00\% \times \$118,350 = \$37,872$
   Year 3:  $19.20\% \times \$118,350 = \$22,723$

5. $\$118,350 - \$23,670 - \$37,872 - \$22,723$
   $= \$34,085$

   The book value at the end of the third year is $34,085.

6. Year 1 Rate:  20.00%
   Year 2 Rate:  32.00%
   Year 3 Rate:  <u>19.20%</u>
                 71.20%

   The percent of the total depreciation that is taken in the first three years is 71.2%.

7. No additional depreciation is allowed after book value reaches salvage value.

## Chapter 14   Test

1. Straight-line rate of depreciation

   $\dfrac{1}{4} = .25 = 25\%$

   Double-declining-balance rate of depreciation

   $\dfrac{1}{4} \times 2 = .25 \times 2 = 25\% \times 2 = 50\%$

   Sum-of-the-Years'-Digits
   Depreciation Fraction
   $\dfrac{n(n+1)}{2} = \dfrac{4(4+1)}{2} = \dfrac{4(5)}{2} = 10; \ r = \dfrac{4}{10}$

2. Straight-line rate of depreciation

   $\dfrac{1}{5} = .20 = 20\%$

   Double-declining-balance rate of depreciation

   $\dfrac{1}{5} \times 2 = .20 \times 2 = 20\% \times 2 = 40\%$

   Sum-of-the-Years'-Digits
   Depreciation Fraction
   $\dfrac{n(n+1)}{2} = \dfrac{5(5+1)}{2} = \dfrac{5(6)}{2} = 15; \ r = \dfrac{5}{15}$

3. Straight-line rate of depreciation

   $\dfrac{1}{8} = .125 = 12.5\%$

   Double-declining-balance rate of depreciation

   $\dfrac{1}{8} \times 2 = .125 \times 2 = 12.5\% \times 2 = 25\%$

   Sum-of-the-Years'-Digits
   Depreciation Fraction
   $\dfrac{n(n+1)}{2} = \dfrac{8(8+1)}{2} = \dfrac{8(9)}{2} = 36; \ r = \dfrac{8}{36}$

4. Straight-line rate of depreciation

   $\dfrac{1}{20} = 0.05 = 5\%$

   Double-declining-balance rate of depreciation

   $\dfrac{1}{20} \times 2 = 0.05 \times 2 = 5\% \times 2 = 10\%$

   Sum-of-the-Years'-Digits
   Depreciation Fraction
   $\dfrac{n(n+1)}{2} = \dfrac{20(20+1)}{2} = \dfrac{20(21)}{2} = 210; \ r = \dfrac{20}{210}$

**5.** $\dfrac{\$82,000-\$3000}{10}=\dfrac{\$79,000}{10}=\$7900$

The annual depreciation is $7900.

**6.** Double-declining-balance rate is 25%.

| Year | Computation | Amount of Depreciation | Accumulated Depreciation | Book Value |
|------|-------------|------------------------|--------------------------|------------|
| 0 | – | – | – | $38,000 |
| 1 | $(25\%\times\$38,000)$ | $9500 | $9500 | $28,500 |
| 2 | $(25\%\times\$28,500)$ | $7125 | $16,625 | $21,375 |

The book value at the end of 2 years is $21,375.

**7.** $\dfrac{n(n+1)}{2}=\dfrac{4(4+1)}{2}=\dfrac{4(5)}{2}=10$

$8250-\$1500=\$6750$

Year 1:   $\dfrac{4}{10}\times\$6750=\$2700$

Year 2:   $\dfrac{3}{10}\times\$6750=\$2025$

Year 3:   $\dfrac{2}{10}\times\$6750=\$1350$

Year 4:   $\dfrac{1}{10}\times\$6750=\$675$

**8.** Cost: $56,000,  Recovery period: 15 years

The third year of a 15-year recovery period has a depreciation rate of 8.55%.
$8.55\%\times\$56,000=\$4788$
The depreciation in the third year is $4788.

**9.** $\dfrac{\$74,000-\$12,000}{20}=\dfrac{\$62,000}{20}=\$3100$

The annual depreciation is $3100.

$\$74,000-\$3100\times10=\$43,000$
The book value at the end of 10 years is $43,000.

**10.** $\dfrac{n(n+1)}{2}=\dfrac{10(10+1)}{2}=\dfrac{10(11)}{2}=55$

$4\times\$2800=\$11,200$
The depreciable amount is $11,200.

Year 1 Rate:   $\dfrac{10}{55}$

Year 2 Rate:   $\dfrac{9}{55}$

Year 3 Rate:   $\dfrac{8}{55}$

$\dfrac{27}{55}$

$\$11,200-\dfrac{27}{55}\times\$11,200=\$5702$

The book value at the end of the third year is $5702.

**11. (a)** $\dfrac{\$20,100-\$1500}{30,000}=\dfrac{\$18,600}{30,000}=\$.62$

The depreciation per unit is $.62.

**(b)**

| Year | Computation | Amount of Depreciation | Accumulated Depreciation | Book Value |
|------|-------------|------------------------|--------------------------|------------|
| 0 | – | – | – | $20,100 |
| 1 | $(7800\times\$.62)$ | $4836 | $ 4,836 | $15,264 |
| 2 | $(4300\times\$.62)$ | $2666 | $ 7,502 | $12,598 |
| 3 | $(4850\times\$.62)$ | $3007 | $10,509 | $ 9,591 |
| 4 | $(7600\times\$.62)$ | $4712 | $15,221 | $ 4,879 |

**12.** Cost: $2,800,000,  Recovery period: 39 years

Year 1 Rate:   2.461%
Year 2 Rate:   2.564%
Year 3 Rate:   2.564%
Year 4 Rate:   2.564%
Year 5 Rate:   2.564%
$\overline{\qquad\quad 12.717\%}$

$\$2,800,000-12.717\%\times\$2,800,000$
$=\$2,443,924$

The book value at the end of the fifth year is $2,443,924.

### 15.1 The Income Statement

1. Net sales = Gross sales − Returns = $685,900 − $2350 = $683,550

   (a) Gross profit = Net sales − Cost of goods sold = $683,550 − $367,200 = $316,350

   (b) Net income before taxes = Gross profit − Operating expenses = $316,350 − $228,300 = $88,050

   (c) Net income after taxes = Income before taxes − Income taxes = $88,050 − $22,700 = $65,350

3.

| JILL'S FASHIONS INCOME STATEMENT YEAR ENDING DECEMBER 31 | | |
|---|---:|---:|
| Gross Sales | | $852,300 |
| Returns | | $42,800 |
| Net Sales | | $809,500 |
| Inventory, January 1 | $174,690 | |
| Cost of Goods Purchased | $345,790 | |
| Freight | $18,107 | |
| Total Cost of Goods Purchased | $363,897 | |
| Total of Goods Available for Sale | $538,587 | |
| Inventory, December 31 | $158,200 | |
| Cost of Goods Sold | | $380,387 |
| Gross Profit | | $429,113 |
| Expenses | | |
| Salaries and Wages | $168,240 | |
| Rent | $48,200 | |
| Advertising | $24,300 | |
| Utilities | $11,600 | |
| Taxes on Inventory and Payroll | $13,880 | |
| Miscellaneous Expenses | $21,900 | |
| Total Expenses | | $288,120 |
| Net Income Before Taxes | | $140,993 |
| Income Taxes | | $34,800 |
| Net Income After Taxes | | $106,193 |

5. Answers will vary.

## 15.2 Analyzing the Income Statement

**1.** Percent cost of goods sold

$$\frac{\$198,400}{\$439,000} = 45.2\%$$

Percent operating expenses

$$\frac{\$143,180}{\$439,000} = 32.6\%$$

**3.** Percent cost of goods sold

$$\frac{\$243,570}{\$480,300} = 50.7\%$$

Percent operating expenses

$$\frac{\$140,450}{\$480,300} = 29.2\%$$

**5.** Gooden Drugs

|  | Amount | Percent | Industry Percent from Table 17.1 |
|---|---|---|---|
| Net sales | $850,000 | 100.0% | 100.0% |
| Cost of goods sold | $570,350 | 67.1% | 67.9% |
| Gross profit | $279,650 | 32.9% | 32.1% |
| Wages | $106,250 | 12.5% | 12.3% |
| Rent | $ 21,250 | 2.5% | 2.4% |
| Advertising | $ 12,750 | 1.5% | 1.4% |
| Total expenses | $209,100 | 24.6% | 23.5% |
| Net income before taxes | $ 70,550 | 8.3% | 8.6% |

**7.** Answers will vary.

**9.** Hernandez Nursery Comparative Income Statement

|  | This Year | | Last Year | |
|---|---|---|---|---|
|  | Amount | Percent | Amount | Percent |
| Gross sales | $1,856,000 | 100.3% | $1,692,000 | 100.7% |
| Returns | $ 6,000 | .3% | $ 12,000 | .7% |
| Net sales | $1,850,000 | 100.0% | $1,680,000 | 100.0% |
| Cost of goods sold | $1,102,000 | 59.6% | $ 950,000 | 56.5% |
| Gross profit | $ 748,000 | 40.4% | $ 730,000 | 43.5% |
| Wages | $ 252,000 | 13.6% | $ 248,000 | 14.8% |
| Rent | $ 82,000 | 4.4% | $ 78,000 | 4.6% |
| Advertising | $ 111,000 | 6.0% | $ 122,000 | 7.3% |
| Utilities | $ 32,000 | 1.7% | $ 17,000 | 1.0% |
| Taxes on inventory, payroll | $ 17,000 | .9% | $ 18,000 | 1.1% |
| Miscellaneous expenses | $ 62,000 | 3.4% | $ 58,000 | 3.5% |
| Total expenses | $ 556,000 | 30.1% | $ 541,000 | 32.2% |
| Net income before taxes | $ 192,000 | 10.4% | $ 189,000 | 11.3% |

**11.**

| Type of Store | Cost of Goods | Gross Profit | Total Operating Expenses | Net Income | Wages | Rent | Advertising |
|---|---|---|---|---|---|---|---|
| Women's apparel | 66.4% | 33.6% | 25.3% | 8.3% | 8.4% | 6.5% | 1.9% |
| | 64.8% | 35.2% | 23.4% | 11.7% | 7.9% | 4.9% | 1.8% |

Cost of goods, total operating expenses, and rent are high, resulting in a low net income.

**13.** Answers will vary.

## 15.3 The Balance Sheet

**1.** (Note that figures are in millions of dollars.)

| BROOKSHIRE'S GROCERY BALANCE SHEET DECEMBER 31 | | |
|---|---|---|
| **Assets** | | |
| Current Assets | | |
| Cash | $273 | |
| Notes Receivable | $312 | |
| Accounts Receivable | $264 | |
| Inventory | $180 | |
| Total Current Assets | | $1029 |
| Plant Assets | | |
| Land | $466 | |
| Buildings | $290 | |
| Fixtures | $ 28 | |
| Total Plant Assets | | $ 784 |
| Total Assets | | $1813 |
| **Liabilities** | | |
| Current Liabilities | | |
| Notes Payable | $312 | |
| Accounts Payable | $ 63 | |
| Total Current Liabilities | | $ 375 |
| Long-term Liabilities | | |
| Mortgages Payable | $212 | |
| Long-term Notes Payable | $ 55 | |
| Total Long-term Liabilities | | $ 267 |
| Total Liabilities | | $ 642 |
| **Owner's Equity** | | |
| Owner's Equity | | $1171 |
| TOTAL LIABILITIES AND OWNER'S EQUITY | | $1813 |

**3.** Answers will vary.

## 15.4 Analyzing the Balance Sheet

**1.** (Note that figures are in thousands of dollars.)

| | This Year | | Last Year | |
|---|---|---|---|---|
| PLEASURE YACHT, INC.<br>COMPARATIVE BALANCE SHEET | Amount | Percent | Amount | Percent |
| **Assets** | | | | |
| Current Assets | | | | |
| Cash | $ 52,000 | 13.0% | $ 42,000 | 13.1% |
| Notes Receivable | $  8,000 | 2.0% | $  6,000 | 1.9% |
| Accounts Receivable | $148,000 | 37.0% | $120,000 | 37.5% |
| Inventory | $153,000 | 38.3% | $120,000 | 37.5% |
| Total Current Assets | $361,000 | 90.3% | $288,000 | 90.0% |
| Plant Assets | | | | |
| Land | $ 10,000 | 2.5% | $  8,000 | 2.5% |
| Buildings | $ 14,000 | 3.5% | $ 11,000 | 3.4% |
| Fixtures | $ 15,000 | 3.8% | $ 13,000 | 4.1% |
| Total Plant Assets | $ 39,000 | 9.8% | $ 32,000 | 10.0% |
| Total Assets | $400,000 | 100.0% | $320,000 | 100.0% |
| **Liabilities** | | | | |
| Current Liabilities | | | | |
| Accounts Payable | $  3,000 | .8% | $  4,000 | 1.3% |
| Notes Payable | $201,000 | 50.3% | $152,000 | 47.5% |
| Total current liabilities | $204,000 | 51.0% | $156,000 | 48.8% |
| Long-term liabilities | | | | |
| Mortgages payable | $ 20,000 | 5.0% | $ 16,000 | 5.0% |
| Long-term notes payable | $ 58,000 | 14.5% | $ 42,000 | 13.1% |
| Total long-term liabilities | $ 78,000 | 19.5% | $ 58,000 | 18.1% |
| Total liabilities | $282,000 | 70.5% | $214,000 | 66.9% |
| Owner's equity | $118,000 | 29.5% | $106,000 | 33.1% |
| Total liabilities and owner's equity | $400,000 | 100.0% | $320,000 | 100.0% |

**3. (a)** Current Ratio

$$\frac{\$361,000}{\$204,000} = 1.77$$

**(b)** Liquid Assets

$$\$52,000 + \$8000 + \$148,000 = \$208,000$$

Acid-test Ratio

$$\frac{\$208,000}{\$204,000} = 1.02$$

**(c)** No, the current ratio is low.

**5. (a)** Current Ratio

$$\frac{\$2,210,350}{\$1,232,500} = 1.79$$

**(b)** Liquid Assets

$$\$480,500 + \$279,050 = \$759,550$$

Acid-test Ratio

$$\frac{\$759,550}{\$1,232,500} = .62$$

**(c)** No, the acid-test ratio is low.

**7.-8.** Western Auto Supply (in thousands)

| | This Year | | Last Year | |
| --- | --- | --- | --- | --- |
| | Amount | Percent | Amount | Percent |
| Current assets | | | | |
| Cash | $12,000 | 15.0% | $15,000 | 20.0% |
| Notes Receivable | $ 4,000 | 5.0% | $ 6,000 | 8.0% |
| Accounts Receivable | $22,000 | 27.5% | $18,000 | 24.0% |
| Inventory | $26,000 | 32.5% | $24,000 | 32.0% |
| Total current assets | $64,000 | 80.0% | $63,000 | 84.0% |
| Total plant assets | $16,000 | 20.0% | $12,000 | 16.0% |
| Total assets | $80,000 | 100.0% | $75,000 | 100.0% |
| Total current liabilities | $30,000 | 37.5% | $25,000 | 33.3% |

**7.** Current Ratio

$$\frac{\$64,000}{\$30,000} = 2.13$$

Liquid Assets

$$\$12,000 + \$4000 + \$22,000 = \$38,000$$

Acid-test Ratio

$$\frac{\$38,000}{\$30,000} = 1.27$$

**9.** Average owner's equity

$$\frac{\$845,000 + \$928,500}{2} = \$886,750$$

Ratio of net income after taxes to average owner's equity

$$\frac{\$54,400}{\$886,750} \approx .061 = 6.1\%$$

**11.** Current Ratio

$$\frac{\$268,700}{\$294,200} = .91, \text{ which is too low}$$

Acid-test Ratio

$$\frac{\$109,900}{\$294,200} = .37, \text{ which is also too low}$$

**13.** Answers will vary.

## Case Study

1.

| SMARTER'S BICYCLE SHOP<br>INCOME STATEMENT<br>YEAR ENDING DECEMBER 31 | | | |
|---|---|---|---|
| Gross Sales | | | $238,300 |
| Returns | | | $3,600 |
| Net Sales | | | $234,700 |
| Inventory, January 1 | | $53,400 | |
| Cost of Goods Purchased | $98,500 | | |
| Freight | $2,300 | | |
| Total Cost of Goods Purchased | | $100,800 | |
| Total of Goods Available for Sale | | $154,200 | |
| Inventory, December 31 | | $48,900 | |
| Cost of Goods Sold | | | $105,300 |
| Gross Profit | | | $129,400 |
| Expenses | | | |
| Salaries and Wages | | $78,690 | |
| Rent & Utilities | | $11,800 | |
| Advertising | | $3,200 | |
| Miscellaneous Expenses | | $4,800 | |
| Total Expenses | | | $98,490 |
| Net Income Before Taxes | | | $30,910 |
| Income Taxes | | | $3,600 |
| Net Income After Taxes | | | $27,310 |

**2.**

| SMARTER'S BICYCLE SHOP | | | |
|---|---|---|---|
| BALANCE SHEET | | | |
| DECEMBER 31 | | | |

| Assets | | | |
|---|---|---|---|
| Current Assets | | | |
| Cash | | $62,000 | |
| Notes Receivable | | $ 0 | |
| Accounts Receivable | | $10,700 | |
| Inventory | | $48,900 | |
| Total Current Assets | | | $121,600 |
| Plant Assets | | | |
| Land and Buildings | | $ 0 | |
| Improvements | | $ 41,500 | |
| Total Plant Assets | | | $ 41,500 |
| Total Assets | | | $163,100 |

| Liabilities | | | |
|---|---|---|---|
| Current Liabilities | | | |
| Notes Payable | | $ 4,300 | |
| Accounts Payable | | $14,800 | |
| Total Current Liabilities | | | $19,100 |
| Long-term Liabilities | | | |
| Mortgages Payable | | $ 0 | |
| Long-term Notes Payable | | $12,300 | |
| Total Long-term Liabilities | | | $12,300 |
| Total Liabilities | | | $ 31,400 |

| Owner's Equity | | | |
|---|---|---|---|
| Owner's Equity | | $131,700 | |
| TOTAL LIABILITIES AND OWNER'S EQUITY | | | $163,100 |

## Case in Point Summary Exercise

1.

| DARLING CONFECTIONARY | | | |
|---|---|---|---|
| **INCOME STATEMENT** | | | |
| **YEAR ENDING DECEMBER 31** | | | |
| Gross Sales | | | $834,200 |
| Returns | | | $4,500 |
| Net Sales | | | $829,700 |
| Inventory, January 1 | | $84,200 | |
| Cost of Goods Purchased | $346,500 | | |
| Freight | $9,100 | | |
| Total Cost of Goods Purchased | | $355,600 | |
| Total of Goods Available for Sale | | $439,800 | |
| Inventory, December 31 | | $96,200 | |
| Cost of Goods Sold | | | $343,600 |
| Gross Profit | | | $486,100 |
| Expenses | | | |
| Salaries and Wages | | $193,200 | |
| Rent & Utilities | | $68,900 | |
| Advertising | | $13,900 | |
| Utilities | | | |
| Insurance and Payroll Taxes | | $19,400 | |
| Miscellaneous Expenses | | $18,700 | |
| Total Expenses | | | $314,100 |
| Net Income Before Taxes | | | $172,000 |
| Income Taxes | | | $37,800 |
| Net Income After Taxes | | | $134,200 |

**2.**

| DARLING CONFECTIONARY<br>BALANCE SHEET<br>DECEMBER 31 | | | |
|---|---|---|---|
| Assets | | | |
| Current Assets | | | |
|   Cash | | $84,500 | |
|   Notes Receivable | | $ 0 | |
|   Accounts Receivable | | $ 2,100 | |
|   Inventory | | $96,200 | |
|     Total Current Assets | | | $182,800 |
| Plant Assets | | | |
|   Land and Buildings | | $186,500 | |
|   Improvements | | $ 82,100 | |
|     Total Plant Assets | | | $268,600 |
|   Total Assets | | | $451,400 |
| Liabilities | | | |
| Current Liabilities | | | |
|   Notes Payable | | $ 4,900 | |
|   Accounts Payable | | $58,400 | |
|     Total Current Liabilities | | | $ 63,300 |
| Long-term Liabilities | | | |
|   Mortgages Payable | | $134,200 | |
|   Long-term Notes Payable | | $ 0 | |
|     Total Long-term Liabilities | | | $134,200 |
|   Total Liabilities | | | $197,500 |
| Owner's Equity | | | |
| Owner's Equity | | $253,900 | |
|     TOTAL LIABILITIES AND<br>    OWNER'S EQUITY | | | $451,400 |

## Chapter 15   Test

1.

| BENNI'S FISH COMPANY INCOME STATEMENT YEAR ENDING DECEMBER 31 | | | |
|---|---|---|---|
| Gross Sales | | | $756,300 |
| Returns | | | $285 |
| Net Sales | | | $756,015 |
| Inventory, January 1 | | $92,370 | |
| Cost of Goods Purchased | $465,920 | | |
| Freight | $1,205 | | |
| Total Cost of Goods Purchased | | $467,125 | |
| Total of Goods Available for Sale | | $559,495 | |
| Inventory, December 31 | | $82,350 | |
| Cost of Goods Sold | | | $477,145 |
| Gross Profit | | | $278,870 |
| Expenses | | | |
| Salaries and Wages | | $84,900 | |
| Rent | | $42,500 | |
| Advertising | | $2,800 | |
| Utilities | | $18,950 | |
| Taxes on Inventory and Payroll | | $4,500 | |
| Miscellaneous Expenses | | $18,400 | |
| Total Expenses | | | $172,050 |
| Net Income Before Taxes | | | $106,820 |
| Income Taxes | | | $25,450 |
| Net Income After Taxes | | | $81,370 |

**2.**

| China Imports, Inc. Comparative Income Statement (in thousands) | | | Increase or (Decrease) | |
|---|---|---|---|---|
| | This Year | Last Year | Amount | Percent |
| Net Sales | $95,000 | $60,000 | $35,000 | 58.3% |
| Cost of Goods Sold | $63,000 | $40,000 | $23,000 | 57.5% |
| Gross Profit | $16,000 | $12,000 | $ 4,000 | 33.3% |

**3.** Alberta Heights Service Station

| | Amount (in thousands) | Percent | Average Percent |
|---|---|---|---|
| Net sales | $1200 | 100.0% | 100.0% |
| Cost of goods sold | $ 875 | 72.9% | 76.8% |
| Gross profit | $ 325 | 27.1% | 23.2% |
| Net Income | $ 112 | 9.3% | 6.3% |
| Wages | $ 129 | 10.8% | 8.5% |
| Rent | $ 72 | 6.0% | 2.3% |
| Total expenses | $213 | 17.8% | 16.9% |

**4. (a)** Current Ratio

$$\frac{\$2,482,500}{\$1,800,200} = 1.38$$

**(b)** Acid-test Ratio

$$\frac{\$850,000+\$680,100}{\$1,800,200}$$
$$= \frac{\$1,530,100}{\$1,800,200} = .85$$

**5. (a)** Current Ratio

$$\frac{\$154,000}{\$146,500} = 1.05$$

**(b)** Acid-test Ratio

$$\frac{\$22,000+\$32,500}{\$146,500}$$
$$= \frac{\$54,500}{\$146,500} = .37$$

**6.** Average owner's equity

$$\frac{\$472,600+\$514,980}{2} = \$493,790$$

Ratio of net income after taxes to average owners' equity

$$\frac{\$148,200}{\$493,790} = 30.0\%$$

**7.** Average owner's equity

$$\frac{\$28,346,000+\$36,450,000}{2} = \$32,398,000$$
$$= \$32,398 \text{ (in thousands)}$$

Ratio of net income after taxes to average owners' equity

$$\frac{\$8465}{\$32,398} = 26.1\%$$

## 16.1 Frequency Distributions and Graphs

**1.** 2100; 9.1 billion

**3.** $8.9 \times 0.24 = 2.136$
There will be 2.136 billion Chinese.

$8.9 \times .04 = .356$
There will be .356 billion Americans.

**5.** The percent of people divorced is increasing during the past 50+ years.

**7.-12.**

| Number of Credits Completed | Number of Employees |
|---|---|
| 0-24 | 4 |
| 25-49 | 3 |
| 50-74 | 6 |
| 75-99 | 3 |
| 100-124 | 5 |
| 125-149 | 9 |

**13.**

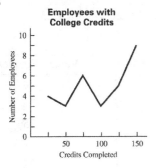

**15.** $6 + 3 + 5 + 9 = 23$
23 employees completed 50 or more credits.

**17.** $4 + 3 = 7$
7 employees completed from 0 to 49 credits.

**18.-26.**

| Sales (in thousands) | Frequency |
|---|---|
| 260-269 | 1 |
| 270-279 | 2 |
| 280-289 | 2 |
| 290-299 | 1 |
| 300-309 | 3 |
| 310-319 | 2 |
| 320-329 | 5 |
| 330-339 | 6 |
| 340-349 | 4 |

**27.**

**29.** $3 + 2 + 5 + 6 + 4 = 20$
Sales equaled or exceeded $300,000 for 20 weeks.

**31.-37.**

| Score | Frequency |
|---|---|
| 30-39 | 1 |
| 40-49 | 6 |
| 50-59 | 13 |
| 60-69 | 22 |
| 70-79 | 17 |
| 80-89 | 13 |
| 90-99 | 8 |

**39.** $17 + 13 + 8 = 38$
38 students passed the test.

**41.** $1 + 6 + 13 + 22 = 42$
42 students failed the test.

**43.** $\dfrac{72°}{360°} = .20 = 20\%$

**45.** $.10 \times 360° = 36°$

**47.** $\dfrac{\$70}{\$1400} = .05 = 5\%$

$.05 \times 360° = 18°$

**49.**

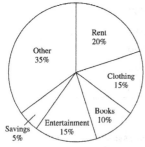

**51.** $5\% + 15\% = 20\%$

Reuben spent 20% on savings and entertainment.

**53.**

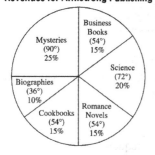

**55.**

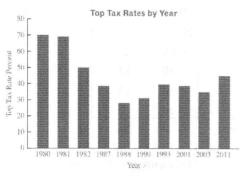

**57.** Answers will vary.

## 16.2  Mean, Median, and Mode

**1.** Mean

$\dfrac{3.5 + 1.1 + 2.8 + .8 + 4.1}{5} = 2.46 \approx 2.5$

**3.** Mean

$\dfrac{40 + 51 + 59 + 62 + 68 + 73 + 49 + 80}{8}$

$= 60.25 \approx 60.3$

**5.** Mean

$\dfrac{21,900 + 22,850 + 24,930 + 29,710 + 28,340 + 40,000}{6}$

$= 27,955$

**7.** Mean

$\dfrac{10.6 + 12.5 + 11.7 + 9.6 + 10.3 + 9.6 + 10.9 + 6.4 + 2.3 + 4.1}{10}$

$= 8.8$

**9.** Answers will vary.

**11.**

| Value | Frequency | Value × Frequency |
|-------|-----------|-------------------|
| 9     | 3         | 27                |
| 12    | 4         | 48                |
| 18    | 2         | 36                |
|       | 9         | 111               |

Weighted Mean $= \dfrac{111}{9} = 12.3$

**13.**

| Value | Frequency | Value × Frequency |
|-------|-----------|-------------------|
| 12    | 4         | 48                |
| 13    | 2         | 26                |
| 15    | 5         | 75                |
| 19    | 3         | 57                |
| 22    | 1         | 22                |
| 23    | 5         | 115               |
|       | 20        | 343               |

Weighted Mean $= \dfrac{343}{20} = 17.2$

**15.**

| Value | Frequency | Value × Frequency |
|-------|-----------|-------------------|
| 104 | 6 | 624 |
| 112 | 14 | 1568 |
| 115 | 21 | 2415 |
| 119 | 13 | 1547 |
| 123 | 22 | 2706 |
| 127 | 6 | 762 |
| 132 | 9 | 1188 |
| | 91 | 10,810 |

$$\text{Weighted Mean} = \frac{10,810}{91} = 118.8$$

**17.**

| Credits | Grade | Grade × Credits |
|---------|-------|-----------------|
| 4 | B($= 3$) | $4 \times 3 = 12$ |
| 2 | A($= 4$) | $2 \times 4 = 8$ |
| 5 | C($= 2$) | $5 \times 2 = 10$ |
| 1 | F($= 0$) | $1 \times 0 = 0$ |
| 3 | B($= 3$) | $3 \times 3 = 9$ |
| 15 | | 39 |

$$\text{GPA} = \frac{39}{15} = 2.6$$

**19.** 85, 98, 114, 122, 140
Median $= 114$

**21.** 100, 114, 125, 135, 150, 172
$$\text{Median} = \frac{125 + 135}{2} = 130$$

**23.** 26, 32, 37, 41, 44, 50, 63, 75, 92
Median $= 44$

**25.** 18%, 21%, 21%, 21%, 22%, 25%, 28%
Mode $= 21\%$

**27.** 53, 64, 64, 64, 72, 72, 80
Mode $= 64$

**29.** 30, 32, 32, 34, 35, 36, 38, 38, 39
Bimodal: 32, 38

**31.** Mean
$$\frac{35 + 33 + 32 + 34 + 35 + 34 + 35 + 35 + 34}{9}$$
$$\approx 34.11$$

**33.** Mean
$$\frac{35 + 33 + 34 + 35 + 34 + 35 + 35 + 34}{8}$$
$$\approx 34.38$$

**35.** Answers will vary.

## Case Study

**1.** Store 1:
6.5, 6.8, 6.9, 7.0, 7.5, 7.6, 7.8, 8.0, 8.2

Store 2:
6.2, 8.2, 8.2, 8.7, 9.6

Store 1 Mean
$$= \frac{6.5 + 6.8 + 6.9 + 7.0 + 7.5 + 7.6 + 7.8 + 8.0 + 8.2}{9}$$
$$= \$7.4$$

Store 2 Mean
$$= \frac{6.2 + 8.2 + 8.2 + 8.7 + 9.6}{5}$$
$$= \$8.2$$

Store 1 Median $= \$7.5$

Store 2 Median $= \$8.2$

Store 1 has no mode

Store 2 Mode $= \$8.2$

**2.**

**3.** Sales at Store 2 are growing faster than at Store 1.

## Case in Point Summary Exercise

**1.** October:

$7.4, $7.4, $8.0, $8.3

Mean

$$\frac{\$7.4+\$7.4+\$8.0+\$8.3}{4}$$

$= \$7.775$ thousand $= \$7775$

$$\frac{\$7.4+\$8.0}{2}$$

$= \$7.7$ thousand $= \$7700$

November:

$8.0, $8.2, $9.8, $10.6

Mean

$$\frac{\$8.0+\$8.2+\$9.8+\$10.6}{4}$$

$= \$9.15$ thousand $= \$9150$

$$\frac{\$8.2+\$9.8}{2}$$

$= \$9$ thousand $= \$9000$

December:

$7.1, $8.9, $8.9, $9.2

Mean

$$\frac{\$7.1+\$8.9+\$8.9+\$9.2}{4}$$

$= \$8.525$ thousand $= \$8525$

$$\frac{\$8.9+\$8.9}{2}$$

$= \$8.9$ thousand $= \$8900$

**2.**

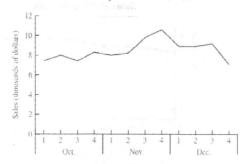

Weekly Sales at Bev's Deli

In the United States sales of many restaurants are typically high during mid- to late November associated with shopping for Christmas and then low during the week of Christmas.

**3.**

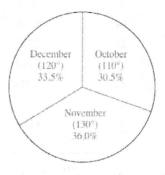

Sales at Bev's Deli

December (120°) 33.5%
October (110°) 30.5%
November (130°) 36.0%

## Chapter 16   Test

**1.**

| Cases of Motor Oil | Number of Weeks |
|---|---|
| 10,000-10,999 | 1 |
| 11,000-11,999 | 3 |
| 12,000-12,999 | 10 |
| 13,000-13,999 | 3 |
| 14,000-14,999 | 2 |
| 15,000-15,999 | 1 |

**2.**  $3+2+1=6$

6 weeks had sales of 13,000 cases or more.

**3.**

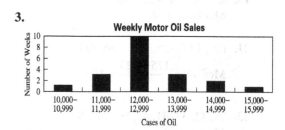

Weekly Motor Oil Sales

**4.**

| Item | Dollar Amount | Percent of Total | Degrees of a Circle |
|---|---|---|---|
| Newsprint | $12,000 | $\frac{\$12,000}{\$60,000}=20\%$ | $.20\times360° = \underline{72°}$ |
| Ink | $ 6,000 | $\frac{\$6000}{\$60,000}=\underline{10\%}$ | $.10\times360° = 36°$ |
| Wire Service | $18,000 | $\frac{\$18,000}{\$60,000}=30\%$ | $.30\times360° =\underline{108°}$ |
| Salaries | $18,000 | $\frac{\$18,000}{\$60,000}=30\%$ | $.30\times360° =\underline{108°}$ |
| Others | $ 6,000 | $\frac{\$6000}{\$60,000}=10\%$ | $.10\times360° = \underline{36°}$ |

**5.**

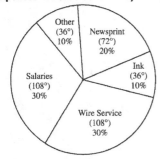

**Expenses at Dallas Community College**

Other (36°) 10%
Newsprint (72°) 20%
Ink (36°) 10%
Salaries (108°) 30%
Wire Service (108°) 30%

**6.** $20\% + 10\% + 30\% = 60\%$

60% of the expenses were for newsprint, ink, and wire service.

**7.** Mean

$$\frac{220 + 275 + 198 + 212 + 233 + 246}{6} \approx 230.7$$

**8.** Mean

$$\frac{12 + 18 + 14 + 17 + 19 + 22 + 23 + 25}{8}$$
$$= 18.75 \approx 18.8 \text{ centimeters}$$

**9.** Mean

$$\frac{458 + 432 + 496 + 491 + 500 + 508 + 512 + 396 + 492 + 504}{10}$$
$$= \$478.90$$

**10.**

| Volume | Frequency | Volume × Frequency |
|--------|-----------|--------------------|
| 6 | 7 | 42 |
| 10 | 3 | 30 |
| 11 | 4 | 44 |
| 14 | 2 | 28 |
| 19 | 3 | 57 |
| 24 | 1 | 24 |
| | 20 | 225 |

Weighted Mean $= \dfrac{225}{20} = 11.3$

**11.**

| Sales | Frequency | Sales × Frequency |
|-------|-----------|-------------------|
| 150 | 15 | 2250 |
| 160 | 17 | 2720 |
| 170 | 21 | 3570 |
| 180 | 28 | 5040 |
| 190 | 19 | 3610 |
| 200 | 7 | 1400 |
| | 107 | 18,590 |

Weighted Mean $= \dfrac{18{,}590}{107} = 173.7$

**12.** 7, 15, 18, 19, 20, 22, 25
Median $= 19$

**13.** 38, 38, 39, 41, 42, 45, 47, 51
Median $= \dfrac{41 + 42}{2} = 41.5$

**14.** 4.2, 5.3, 7.1, 7.6, 8.3, 9.0. 9.3. 10.4, 11.8
Median $= 8.3$

**15.** 29, 34, 38, 41, 51, 58, 76, 83, 91, 92
Median $= \dfrac{51 + 58}{2} = 54.5$

**16.** 32, 47, 47, 47, 48, 51, 71, 82
Mode $= 47$

**17.** 19, 25, 32, 43, 51, 74, 75, 82, 98, 100
No mode

**18.** 74, 91, 96, 103, 103, 103, 104, 104, 104
Bimodal: 103, 104

**19.**

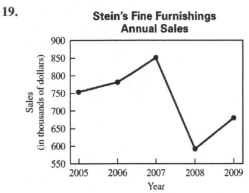

**Stein's Fine Furnishings Annual Sales**

It appears that the recession had an effect on the business.

**20.**

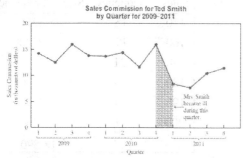

It appears that Mr. Smith's work was affected.

**1.** $68 \text{ cm} = \dfrac{68}{100} = .68 \text{ m}$

**2.** $934 \text{ mm} = \dfrac{934}{1000} = .934 \text{ m}$

**3.** $4.7 \text{ m} = 4.7 \times 1000 = 4700 \text{ mm}$

**4.** $7.43 \text{ m} = 7.43 \times 100 = 743 \text{ cm}$

**5.** $8.9 \text{ kg} = 8.9 \times 1000 = 8900 \text{ g}$

**6.** $4.32 \text{ kg} = 4.32 \times 1000 = 4320 \text{ g}$

**7.** $39 \text{ cL} = \dfrac{39}{100} = .39 \text{ L}$

**8.** $469 \text{ cL} = \dfrac{469}{100} = 4.69 \text{ L}$

**9.** $46,000 \text{ g} = \dfrac{46,000}{1000} = 46 \text{ kg}$

**10.** $35,800 \text{ g} = \dfrac{35,800}{1000} = 35.8 \text{ kg}$

**11.** $.976 \text{ kg} = .976 \times 1000 = 976 \text{ g}$

**12.** $.137 \text{ kg} = .137 \times 1000 = 137 \text{ g}$

**13.** $36 \text{ m} = 36 \times 1.09 = 39.2 \text{ yards}$

**14.** $76.2 \text{ m} = 76.2 \times 1.09 = 83.1 \text{ yards}$

**15.** $55 \text{ yards} = 55 \times 0.914 = 50.3 \text{ m}$

**16.** $89.3 \text{ yards} = 89.3 \times .914 = 81.6 \text{ m}$

**17.** $4.7 \text{ m} = 4.7 \times 3.28 = 15.4 \text{ feet}$

**18.** $1.92 \text{ m} = 1.92 \times 3.28 = 6.3 \text{ feet}$

**19.** $3.6 \text{ feet} = 3.6 \times .305 = 1.1 \text{ m}$

**20.** $12.8 \text{ feet} = 12.8 \times .305 = 3.9 \text{ m}$

**21.** $496 \text{ km} = 496 \times .62 = 307.5 \text{ miles}$

**22.** $138 \text{ km} = 138 \times .62 = 85.6 \text{ miles}$

**23.** $768 \text{ miles} = 768 \times 1.609 = 1235.7 \text{ km}$

**24.** $1042 \text{ miles} = 1042 \times 1.609 = 1676.6 \text{ km}$

**25.** $683 \text{ g} = 683 \times .00220 = 1.5 \text{ pounds}$

**26.** $1792 \text{ g} = 1792 \times .00220 = 3.9 \text{ pounds}$

**27.** $4.1 \text{ pounds} = 4.1 \times 454 = 1861.4 \text{ g}$

**28.** $12.9 \text{ pounds} = 12.9 \times 454 = 5856.6 \text{ g}$

**29.** $38.9 \text{ kg} = 38.9 \times 2.20 = 85.6 \text{ pounds}$

**30.** $40.3 \text{ kg} = 40.3 \times 2.20 = 88.7 \text{ pounds}$

**31.** $1 \text{ kg} = 1 \times 1000 = 1000 \text{ g}$

$\dfrac{1000 \text{ g}}{5 \text{ g}} = 200$

There are 200 nickels in 1 kilogram of nickels.

**32.** $5 \text{ L} = 5 \times 1000 = 5000 \text{ mL}$

$5000 \text{ mL} \times \dfrac{3.5 \text{ g}}{1000 \text{ mL}} = 17.5 \text{ g}$

5 liters of seawater contain 17.5 grams of salt.

**33.** $3 \text{ L} = 3 \times 1000 = 3000 \text{ mL}$

$3000 \text{ mL} \times \dfrac{.0002 \text{ g}}{1 \text{ mL}} = .6 \text{ g}$

The helium weighs .6 grams.

**34.** $1 \text{ mL} = \dfrac{1}{1000} = .001 \text{ L}$

$.001 \text{ L} \times \dfrac{1500 \text{ g}}{1 \text{ L}} = 1.5 \text{ g}$

1.5 grams of sugar could be dissolved in 1 milliliter of warm water.

**35.** Answers will vary.

**36.** Answers will vary.

**37.** $C = \dfrac{5(104-32)}{9} = \dfrac{5(72)}{9} = \dfrac{360}{9} = 40°C$

**38.** $C = \dfrac{5(86-32)}{9} = \dfrac{5(54)}{9} = \dfrac{270}{9} = 30°C$

**39.** $C = \dfrac{5(536-32)}{9} = \dfrac{5(504)}{9} = \dfrac{2520}{9} = 280°C$

**40.** $C = \dfrac{5(464-32)}{9} = \dfrac{5(432)}{9} = \dfrac{2160}{9} = 240°C$

**41.** $C = \dfrac{5(98-32)}{9} = \dfrac{5(66)}{9} = \dfrac{330}{9} \approx 37°C$

**42.** $C = \dfrac{5(114-32)}{9} = \dfrac{5(82)}{9} = \dfrac{410}{9} \approx 46°C$

**43.** $F = \dfrac{9 \times 35}{5} + 32 = \dfrac{315}{5} + 32$
$= 63 + 32 = 95°F$

**44.** $F = \dfrac{9 \times 100}{5} + 32 = \dfrac{900}{5} + 32$
$= 180 + 32 = 212°F$

**45.** $F = \dfrac{9 \times 10}{5} + 32 = \dfrac{90}{5} + 32$
$= 18 + 32 = 50°F$

**46.** $F = \dfrac{9 \times 25}{5} + 32 = \dfrac{225}{5} + 32$
$= 45 + 32 = 77°F$

**47.** $F = \dfrac{9 \times 135}{5} + 32 = \dfrac{1215}{5} + 32$
$= 243 + 32 = 275°F$

**48.** $F = \dfrac{9 \times 215}{5} + 32 = \dfrac{1935}{5} + 32$
$= 387 + 32 = 419°F$

**49.** $1940 \text{ g} = 1940 \times .0022 = 4.268$ pounds
Unreasonable

**50.** $76.8 \text{ cL} = \dfrac{76.8}{100} = .768 \text{ L};$
$.768 \times 1.06 = .814$ quart
Unreasonable

**51.** $943 \text{ mL} = \dfrac{943}{1000} = .943 \text{ L};$
$.943 \times 1.06 = .99958$ quart
Reasonable

**52.** $1.4 \text{ kg} = 1.4 \times 2.20 = 3.08$ pounds
Unreasonable

**1.** 384.92 + 407.61 + 351.14 + 27.93 = 1171.6

**2.** 85.76 + 21.94 + 39.89 = 147.59

**3.** 6850 + 321 + 4207 = 11,378

**4.** 781.42 + 304.59 + 261.35 = 1347.36

**5.** 4270.41 − 365.09 = 3905.32

**6.** 3000.07 − 48.12 = 2951.95

**7.** 384.96 − 129.72 = 255.24

**8.** 36.84 − 12.17 = 24.67

**9.** 365 × 43 = 15,695

**10.** 27.51 × 1.18 = 32.4618,
which rounds to 32.46.

**11.** 3.7 × 8.4 = 31.08

**12.** 62.5 × 81 = 5062.5

**13.** 375.4 ÷ 10.6 = 35.41509434,
which rounds to 35.42.

**14.** 9625 ÷ 400 = 24.0625,
which rounds to 24.06.

**15.** 96.7 ÷ 3.5 = 27.62857143,
which rounds to 27.63.

**16.** 103.7 ÷ 0.35 = 296.2857143,
which rounds to 296.29.

**17.** ( 9 × 9 ) ÷ ( 2 × 5 )
= 8.1

**18.** ( 15 × 8 × 3 ) ÷
( 11 × 7 × 4 ) =
1.168831169, which rounds to 1.17.

**19.** ( 87 × 24 × 47.2 ) ÷
( 13.6 × 12.8 ) =
566.1397059, which rounds to 566.14.

**20.** ( 2 × ( 3 + 4 ) ) ÷
( 6 + 10 ) = 0.875,
which rounds to 0.88.

**21.** ( 2 × 3 + 4 ) ÷
( 6 + 10 ) = 0.625,
which rounds to 0.63.

**22.** ( 4200 × 0.12 × 90 )
÷ 365 ENTER 124.2739726,
which rounds to 124.27.

**23.** ( 640 − 0.6 × 12 ) ÷
( 17.5 + 3.2 ) =
30.57004831, which rounds to 30.57.

**24.** ( 16 × 18 ÷ .42 ) ÷
( 95.4 × 3 − .8 ) =
2.402642907, which rounds to 2.40.

**25.** ( 14 $x^2$ − 3.6 × 6 ) ÷
( 95.2 ÷ 0.5 ) =
0.9159663866, which rounds to 0.92.

**26.** ( 9 $x^2$ + 3.8 ÷ 2 ) ÷
( 14 + 7.5 ) =
3.855813953, which rounds to 3.86.

**27.** 7 $\boxed{a^{b/c}}$ 5 $\boxed{a^{b/c}}$ 8 $\boxed{÷}$
$\boxed{(}$ $\boxed{1}$ $\boxed{+}$ 3 $\boxed{a^{b/c}}$ 8 $\boxed{)}$ $\boxed{=}$

$\dfrac{61}{11} = 5\dfrac{6}{11}$

**28.** 5 $\boxed{a^{b/c}}$ 1 $\boxed{a^{b/c}}$ 4 $\boxed{x^2}$ $\boxed{×}$ 3.65 $\boxed{=}$
$100.603125 \approx 100.60$

**29.** $\boxed{(}$ 3 $\boxed{a^{b/c}}$ 4 $\boxed{÷}$ 5 $\boxed{a^{b/c}}$ 8 $\boxed{)}$
$\boxed{y^x}$ 3 $\boxed{÷}$ 3 $\boxed{a^{b/c}}$ 1 $\boxed{a^{b/c}}$ 2 $\boxed{=}$
$0.493714286 \approx 0.49$.

**30.** 6 $\boxed{\sqrt{x}}$ $\boxed{×}$ $\boxed{(}$ 3 $\boxed{x^2}$ $\boxed{+}$ 2 $\boxed{a^{b/c}}$ 1 $\boxed{a^{b/c}}$ 2 $\boxed{)}$
$\boxed{÷}$ $\boxed{(}$ 7 $\boxed{×}$ 5 $\boxed{a^{b/c}}$ 6 $\boxed{)}$ $\boxed{=}$
$4.828994064 \approx 4.83$

**31.** Answers will vary.

**32.** Answers will vary.

**33.** 397 $\boxed{×}$ 46.40 $\boxed{+}$ 125 $\boxed{×}$ 38.40
$\boxed{+}$ 740 $\boxed{×}$ 28.30 $\boxed{=}$ 44,162.80
The total paid by the bookstore is $44,162.80.

**34.** 5 $\boxed{×}$ 104.19 $\boxed{+}$ 4 $\boxed{×}$ 86.80 $\boxed{+}$
8 $\boxed{×}$ 36.40 $\boxed{+}$ 916 $\boxed{×}$ .28 $\boxed{=}$ 1415.83
Judy's total expenses were $1415.83.

**35. (a)** 17,908.43 $\boxed{×}$ .065 $\boxed{=}$
$1164.04795 \approx 1164.05$
The tax on the new car is $1164.05.

**(b)** 1463.58 $\boxed{×}$ .065 $\boxed{=}$
$95.1327 \approx 95.13$
The tax on the computer is $95.13.

**36.** She will borrow $1 - \dfrac{1}{3} = \dfrac{2}{3}$ of the money.
$\boxed{(}$ $\boxed{(}$ 78,250 $\boxed{+}$ 4820 $\boxed{)}$
$\boxed{×}$ 1.0725 $\boxed{+}$ 1135 $\boxed{+}$ 428 $\boxed{)}$
$\boxed{×}$ $\boxed{(}$ 2 $\boxed{a^{b/c}}$ 3 $\boxed{)}$ $\boxed{=}$ 60,437.05
Strutz will borrow $60,437.05.

**37.** 8000 $\boxed{+}$ 30 $\boxed{×}$ 12 $\boxed{×}$ 1002.80
$\boxed{-}$ 155,000 $\boxed{=}$ 214,008
The down payment and the sum of the monthly payments exceeds the purchase price by $214,008.

**38.** 150,000 $\boxed{+}$ 15 $\boxed{×}$ 12 $\boxed{×}$ 5050
$\boxed{-}$ 620,000 $\boxed{=}$ 439,000
The down payment and the sum of the monthly payments exceeds the purchase price by $439,000.

**39.** 15,000 $\boxed{+}$ 2800 $\boxed{+}$ 28,000
$\boxed{-}$ 32,400 $\boxed{=}$ 13,400
Ben needs additional funding of $13,400.

**40.** 52,000 $\boxed{+}$ 240,000 $\boxed{+}$ 57,000
$\boxed{-}$ 100,000 $\boxed{=}$ 249,000
Koplan Kitchens must borrow $249,000.

**41.** 60 $\boxed{-}$ 24.50 $\boxed{=}$ 35.50 $\boxed{÷}$ 60
$\boxed{=}$ .5916 $\approx 59\%$
There is a 59% markup on selling price.

**42.** 37,800 $\boxed{+}$ 59,600 $\boxed{+}$ 24,300
$\boxed{=}$ 121,700 $\boxed{STO}$
136,500 $\boxed{-}$ $\boxed{RCL}$ $\boxed{=}$ 14,800
$\boxed{÷}$ $\boxed{RCL}$ $\boxed{=}$
$.12161 \approx 12\%$
There is a 12% markup over cost.

**1.** 20 [n] 10 [i] −5800 [PV] [FV] 39019.50
$39,019.50

**2.** 7 [n] 8 [i] −8900 [PV] [FV] 15253.04
$15,253.04

**3.** 10 [n] 3 [i] 12000 [FV] [PV] −8929.13
$8929.13

**4.** 16 [n] 4 [i] 8200 [FV] [PV] −4378.05
$4378.05

**5.** 7 [n] 8 [i] −300 [PMT] [FV] 2676.84
$2676.84

**6.** 25 [n] 2 [i] −1000 [PMT] [FV] 32030.30
$32,030.30

**7.** 30 [n] 12000 [FV] −319.67 [PMT] [i] 1.5
1.5%

**8.** 50 [n] 285000 [FV] −4718.99 [PMT] [i] .75
.75%

**9.** 360 [n] 1 [i] −83500 [PV] [PMT] 858.89
$858.89

**10.** 180 [n] .5 [i] −125000 [PV] [PMT] 1054.82
$1054.82

**11.** 4 [i] −85383 [PV] 5600 [PMT] [n] 24
24 payments

**12.** 2 [i] −3822 [PV] 100 [PMT] [n] 73
73 payments

**13.** $4 \times 5 = 20$ quarters; $\dfrac{6\%}{4} = 1.5\%$ per quarter
20 [n] 1.5 [i] −23500 [PV] [FV] 31651.09
The future value at the end of 5 years is
$31,651.09.

**14.** $14 \times 12 = 168$ payments
168 [n] .5 [i] −50 [PMT] [FV] 13115.24
The future value at the end of 4 years is
$13,115.24.

**15.** $30 \times 12 = 360$ payments; $\dfrac{9\%}{12} = .75\%$ per month
86500 [PV] .75 [i] 360 [n] [PMT] −696
The monthly payment is $696.

**16.** $10 \times 4 = 40$ payments; $\dfrac{10\%}{4} = 2.5\%$ per quarter
40 [n] 2.5 [i] 20000 [FV] [PMT] −296.72
Walker must make a payment of 296.72 at the
end of each quarter.

**17.** .8 [i] −12000 [PMT] 340000 [FV] [n] 26
26 payments must be paid before reaching its
goal.

**18.** $\dfrac{7\%}{12} = .583333\%$ per month
.583333 [i] 70000 [FV] −500 [PMT] [n] 103
$103 \div 12 \approx 8.6$
103 months of 8.6 years

**19.** $30 \times 12 = 360$ payments
360 [n] 110000 [PV] −845 [PMT] [i] .70747
$.70747\% \times 12 = 8.48964\% \approx 8.5\%$
The highest acceptable annual interest rate
is 8.5%.

**20.** $4 \times 12 = 48$ payments
28000 [PV] −700 [PMT] 48 [n] [i] .770147
$.770147\% \times 12 = 9.241764\% \approx 9.2\%$
The maximum interest rate Blalock can afford
is 9.2%.